D0204239

Criminal Justice and Political Cultures

Criminal Justice and Political Cultures

National and international dimensions of crime control

Edited by

Tim Newburn and Richard Sparks

WILLAN
PUBLISHING

Published by

Willan Publishing
Culmcott House
Mill Street, Uffculme
Cullompton, Devon
EX15 3AT, UK
Tel: +44(0)1884 840337
Fax: +44(0)1884 840251
e-mail: info@willanpublishing.co.uk
website: www.willanpublishing.co.uk

Published simultaneously in the USA and Canada by

Willan Publishing
c/o ISBS, 920 NE 58th Ave, Suite 300,
Portland, Oregon 97213-3786, USA
Tel: +001(0)503 287 3093
Fax: +001(0)503 280 8832
e-mail: info@isbs.com
website: www.isbs.com

First published 2004

ISBN 1-84392-026-3 (hardback)
ISBN 1-84392-054-9 (paperback)

British Library Cataloguing-in-Publication Data
A catalogue record for this book is available from the British Library

Project management by Deer Park Productions, Tavistock, Devon
Typeset by GCS, Leighton Buzzard, Beds
Printed and bound by T.J. International, Padstow, Cornwall

Contents

Acknowledgements

Particular thanks are due to Professor Ed Page who, as Director of the ESRC's Future Governance Programme, provided both financial and moral support for the 'How Crime Policy Travels' symposium at Keele in June 2001 which gave rise to many of the papers that appear in this book. The chapters by Susanne Karstedt, Ian Loader, Pat Carlen, Trevor Jones and Tim Newburn, and Pat O'Malley first appeared in a special edition of the journal *Criminal Justice*, and the chapter by Dario Melossi first appeared in *Theoretical Criminology*. All are reproduced with permission and thanks are due to Sage Publications and to the editors of the journals for their support. As ever, Brian Willan has been an encouraging and enthusiastic publisher and we are grateful to all at Willan Publishing and at Deer Park Productions, for their efficiency and professionalism.

Notes on contributors

Pat Carlen is Honorary Professor of Criminology at Keele University, Staffordshire, and Visiting Professor of Criminology at Westminster University, London. She has published 15 books and many articles on the relationships between criminal and social justice, the latest being *Women and Punishment: The Struggle for Justice* (Willan, 2002). Presently engaged in an EC-funded 6 nation project on social exclusion and women prisoners, she is also an Editor of the *British Journal of Criminology* and Book Review Editor of *Punishment and Society.* In 1997 she was awarded the Sellin-Glueck Prize by the American Society of Criminology for outstanding international contributions to Criminology.

David Dixon is Associate Dean (Research) in the Faculty of Law, University of New South Wales, Sydney, Australia. He has researched and published widely on policing and crime control in Britain, Australia, and the USA. His publications include *From Prohibition to Regulation: Bookmaking, Anti-Gambling and the Law* (Oxford University Press); *Law in Policing: Legal Regulation and Police Practices* (Oxford University Press); and *A Culture of Corruption: Changing an Australian Police Service* (Hawkins Press). His current research includes 'Q&A: Police Interviewing of Suspects' – a study of videorecorded police interrogations – and 'Policing, Law, and Order'– a comparative study of developing crime control strategies.

Adam Edwards is Senior Lecturer in Criminology at Nottingham Trent University and Deputy Director of the Nottingham Crime Research Unit. He has published widely on such topics as the politics of crime control, organised crime, crime prevention and crime control policy transfer and has also co edited two volumes entitled *Crime Control and Community* (Willan, 2002 with Gordon Hughes) and *Transnational Organised Crime* (Routledge, 2003 with Pete Gill).

Trevor Jones teaches criminology in the School of Social Sciences at the University of Cardiff, Wales. He has published widely in the areas of policing, community safety and criminal justice policy-making. His research has explored the relationship between policing and democratic institutions in England/Wales and in the Netherlands, and also includes the first national empirical study of the commercial security industry in the UK. In collaboration with Tim Newburn, he is currently engaged in a major ESRC-funded study of comparative criminal justice policy-making.

Susanne Karstedt is Professor of Criminology at Keele University. Her current research focuses on cross-national and cross-cultural comparisons in criminology. Recent publications include *Social Dynamics of Crime and Control: New Theories for a World in Transition* (edited with K.D. Bussmann, 2000); 'Comparing Cultures, Comparing Crime: Challenges, Prospects and Problems for a Global Criminology in *Crime, Law and Social Change*, 36 (2001); 'Die moralische Stärke schwacher Bindungen: Individualismus und Gewalt im Kulturvergleich (The Moral Strength of Weak Ties: A Cross-Cultural Comparison of Individualism and Violence) in *Monatsschrift fuer Kriminologie und Strafrechtsreform*, 84; 'Legacies of a Culture of Inequality: The Janus-Face of Crime in Post-Communist Societies', *Crime, Law and Social Change*, 2003.

Ian Loader is Reader in the Department of Criminology, Keele University. In addition to various articles on contemporary trans-formations in policing and security he has written *Crime and Social Change in Middle England* (Routledge, 2000, with Evi Girling and Richard Sparks) and *Policing and the Condition of England: Memory, Politics and Culture* (Oxford University Press, 2003 with Aogán Mulcahy).

Lisa Maher is an Associate Professor in the School of Public Health and Community Medicine at the University of New South Wales and an Honorary Fellow of the Centre for Harm Reduction, Macfarlane Burnet. She has international experience in research, program development and service delivery with injecting drug users, sex workers, people living with HIV/AIDS and marginalised youth in North America, South East Asia and Australia, and has published extensively. Since 1995, she has been conducting research in south-west Sydney on risk-taking behaviours, blood-borne viruses and the social, cultural and environmental contexts of drug-related harms.

Dario Melossi is Professor of Criminology at the Faculty of Law of the University of Bologna. He has also taught for many years at the University of California, Davis. His main works are *The Prison and the Factory* (with Massimo Pavarini) and *The State of Social Control: A Sociological Study of Concepts of State and Social Control in the Making of Democracy.* He is currently doing research and writing on the relationship between migratory movements and representations and practices of crime and punishment.

John Muncie is Professor of Criminology at the Open University. He is the author of *Youth and Crime: A Critical Introduction,* 1999, and currently working on a second edition for publication in 2004. His latest books are the co-edited works: *The Problem of Crime, 2001; Controlling Crime, 2001; The Sage Dictionary* of *Criminology, 2001* (with Eugene McLaughlin) and *Criminological Perspectives: Essential readings, 2003, Youth Justice: Critical readings, 2002* and *Crime Prevention and Community Safety: New Directions,* 2002 (with Gordon Hughes and Eugene McLaughlin).

Tim Newburn is Professor of Criminology and Social Policy and Director of the Mannheim Centre for Criminology at the London School of Economics. He has written and researched widely on issues of crime and justice and, in particular, on policing and security. His recent work includes *Policing, Surveillance and Social Control* (with Stephanie Hayman, 2001); *Youth Offending and Restorative Justice* (with Adam Crawford, 2003); *Criminology, Conflict Resolution and Restorative Justice* (with Kieran McEvoy, 2003); *Crime and Criminal Justice Policy* (2003) and *Handbook of Policing* (2003). He is currently working with Trevor Jones on a study of the relationship between US and UK crime control systems and rhetorics.

Pat O'Malley is a Canada Research Chair in Criminology and Criminal Justice at Carleton University, Ottawa. Much of his work over the past decade has focused on frameworks of government, focusing on the governance of risk and uncertainty, most especially with reference to criminal justice. Other research has examined the sociology of drug consumption and drug policy, and the place of excitement and pleasure as discourses of regulation. A monograph on *Risk, Uncertainty and Government* will be published by Cavendish in 2004.

Richard Sparks is Professor of Criminology at Keele University. His main research interests lie in the sociology of punishment (especially imprisonment); penal politics; and public responses to crime and punishment. Recent and current research projects have included an account (with Marion Smith and Evi Girling) of nine-year old children's conversations about justice and punishment and (with Elaine Crawley) a study of older men in English prisons. Richard is the author of *Television and the Drama of Crime* (1992) and co-author (with Tony Bottoms and Will Hay) of *Prisons and the Problem of Order* (1996) and (with Evi Girling and Ian Loader) of *Crime and Social Change in Middle England* (2000). He has also co-edited (with David Garland) *Criminology and Social Theory* (2000), and (with Tim Hope) *Crime, Risk and Insecurity* (2000). He is currently Editor-in-Chief of the journal *Punishment and Society.*

Kevin Stenson is Professor of Criminology at Buckinghamshire Chilterns University College, UK. His research interests are mainly in the fields of policing, community safety and the new modes of liberal governance. He has written extensively on these issues and his publications include *Crime, Risk and Justice*, co-edited with Robert Sullivan (Willan, 2001).

Elrena van der Spuy is a Senior Lecturer attached to the Department of Criminal Justice and former Director of the Institute of Criminology at the University of Cape Town, South Africa. She has published in the area of police reform. More recently she has conducted research into the role of the international donor community on criminal justice reform in southern Africa. Together with Bill Dixon, she is co-editor of *Justice Gained? Crime and Crime Control in South Africa's Transition* to be published by UCT Press (SA) and Willan Publishing (UK) in 2004.

Dirk van Zyl Smit holds joint appointments as Professor of International and Comparative Penal Law at the University of Nottingham and Professor of Criminology at the University of Cape Town. His books include *Taking Life Imprisonment Seriously in National and International Law (2002), Prison Labour: Salvation or Slavery? International Perspectives* (1999) and *Imprisonment Today and Tomorrow – International Perspectives on Prisoners' Rights and Prison Conditions* (2nd ed. 2001), both edited together with Frieder Dünkel, as well as *South African Prison Law and Practice* (1992). In South Africa he assisted in drafting the Correctional Services Act 1998. He was also project leader of the committee of the South African Law Commission investigating a new sentencing framework.

Chapter 1

Criminal justice and political cultures

Tim Newburn and Richard Sparks

Introduction

This book develops a discussion in which we and others have been engaged in recent years about the changing relationships between national cultures or traditions in criminal justice, on one hand and, on the other, influences on knowledge and practice that exceed or subvert the boundaries of these systems as we conventionally understand them. The first staging-post in the production of this book was a symposium we convened at Keele University in 2001 under the title 'How does crime policy travel?'[1] Five of the papers from that event were subsequently published in a special edition of the journal *Criminal Justice* and one in *Theoretical Criminology*. Those six papers all reappear here alongside a number of new contributions that we have commissioned in an attempt to extend the scope of this discussion and make its key arguments more accessible. We are very far from claiming that the contributors to this volume are alone in facing up to these concerns or that we were the first people to notice them. Neither is criminology unique among the social sciences in needing to confront anew the dialectic between national particularity and inter- or trans- or supranational mobilities now. Rather it is precisely the fact that it shares these characteristics with so many fields of governance and policy that makes the task of reappraisal timely and necessary.

The focus of the Keele symposium was on the interdependence of criminal justice systems and criminological commodities. More particularly, participants were concerned with the issue of how crime control policies, practices, ideas and ideologies flow within and between nation-states. This is not a new subject (see Chapter 2) but it is, we feel, undoubtedly one whose 'moment' has arrived. This book is an extension of that original project, adding a further five papers that seek to map out and broaden the scope and focus of the project with a view to developing, or at least identifying the possibility of, a theoretical vocabulary with which to explore issues of transfer, mobility and exchange in criminal justice and penal policy.

The imperative to think about contemporary social analysis in terms of 'flows' and 'edges' has latterly become part of the common currency of much social theory and substantive research (Lash and Urry 1993; Urry 1999; Castells 2000; Bauman 2001b). The way in which the notion of globalization has burst the bounds of technical discussion (in which it was itself a fairly novel coinage only ten or fifteen years ago) and has become a standard term of public debate attests to the receptiveness of our wider political culture to these concerns, even if the concept of globalisation has lost something in precision or specificity in the process. The case of criminal justice is an especially vexed and interesting one here, however. While it seems clear that policy-makers and senior practitioners increasingly occupy the 'space of flows' (Castells 2001) it is also the case that many of the key concerns of criminology and criminal justice – with police powers or with the punishment of offenders, for example – have classically been regarded as integral to, and even definitve of, the capacities and legitimation claims of the nation-state (Weber 1978). There are questions of sovereignty, of democratic account-ability and, indeed, of national self-definition at stake in this field. We should therefore be ready to confront a quite complicated and con-tentious arena in which examples of 'policy transfer' and convergence, and the creation of specifically supranational institutions, jostle against restatements of state sovereignty and assertions of identity. David Garland (1996) has famously identified and analysed one half of this dialectic, namely the sense of a withering of state capacity in crime control and the menace this poses to the power to rule by sovereign command, as central to explaining the amplified importance of con-temporary penal politics. We share this concern but think that the time is also ripe for a wider attempt at reorientation. In other words in seeking to pose contemporary and demanding questions about 'what is going on?' (let alone about 'what is to be done?') criminology and criminal justice as fields of study will have to address the tense and contradictory intersection between 'the space of flows' and 'the space of places', for it is here that new institutional forms emerge and political energies are generated.

Two basic premises thus run through this book. First, that there is increasing evidence of certain forms of convergence in the languages and practices of crime control (Garland 2001). We plainly need to confront the emergence and promulgation of supranational legal orders, international standards and common intellectual currencies. Secondly, the mechanisms, directions and outcomes of such flows and transfers are both more complex and less well elucidated empirically and theoretically than is commonly assumed.

'Policy transfer' and 'lesson drawing'

As we have noted, an early starting point in this project was a fairly narrow focus upon 'policy transfer' within the crime control arena. The idea that policies and practices in one jurisdiction are affected, more or less directly, by those in another is by no means new. In the context of the broad sweep of changes associated with the idea of globalisation it is, however, of increasing importance across the social sciences. There has, in this regard, been a developing interest within the fields of comparative politics and international relations in the idea of 'policy transfer' (Stone 1999; Dolowitz and Marsh 1996) and related but distinct ideas, including 'lesson-drawing' (Rose 1993), 'policy convergence' (Bennett 1991) and 'policy diffusion' (Eyestone 1977).

As we have separately noted elsewhere (Sparks 2001; Newburn 2002) the impulse to look across, to import novel ideas and replicate models encountered elsewhere can be traced back more or less to the inception of criminal justice institutions in their 'modern' forms. This is perhaps best attested in relation to penitentiary imprisonment. It stands behind John Howard's epic pilgrimage through the prisons of Britain and Europe or Beaumont and de Tocqueville's epistles home from the USA. Salvatore and Aguirre (1996) have, for example, provided a compelling account of the introduction of the penitentiary form in Latin America. One could multiply instances and consider their relation to modernity and to empire almost indefinitely. Radzinowicz's (1999) account of his peripatetic early career and its context in the professional congresses of early twentieth-century European and Latin American penology is a revealing case in point. According to Tarde (1903) the purpose of scholarship in this area was 'to learn why, given one hundred innovations conceived at the same time – innovations in the form of words, in mythological ideas, in industrial processes, etc. – ten will spread abroad while ninety will be forgotten' (cited in Rogers 1995: 40). One question before us now concerns the ways in which such processes of exchange may have intensified, accelerated and altered their media of transmission in recent times.

In its narrow form, the question can be reduced to the idea of 'policy transfer'. This may be seen as 'a process in which knowledge about policies, administrative arrangements, institutions etc. in one time and/ or place is used in the development of policies, administrative arrangements and institutions in another time and/or place' (Dolowitz and Marsh 1996: 344). This definition of the process of policy transfer is broad enough to encompass essentially voluntary processes such as 'lesson drawing' and more structurally influenced notions such as 'convergence'. Previous work in this area has highlighted at least seven major questions. Though they don't necessarily form an explicit focus here, they nevertheless run through the book and, to differing degrees, the chapters in this volume help throw some light on potential answers to each of them.

The first of the questions concerns the reasons why particular policies, practices or ideas are transferred. Crudely, transfer may be analysed along a continuum from the broadly voluntary to the more coercive. At the largely voluntary end one example would be the many visits by politicians and professionals to the New York Police Department, particularly during the 'crime drop' of the 1990s, to examine the possibility of replicating the NYPD's use of information technology for the management of police performance (known locally as Compstat) to domestic forces (see Chapter 11). At the more coercive end are the changes wrought as a result of the existence of international treaties and other obligations. One of the most visible sites of such changes in the crime control sphere is the transnationalising effect of the processes and practices central to increasing European co-operation in field of policing (Chapter 4) and the impact of donor assistance on police reform in South Africa (Chapter 9).

Secondly, any analysis of these processes requires us to ask: who is involved in the transfer of ideas, policies and practices? As Rogers (1995: 7) puts it, 'innovations do not sell themselves'. A number of actors, agencies and institutions may be involved in different ways in the process of transfer. They may include, *inter alia*, politicians, parties and governments (Chapter 7), pressure groups and think-tanks (Chapter 10), policy entrepreneurs and experts (Chapters 7, 10 and 11) and transnational corporations and non-governmental institutions/networks (Chapters 2 and 4). Though it may seem obvious to note that there are people, agencies and institutions involved in such processes, all too often work in this area talks of emergent systems of crime control as if they were entirely the product of structural forces that underpin them. While we don't for a moment deny the importance of structural forms of explanation, we need also to move beyond what Karstedt (Chapter 2) suggests are approaches that involve unilateral or deterministic concepts towards those that also recognise the 'path dependency' inherent in the notion of travel: 'decisions taken at crossroads, different destinations and different points of departure.'

Thirdly, there is the issue of *what* is transferred. Though the focus of much extant work in this area has tended to be on the most formal aspects of policy – programmes, instruments and institutions – as several of the chapters remind us, symbols and rhetoric may be at least if not more important. This is particularly the case, it would appear, in the crime control arena. Moreover, the fact that transfer might be more common at the level of symbol than substance should not be taken as an indication of its relative unimportance, for as Muncie (Chapter 8) notes, 'it is vital not to lose sight of the fact that the discursive also has material effects'. Finally in this regard there is also what might be thought of as 'negative policy transfer' (Chapter 11) where the result of a particular influence is the non-adoption of a particular policy.

Fourthly is the question of from where are lessons drawn. Influences may be domestic and international. In terms of the topography of contemporary crime control it is undoubtedly the case that the USA is perceived to be the source of the greatest number of exported ideas and practices. Two of the most powerful and insightful analyses of the developments of a late modern system of crime control – that by David Garland (1996, 2001) and by Jock Young (1999) – have focused specifically on the parallels between USA and UK developments and, though to a lesser extent, on the influence of the former on the latter. As a number of contributions to this volume indicate, the influence of ideas, policies and practices that appear to have their origins in the US extends across the globe. However, one of the other key narratives running through the contributions to this book concerns the ease with which this can, and has been, misunderstood, misrepresented, exaggerated or simplified. Much of the political science literature focuses on the nature of the policies being transferred and how their complexity and feasibility affect the extent of transfer. By contrast, we argue that while these factors are undoubtedly important, it is the sociopolitical and cultural context in which 'transfer' occurs, or is attempted, that has the most profound effect on the eventual shape and style of the policy concerned. This raises two further questions about policy transfer. What are the constraints on such transfer and, linked to this, what are the different degrees of transfer or, put another way, how complete is the process? Is what is occurring something akin to 'copying' or, rather, is it a vaguer process of emulation in which inspiration is taken from a set of ideas or practices, but where the eventual result is the production of something quite distinctive? In part, as we have intimated, the likely answer to the latter question is, in particular cases, a product, at least in part, of the socio-political circumstances under which 'policy transfer' takes place.

Finally there is the question of how the process is related to policy 'success' or 'failure'. In part, this could be interpreted as simply a different way of assessing the degree of fidelity in the process of transfer. Seen more broadly, the question concerns the more general results of the spread of particular policies. Were they fully implemented? When implemented, did they achieve their intended goals? And so on. These, however, are not really questions addressed in this volume. It is not that they are not, or could not be, important. Rather, that they are rather narrowly technical in scope and lead us away from many of the broader political and normative questions that a focus on the spread of ideas, policies and practices can raise. Moreover, questions of policy 'success' or 'failure' also lead us quite quickly to some of the difficulties of the very idea of policy transfer.

As we said earlier, we could limit our focus to the narrow question of policy transfer. The notion is a suggestive and interesting one and, as we hope we have illustrated, raises some important questions. Yet it is insufficiently broad to allow some of the distinctive structural and cultural issues to come fully into play. It also suffers from a number of other difficulties. First, as Jones and Newburn (Chapter 7) outline, the term 'policy' is often rather taken for granted; it tends to be insufficiently specified in studies of 'transfer'. Related to this, 'transfer' is itself a somewhat problematic concept, inviting the assumption that there are conscious, intended processes at work. As a consequence it draws attention away from unintended consequences and, crucially, is generally based on a model of policy-making and policy development that is overly rational and which tends, either explicitly or implicitly, to see policy-making as a set of stages involving the creation of agendas, the selection between alternatives, the implementation (possibly following transfer) of the selected policy, followed by some assessment of its success or failure. Now there may be occasions where policy-making does indeed look like this. However, and this may be something specifically to do with criminal justice and penal policy – though we very much doubt it – the emergence and adoption of crime control practices, policies and technologies are subject to a much more complex mix of structural, subjective and simply serendipitous influences. And it is these as much as the more obvious accoutrements of policy-making (and transfer) that concern us here. Thus, while one of the central narratives of this volume concerns the movement of criminological commodities, the contributors individually and collectively have sought to move beyond the limiting vocabulary of policy transfer towards a more broadly conceptualised idea of comparative policy analysis. Such a project is itself, of course, far from unproblematic.

Some problems of comparative criminology

For all the reasons already stated, students of crime, punishment and control increasingly address the transnational scope of their subject, and are bound to do so with increasing urgency in coming years. This in no sense means that the traditions of comparative criminology (the contrastive exploration of problems, priorities, legal cultures, elite networks, public sensibilities and so on) are anywhere near being exhausted. Indeed, Nelken, in some of the most elegant and authoritative commentaries on the problems and prospects of comparative study in criminology and criminal justice (see, *inter alia*, Nelken 1994, 1997, 2000), more often suggests that this style of work is embryonic and unfulfilled than that it is, in any sense of the term, *finished*.

We expressly do not, therefore, suggest that a concern with flux, mobility and transfer simply supercedes one with difference, diversity or intercultural understanding. The cognitive, explanatory and ethical challenges posed by comparative research remain both daunting and exciting. Indeed, given that it has very often been suggested (for example, here in terms suggested by Giddens 1991) that one of the primary purposes of sociological work is to 'think oneself away' from the immediacy of local experience, there remains an abiding place for comparative reflection at every level of theory and research. Moreover, comparative study retains its essential role simply as a corrective against sweeping assertions of either difference or sameness. Many of the generalisations that we commonly use to divide up the world ('the Anglo-Saxon' versus 'the continental' and so on) do refer to real distinctions of history and generative tradition but become blocks against insight when used in lieu of more particular and grounded accounts. In these respects the ethnographic moment of *surprise* (Willis 2000: 78) in the researcher's encounters with the complexity and variety of the real is no less relevant and powerful than it ever was.

Similarly the conceptual and practical problems of translation remain central (Sozzo 2001; see Chapter 5). Among the more salutary discoveries of recent comparative research is that terms and institutions that at first blush look strikingly similar (indeed often consciously adopted or adapted from an imported model) turn out on closer examination to be distinct in interesting and meaningful ways. Thus for example the important work of Lacey and Zedner on concepts of 'security' and 'community' in Britain and Germany (1995, 1998; see also Bauman 2001a), and the growing international literature on 'prevention' and 'safety' (King 1989; Crawford 2000; Melossi and Selmini 2000), disclose both subtle and basic differences of meaning and application. On some occasions while there is a surface similarity – in terms of symbolism or of diction – deeper analysis reveals often quite profound differences at the level of substance. Work in the area of policing, for example, while revealing a number of shared attributes in the changes apparently now affecting many developed economies (Bayley and Shearing 1996), has also served to remind us of the continuing divergences (Jones and Newburn, 2002) and of the need to be 'wary of taking histories from one country as unambiguous lessons for another' (Lacey, 2003: 104). As Muncie (Chapter 8) argues, it is by no means always clear whether 'globalisation' and its synonyms have broad applicability or merely serve to direct our attention to those trans-formations that fit neatly within our narrowly ethnocentric view of the world.

At the same time, and as we have implied, the future of comparative criminology is increasingly complicated by both those illegal flows and markets (movements of people, drugs, weapons, money and information) that expressly puncture national and jurisdictional boundaries and the varieties of police co-operation, international treaties, protocols and conventions designed to impede their mobility and promote common standards and practices. In many of their aspects these dialectics of crime and control systems are now familiar (if none the less bewildering) features of policy networks and of academic discourse. What remain arguably less well understood are the means whereby cultural and conceptual resources also escape their points of origin and become naturalised (and hence variously translated, inflected or hybridised) in other locations. Wacquant, for example, has written on the 'globalisation of zero tolerance' and on how (American) penal 'common sense' comes to Europeans (Wacquant 1999). His account raises a range of problems for anatomising the channels of influence and propagation which enable the spread of particular slogans, gadgets, technical vocabularies and rhetorics. Who are their sponsors and entrepreneurs? How is a certain field made fertile for their reception?

And what of less flagrant or less overt sharings of knowledge or experimentation or innovation – a certain 'take' on risk, for instance, or a certain set of demands for auditing or accountability? Such questions also demand attention to the travels undertaken by criminological theories, explanatory models and terms as much as to policy enterprises as such. The international reach of certain of these (Braithwaite's (1989) account of shaming and reintegration springs to mind here) has been striking recently – but how are such effects accomplished and with what consequences? Indeed, this may be one of the more powerful illustrations of the power of criminology. For, despite the oft-lamented refrain that criminology and criminologists have remarkably little influence on their domestic policy-makers and practitioners, a shift of focus away from the minutiae of policy towards the narratives, rhetorics and metaphors developed by criminologists may provide more obvious examples of influence, particularly perhaps when their spread cross-nationally is taken into account. As Zedner (2003) has recently argued, the larger contribution of criminology is to be found not just in empirical research but also in the language and vocabulary it provides for enabling us to think about crime and justice. The ideas, the language and the conceptual frameworks developed by criminologists can, and some-times do, have a profound influence on politicians and policy-makers and, moreover, may do so far beyond local state boundaries, and the processes that underpin this deserve our attention just as much as those that lie behind the movement of the formal instruments of policy.

However, there is an inherent danger in all such activity. It is that in thinking about the global reach of ideas, policies and practices, our attention will tend to be drawn to convergence rather than divergence, to similarity rather than difference and to homogeneity rather than heterogeneity. Influential models and dictions meet resistances, counter-discourses and extant traditions and sensibilities. A crucial question for us, therefore, is how different are the ways in which ostensibly similar vocabularies are taken up and applied in the distinct settings they encounter? Just how diverse in terms of their social organisation, intellectual formation, political temper and points of intersection with policy networks and the wider public sphere are the 'criminologies' of contemporary European societies? How in turn do the latter intersect with and differ from the language and practice of crime control in North America or other regions of the world?

As should already be clear, a very significant focus of the concerns addressed in this book is with the USA and, more particularly, with the apparent influence that the culture of control that has emerged in the USA has exercised in other parts of the world. One immediate question, of course, is why the USA should be, or should appear to be, so dominant in this regard. One possibility, is that the federal and devolved nature of much American government has made the States, as many com-mentators have observed, the laboratories of democracy (Jenkins 2001: 162) or, more particularly, the penal workshop of the world. A second possible explanation is, as Muncie and others have noted, that what appears as 'globalisation' is in fact in many respects merely 'Americanisation' – the global spread and increasingly hegemonic influence of American cultural forms.

Though the 'presence' and influence of the USA on the cultures of control in other parts of the globe seem undeniable, we should also recognise that this focus may be somewhat misleading in helping make sense of current trajectories in crime control – what one of us has previously referred to as 'the distracting sway of the American case as a pole of attraction' (Sparks 2001: 165). What many of the contributions to this volume helpfully illustrate, in fact, are the limits of globalisation and, more particularly, its more particular associate, Americanisation. Indeed, the contributions from the UK, Australia and South Africa all illustrate the points of difference, the sites of resistance and the mediating influence of local political cultures.

The importance of politics and political culture

The central theme of many of the contributions to this volume (see, for example, Chapter 5) is that while much that is common to the cultures of control in contemporary advanced economies is the result of broad social, cultural, political and economic pressures, so it is also the case that particular socioeconomic, cultural and political contexts frame and shape in very different ways apparently mobile policy ideas. Moreover, it is clear that the nature of the politico-cultural environment to which ideas, practices and policies travel has a very significant impact on the eventual shape and destiny of the 'import'; or even if there is any import at all. As Lacey (2003: 86) observes, it is crucial for us to recognise 'that the salience and politicisation of criminal justice vary from country to country' and that our understanding of this variation remains far from developed (Tonry 2001). Understanding similarities and differences in the pattern of contemporary systems of crime control – and understanding the movement and translation of commodities between and within these systems – is therefore arguably one of the key tasks facing criminology.

Strictly speaking, translation, Melossi argues, is impossible. Rather, 'generally speaking any term, even the simplest, is embedded within a cultural context, or milieu, that gives it its meaning' (2000: 144). Of course, cultures are not hermetically sealed and it is the case that practices, policies and rhetorics travel and that, within limits, there can be, and are, common understandings. Nevertheless, his central argument, that we cannot and should not take for granted that surface similarities necessarily imply deeper convergences, is borne out in numerous examples throughout this book. A number of commentators have recently suggested that those criminological theories that focus on the broad swathe of changes being wrought by late modernity in systems of crime control pay insufficient regard to the variation in political cultures that exists, for example, within continental Europe (Nelken 2002; Lacey 2003). As Nelken (2002: 175) has noted, ' "penality" is as much a matter of cultural meaning as of instrumental effectivity ... But it is obvious that such meaning will vary from culture to culture (as well as within cultures)'.

As we have already implied, there is a balance to be struck between analysing and emphasising the extent to which these forces change and mould local systems and structures, on the one hand, and examining and charting the extent to which the impact of these forces differs and is played out in different forms in varying social, political and economic contexts. Given the very strong case made by David Garland for the importance of understanding the shared pattern of experience in the USA and UK (and by implication quite likely elsewhere), we have taken a slightly contrasting approach in this volume, and have sought to draw attention to the ways in which crime control *varies* under conditions of late modernity and, more particularly, to highlight the importance of considering how these differences relate to local political cultures.

How to approach such questions and, more particularly, how to investigate such variation, is a particularly challenging task. A recent interesting addition to the literature exploring this tension between broad structural changes and local socioeconomic circumstances is what Hall and Soskice (2001: 57) have called their 'Varieties of Capitalism' approach.[2] This, they suggest, 'calls into question the monolithic political dynamic conventionally associated with globalisation'. In this thesis they identify two ideal types that they refer to as 'liberal market economies' and 'co-ordinated market economies'. These are distinguished by the way in which firms within such economies resolve the co-ordination problems they face in the spheres of industrial relations, vocational training and education, corporate governance, interfirm relations and in relation to their own employees. In Hall and Soskice's distinction, liberal market economies are ones in which firms primarily co-ordinate their activities through hierarchies and competitive market arrangements. By contrast, co-ordinated market economies are ones in which firms rely to a greater extent on non-market relationships for co-ordination – they are more collaborative than the competitive liberal market economy. For Hall and Soskice, the advantage of this approach is that it helps to explain some of the key questions in comparative political economy, in particular why some states respond differently to the pressures of globalisation and convergence and, more particularly, how some appear to have a 'comparative institutional advantage' over others. For the criminologist, this approach – or some variant of it – directs our attention to possible means of exploring international differences in levels of crime, insecurity and the nature of the political and social responses to them.

One of the potential benefits of paying close attention to the role and impact of political cultures in the diffusion and exchange of crime control ideas is that it will temper the tendency to impose too much order and rationality on the process of policy formation. As most students of policy-making will attest, the emergence of particular ideas is rarely the product of a process which bears any relation to a rational choice model. Rather, at best they tend to be the product of messy compromises and uneasy and temporary alliances and exigencies. One of the most astute observations made by one of the more interesting commentators in this field, John Kingdon (see Kingdon 1995), is that solutions and answers, and problems and questions circulate in what he calls the 'political stream', often remarkably independently of each other. In this regard, solutions seek problems just as much as problems seek solutions. This is not to say that our task as analysts is not to seek, or to impose, a degree of analytical order on these processes. What we are attempting to encourage here, however, is the acceptance of the existence of a greater degree of disorder, disharmony and incompatibility of explanation than is often allowed for in this particular social scientific terrain.

Concluding comments

There are a number of analytically separable, but inextricably linked, tensions running through current work around, and conceptualisations of, convergence and divergence in crime control in the west. First, and crudely, there is the tension between work which on the one hand tends to focus on the broad sweep of structural change and that which, on the other hand, considers the more particular concerns of policy development and change within particular jurisdictions. Secondly, there is the related tension between literatures which focus upon the macro-level concerns of globalisation – and its related concepts and processes – and those which are more concerned with the meso- and micro-level issues of governance and governmentality. Thirdly, work of a more broadly structural character, concerned with globalisation is, for the most part, primarily theoretical in character and, ironically given its overarching focus, somewhat 'placeless' in its concerns. As such, it is often quite distinct from, and in a certain amount of tension with, work that is more obviously concerned with politics and political culture which is heavy with meaning, tradition and symbol, very particularly located and, at least some of the time, more richly empirical in character. Now, clearly, we caricature somewhat in outlining these tensions and divergences for in practice the differences are not so visible or entrenched. Nevertheless, in taking forward the criminological enterprise in this area it is, we would suggest, necessary to recognise and seek to begin to overcome the difficulties inherent in marrying concerns which of necessity are simultaneously broadly generalised and empirically particular.

Notes

1   The original genesis of this book lies a bit further in the past in a conversation we had outside a café during a large thematic criminology conference in November 2000. We were both reflecting on the nature of such events and how difficult it often seems to develop any form of lengthy dialogue around particular issues of criminological concern. All too often one finds oneself in a 90-minute session in which not only are four papers to be delivered but also in subject-matter and approach they may bear relatively little relation to each other. We both felt that it would be fruitful to hold some form of contrasting event, involving only a small number of people, over two days, in which a limited number of papers would be given and discussed. Sometimes it seems that attempts to shift the disciplinary conversation on to slightly different ground need to take place in other venues and formats.
2   We are grateful to Nicola Lacey for drawing this to our attention.

References

Bauman, Z. (2001a) *Community: Seeking Safety in an Insecure World*. Cambridge: Polity Press.

Bauman, Z. (2001b) *The Individualized Society*. Cambridge: Polity Press.

Bayley, D. and Shearing, C. (1996) 'The future of policing', *Law and Society Review*, 30(3): 586–606.

Bennett, C. (1991) 'What is policy convergence and what causes it?', *British Journal of Political Science*, 21: 215–233

Best, J. (2001) 'The diffusion of social problems', in J. Best (ed.) *How Claims Spread: Cross-national Diffusion of Social Problems*. New York, NY: Aldine de Gruyter.

Braithwaite, J. (1989) *Crime, Shame and Reintegration*. Cambridge: Cambridge University Press.

Castells, M. (2000) *The Rise of the Network Society*. Oxford: Blackwell.

Castells, M. (2001) *The Internet Galaxy: Reflections on the Internet, Business and Society*. Oxford: Oxford University Press.

Crawford, A. (2000) 'Contrasts in victim/offender mediation and appeals to community in comparative cultural contexts: France and England and Wales', in D. Nelken (ed.) *Contrasting Criminal Justice*. Aldershot: Dartmouth.

Dolowitz, D. (2000) 'Policy transfer: a new framework of policy analysis?', in D. Dolowitz (ed.) *Policy Transfer and British Social Policy: Learning from the USA?*. Buckingham: Open University Press.

Dolowitz, D. and Marsh, D. (1996) 'Who learns what from whom? A review of the policy transfer literature', *Political Studies*, 44: 343–57.

Eyestone, R. (1977) 'Confusion, diffusion and innovation', *American Political Science Review*, 71: 441–53.

Garland, D. (1996) 'The limits of the sovereign state: strategies of crime control in contemporary society', *British Journal of Criminology*, 36(4): 445–71.

Garland, D. (2001) *The Culture of Control*. Oxford: Oxford University Press.

Giddens, A. (1991) *Modernity and Self-identity: Self and Society in the Late Modern Age*. Cambridge: Polity Press.

Hall, P.A. and Soskice, D. (2001) 'Introduction', in P.A. Hall and D. Soskice (eds) *Varieties of Capitalism: The Institutional Foundations of Comparative Advantage*. Oxford: Oxford University Press.

Jenkins, P. (2001) 'How Europe discovered its sex-offender crisis', in J. Best (ed.) *How Claims Spread: Cross-national Diffusion of Social Problems*. New York, NY: Aldine de Gruyter.

Jones, T. and Newburn, T. (1999) 'Urban change and policing: mass private property reconsidered', *European Journal on Criminal Policy and Research*, 7: 225–44.

Jones, T. and Newburn, T. (2002) 'The transformation of policing? Understanding current trends in policing systems', *British Journal of Criminology*, 42: 129–46.

King, M. (1989) 'Social crime prevention *a la* Thatcher', *Howard Journal of Criminal Justice*, 28: 291–312.

Kingdon, J. (1995) *Agendas, Alternatives and Public Policies* (2nd edn.) New York, NY: HarperCollins.

Lacey, N. (2003) 'Principles, politics and criminal justice', in L. Zedner and A. Ashworth (eds) *The Criminological Foundations of Penal Policy: Essays in Honour of Roger Hood*. Oxford: Clarendon Press.

Lacey, N. and Zedner, L. (1995) 'Discourses of community in criminal justice', *Journal of Law and Society*, 22(1): 301–20.

Lacey, N. and Zedner, L. (1998) 'Community in German criminal justice: a significant absence?' *Social and Legal Studies*, 7: 7–25.

Lash, S. and Urry, J. (1993) *Economies of Signs and Space*. London: Sage.

Melossi, D. (2000) 'Translating social control: reflections on the comparison of Italian and North American cultures concerning social control, with a few consequences for "critical" criminology', in S. Karstedt and K.-D. Bussmann (eds) *Social Dynamics of Crime and Control*. Oxford: Hart Publishing.

Melossi, D. and Selmini, R. (2000) 'Social conflict and the microphysics of crime. The experience of the Emulia-Romagna Citta sicure project', in T. Hope and R. Sparks (eds) *Crime, Risk and Insecurity*. London: Routledge.

Nelken, D. (ed) (1994) *The Futures of Criminology*. London: Sage.

Nelken, D. (1997) *Comparing Legal Cultures*. Aldershot: Dartmouth.

Nelken, D. (2000) *Contrasting Criminal Justice*. Aldershot: Dartmouth.

Nelken, D. (2002) 'Comparing Criminal Justice', in M. Maguire *et al.* (eds) *The Oxford Handbook of Criminology* (3rd edn). Oxford: Oxford University Press.

Newburn, T. (2002) 'Atlantic crossings: 'policy transfer' and crime control in the USA and Britain', *Punishment and Society*, 4(2): 169–94.

Radzinowicz, Sir L. (1999) *Adventures in Criminology*, London: Routledge.

Rogers, E.M. (1995) *The Diffusion of Innovations* (4th edn). New York, NY: The Free Press.

Rose, R. (1993) 'What is lesson drawing?', *Journal of Public Policy*, 11: 3–30.

Salvatore, R.D. and Aguirre, C. (1996) *The Birth of the Penitentiary in Latin America: Essays on Criminology, Prison Reform, and Social Control, 1830–1940*. Austin, TX: University of Texas Press.

Sozzo, M. (2001) ' "Traduttore Traditore". Traducción, importación cultural e historia del presente de la criminología en América Latina', *Cuadernos de doctrina y jurisprudencia penal*, 13.

Sparks, R. (2001) 'Degrees of estrangement: the cultural theory of risk and comparative penology', *Theoretical Criminology*, 5(2): 159–76.

Stone, D. (1999) 'Learning lessons and transferring policy across time, space and disciplines', *Politics*, 19(1): 51–9.

Tarde, G. (1903) *The Laws of Imitation*. New York, NY: Holt.

Tonry, M. (2001) 'Symbol, substance and severity in western penal policies', *Punishment and Society*, 3(4): 417–36.

Urry, J. (1999) *Sociology beyond Societies*. London: Routledge.

Wacquant, L. (1999) 'How penal common sense comes to Europeans: notes on the transatlantic diffusion of the neoliberal doxa', *European Societies*, 1(3): 319–52.

Weber, M. (1978) *Economy and Society. Vol. 1*. Berkeley, CA: University of California Press.

Willis, P. (2000) *The Ethnographic Imagination*. Cambridge: Polity Press.

Young, J. (1999) *The Exclusive Society: Social Exclusion, Crime and Difference in Late Modernity*. London: Sage.

Zedner, L. (2003) 'Useful knowledge? Debating the role of criminology in post-war Britain', in L. Zedner and A. Ashworth (eds) *The Criminological Foundations of Penal Policy: Essays in Honour of Roger Hood*. Oxford: Clarendon Press.

Chapter 2

Durkheim, Tarde and beyond: the global travel of crime policies

Susanne Karstedt

Travelling institutions

Despite his mostly pessimistic views on humankind, the philosopher Voltaire had his moments of optimism. Obviously, he was optimistic as an anglophile, when he explored how British institutions could help the continent to develop the liberties and the political institutions which the British people enjoyed in contrast to the French and other nations on the continent in his time. He was the most famous among eighteenth-century European intellectuals for whom Britain was a model of political institutions and the liberties they guaranteed, which was the more attractive since it was combined with economic success, industrial innovations and all the insignia of a rising hegemonic power. From the eighteenth century, Britain emerged as a provider and exporter of institutional models, not only as a colonial power but because of the attraction and attractiveness of a wide range of its institutions, a process which was certainly fuelled by its world hegemony during the nineteenth century. Its political institutions were widely admired, even by revolutionaries like Marx, its business institutions and regulatory bodies eagerly adopted. In particular, the 'Gentleman' emerged as a model that fired the imagination of continental intellectuals. Thus, Baron de Coubertin, inventor and promoter of the Olympics, was first of all inspired by the model of the 'gentleman' and his education, in particular sports and fair play as in the regime of Dr Arnold in Rugby whom he worshipped in a quite effusive way. The Olympic Games originally were a hybrid of Dr Arnold's regime and French nationalism, which today suffers from an additional layer of McDonaldisation imposed by the most recent hegemonic model. When Theodor Herzl, the founder and first leader of the Zionist movement, looked for an institutional model for the future Jewish nation-state, he turned to Britain for inspiration, but not to the cherished institutions of Parliament, the press or a kind of constitutional monarchy. The institution he had in mind as a cornerstone of his vision of the Jewish nation-state was the British gentleman and aristocrat, and he conceptualised a Jewish aristocracy in 'Altneuland' just like the one that he had found and admired in Britain (Buruma 2000).[1]

There are several lessons to be learnt from Ian Buruma's collection of intriguing accounts how British models travelled across the globe.[2] First and most obvious, the models of the hegemonic power travel well, though they do neither by sheer power, nor by military or economic coercion, as Braithwaite and Drahos (2000) point out. It is a process that involves a diverse set of mechanisms, amongst them the amount of accumulated expertise and intellectual leadership in many fields. Secondly, institutions and models might change their shape considerably in travelling, and even might be hardly recognisable when embedded into a foreign structure and institutional design. Finally, attempts to send institutions and models abroad might be utterly unsuccessful, and they never arrive at foreign shores.

These lessons apply equally to the ways and routes that crime policies take when travelling around the globe. In their chapter on convergence, Jones and Newburn (Chapter 7) give a brilliant account of how the transport of a crime control model from the USA to the UK failed, notwithstanding a powerful rhetoric and obvious interests in such a transport of Megan's law. None the less, there can be no doubt that the exchange and transport of criminal justice policies take place on a global scale today. New strategies of crime prevention, procedures of dealing with offences, offenders and victims, models of institutions and interventions for juvenile and adult offenders rapidly spread around the globe, and knowledge is shared among the 'epistemic communities' of criminologists, criminal justice and policing experts, and practitioners. More than a decade ago this seemed to be a one-way and dead-end road from western industrialised countries mainly to those in the Third World, from the centre to the periphery. This has considerably changed, the model of restorative justice being a leader in reversing the direction. More space and attention are given to indigenous developments of crime prevention and the criminal justice system. Programmes of restorative justice, community policing and crime prevention, and situational crime prevention were implemented in many countries and different cultures, but it became more and more obvious that the process

17

of transport and implementation was in many ways shaped by the specific cultures of control that were involved in this process as 'exporters' as well as 'importers' (Karstedt 2001).

Long before the contours of the global travelling of crime policies became visible, Stanley Cohen (1982) had warned criminologists about the dangers of such a transport, in particular when western crime control models were implemented in the Third World. He strongly criticised that at a time when community crime control and the dispersal of control into the community were favoured in western countries, the traditional community control in Third World countries was increasingly destroyed by bringing in more police, courts and prisons. He pointed to the naïvety and lack of sensitivity of western criminologists who not only transported what they thought were general theories of crime, but also in conclusion from their findings recommended crime prevention policies which restricted rural–urban migration and exactly mirrored those that were enforced in apartheid South Africa at that time. But even if the distance of travel is much shorter and the exporting and importing countries share at least some dominant characteristics of western culture, the distinct institutional and political cultures decisively shape the process of adoption and implementation. Lacey and Zedner (2000) compared the development of locally based prevention initiatives in Britain and Germany, Germany being the 'importing' country. In Germany, the typical corporatist political culture and the ideology of professionalism significantly restricted volunteer involvement, in contrast to Britain. Rhetorics of community were much more subdued than in Britain, and the decentralised political structure in Germany finally gave rise to a very different system of partnerships and co-operation of agencies in communities.[3]

However, crime policies do not only take single routes from country to country, or from culture to culture in the global exchange. They increasingly travel within a transnational and global institutional context. The development of transnational policing in the EU provides such a context that is characterised by 'a complex, ever-shifting mix of informal professional networks, intergovernmental co-operation and novel supranational institutions (Europol)' (Loader, see Chapter 4). This will change the process of transport and adoption of crime policies into one of standardisation and unification which considerably disempowers those on whom such new crime policies are imposed. Consequently, Loader in particular questions the democratic legitimacy of this process. In addition, crime policies are on their routes of travelling increasingly subject to international institutions and human rights regimes, including non-governmental organisations, and international criminal justice institutions might become increasingly powerful in imposing standards of criminal justice and crime prevention.

In this chapter I want to explore how we can conceptualise these modes and routes of travelling. I start with the question: what exactly is travelling when 'crime policies' travel? Next, I analyse the concepts that underlie our notion of such travelling, and explore the problems of 'overarching' concepts which play a decisive role in recent analyses of the globalisation of criminal justice policies. Finally, I contrast these with loosely coupled concepts as has been suggested by Braithwaite and Drahos (2000) in their analysis of global business regulation.

What travels with crime policies?

We find practices, strategies and technologies of crime prevention travelling around the globe. CCTV is a technology that has been widely adopted by communities and business in many countries, though perhaps much less on the continent than in Britain. Private policing has risen to or even overtaken the number of public police nearly every-where (Braithwaite 2000). Private prisons or electronic monitoring obviously travel at a much slower pace, with some tentative implemen-tation in Britain and first 'experiments' in Germany, though private prisons are now discussed in this country. Neighbourhood Watch is a quite common feature of community crime prevention in Britain, but has never been implemented in Germany with the exception of some projects that by no way can be rated as a success. The very idea of community volunteers who take up a mission of crime watch seems to appeal much less to the German public, which has a collective memory of such 'volunteers' in its totalitarian past, in particular in post-communist Eastern Germany.

Even if practices and technologies travel more or less on their own they need an institutional link to be 'plugged in', and these are existing practices and institutional patterns as well as the legal system that allow for or restrict their implementation. The adoption of strategies and techniques of policing might become quite dangerous if institutional checks and balances are missing. Private policing might become a nightmare if the public police already operates as a kind of private enterprise and with little restriction and regulation, and zero tolerance might become a tool for repression and justification of unrestricted use of force when executed by a police who exert it according to their own rules against a public that has no chance to check such practices.

Crime policies comprise more than a technology, a practice or a strategy. They have to be conceptualised as integrated concepts, which have emerged in a particular institutional setting and in a legal and public culture of crime prevention and control. They are decisively local and national. Specific values and symbolic meanings are as much part of them as are particular institutional designs. The difficulties of even literally 'translating' these concepts (see Chapter 5) make the problems of 'transport', 'import' and 'export' obvious. There is no proper term in German for 'community crime prevention' that can grasp its semantic, in particular not the context of the social fabric of a neighbourhood and community. The translation only refers to the political body of the municipality, but misses out on the sense it has in the context of the UK and the USA. Lacey and Zedner's research testifies to these problems and, notwithstanding the fact that the concept of community crime prevention was a very successful traveller, it definitely changed its shape and lost some of its meaning when implemented in Germany. Crime policies often travel as ideas and concepts, and consequently become part of an emerging rhetoric among politicians (see Chapter 7), or within networks of experts. Even if they finally do not arrive in other nations in their original shape, the widespread adoption of community crime prevention schemes in nearly all European countries shows that ideas and concepts are quite powerful travellers, as well within polity and expert networks as in social movements and NGOs.[4]

Crime policies as concepts and ideas travel on the routes of cross-cultural exchange, and consequently all problems of such exchange are involved here. They have to be checked for differences as well as common ground with the cultural practices of control into which they are going to be integrated. None the less, the problem of travelling crime policies would be unduly restricted if cast as a problem of cross-cultural exchange with its specific burdens (Karstedt 2001).[5] In the present discussion about the 'culture of control' (Garland 2001), the institutional pattern and in particular the structure of political institutions and their impact on the transport and exchange of crime policies needs equal attention. The fact that countries differ with regard to the centralisation/decentralisation of their political and institutional structure might account for the differences in the adoption of crime policies and practices. The USA is but one example with considerable differences in criminal justice policies between the federal states. In Germany, the federal states (*Länder*) have responsibility for their police forces. In addition, many if not a majority of the *Länder* have a government formed by the party in opposition to the one in power at the federal level. Consequently, the adoption of new crime policies will be decentralised, and influence of the federal government fairly restricted, which might account for the comparatively minor role which crime polices have in federal election campaigns. Thus electronic monitoring and tagging were first introduced by a newly elected conservative government in one of the states but have not yet spread to other states on a considerable scale.

The continental 'consensus model of democracy' (Lijphart 1999) with governments formed by coalitions of a broad range of parties had an impact on the adoption as well as on the change of welfare policies, in particular on the implementation of more neoliberal policies in these countries during recent decades. We can assume a comparable impact on the adoption of crime policies. Though all European countries introduced new welfare policies clearly inspired by neoliberalism, they mitigated the original 'welfare-to-work' model and came up with new and inventive practices that neither precisely mirrored those in the USA nor those in the UK (in particular, Denmark and the Netherlands; see Lijphart 1999). From this perspective, the 'culture of control' which Garland describes as the general road that crime policies have taken in the USA and the UK seems to be the product of a two-party system which in particular fuels the punitiveness of political and public discourse on crime policies, and of an institutional pattern that allows for easy travelling of increasingly punitive policies.

Legal culture, constitutions and the decisions of higher and the constitutional courts form another, decisive part of the institutional pattern in which crime policies are travelling and which defines their adoption. The European Court is taking an increasingly active role in ruling on human rights issues, and this development will certainly affect how crime policies travel in particular to and within Europe, including the UK.

Which routes do crime policies take when they are travelling? Crime policies are obviously not disseminated in a process of diffusion or by mere imitation, but within 'epistemic communities' that are linked across borders, but locally embedded. They travel between different institutionalised and established discourses: political discourses, legal and public discourses, professional and social movement discourses. None the less, these are highly structured networks, dense in some parts, and only loosely coupled or clearly disconnected in other parts. Jones and Newburn (Chapter 7) describe the political networks that had a decisive impact in facilitating American influences on crime control in the UK during the past decade. Though the German social-democratic candidate, Gerhard Schröder, was eager to copy the successful election campaign of New Labour, crime policies never had a prominent role in his own campaign, which brought him and his party to power in 1998.

For a more neoliberal approach to welfare, the German government went model-shopping to the Netherlands and Denmark. Concepts of crime policies do not diffuse throughout networks but take traditional and established trajectories of cultural exchange.

In particular during the last decade, crime policies took two-way roads instead of the one from the hegemonic centre to the periphery. Restorative justice is the most prominent example of a concept that took up peripheral concepts and values, and transported them back to the centre. The South African Truth and Reconciliation Commission was based on this concept and now serves as a model, a process in which international organisations have a decisive role. Local traditions of social control have emerged as a source to tap in the exchange of crime control models, and they need a positive defence and strong reinforcement which – paradoxically – today often comes from the centre. The travel mode of 'indigenisation' of crime policies – a term borrowed from cross-cultural psychology (see Karstedt 2001: 295ff.) – seems to become increasingly important. It implies that concepts are adapted and blended into the existing culture of control, on the one hand, and that indigenous concepts or 'blended ones' travel from the periphery to the centre on the other hand.

Conceptualising the movement of crime policies

The notion that crime policies are 'travelling' indicates a considerable shift away from one of the strongest and most thriving intellectual traditions of criminology. Starting with Durkheim, the development of penal laws, penal institutions and the modes of social control have been linked – in functionalist and quite deterministic ways – to the process of modernisation. The change of the system of criminal justice and of its most important part – the emergence of the modern prison – was the result and simultaneously signified the structural, economic and cultural changes that societies experienced on their path towards modernity. Changes of the penal system not only illuminated these structural changes but the system itself and its institutions also seemed to emerge as central institutions in modern societies that absorbed these changes and condensed them into the symbols of control in industrial society. Crime policies and penal institutions develop as a necessary product of the political economy, the 'civilising process' or a process of concentration of power and diffusion of discipline, and consequently they converge during this process, from the core to the periphery.

The adoption of such unilateral models in criminology has been underpinned by a shared and common notion that the state acquired and possessed quite unrestricted power and domination, and consequently the penal system should be highly sensitive to any shifts in this power. Though a 'Leviathan' model of the state was contrasted with the 'penology model' of the Keynesian and welfare state, both were equally invested with power and domination, and the state was seen as being capable of controlling society either by discipline or by welfare or a mixture of both. Being linked in such a way to the central mechanisms of the modern state, the penal system emerged as part of its centre (for a discussion of the Keynesian model, see Braithwaite 2000).

Without any doubt these concepts have enhanced our understanding of the historical process that produced modern penal systems, but they are based on a unilateral perspective of the process of modernisation, and presumably on an exaggeration of the role of penal institutions in this process, both questioned today. The forces of penal change might have shifted and presently produce a much more diverse universe of penal institutions, even under the same conditions of 'neoliberalism', 'risk society' and 'market societies' (see O'Malley 1999, 2001; see Chapter 3). On the other hand, the processes by which penal institutions become similar under specific conditions might be more complicated as such 'iron-cage' models contend.

In socioeconomic theories of modernisation the unilateral model and the idea of convergence have been substituted by the concept of 'path dependent' modernisation. The rise of southeast Asian economies showed that not only different conditions at the start but also traditions preserved or abandoned, decisions taken and models adopted shaped the highly diverse trajectories of modernisation. On the other hand the similarity of organisations and institutions that emerge in the globalised economy is the outcome of processes as different as competition, adaption, normative pressure and imitation.[6] The trajectories of modernity are defined by loosely coupled causal patterns, and not driven by a single force.

Criminology has accepted the idea of path dependency and diverse trajectories in the term 'genealogy', but simultaneously new 'over-arching' concepts have been developed and old ones have been revived. In particular, the emergence of 'actuarial justice' has been linked to neoliberal policies and the specific characteristics of modern 'risk societies', the central role of imprisonment in recent crime policies to the political economy of immigrant labour (Melossi 2001), and the convergence of crime policies into an overarching 'culture of control' to post-welfare policies. But the evidence from such diverse trajectories of change that criminal policies take in the Netherlands, Australia or the Scandinavian countries strongly suggests the path dependency of such developments, and this is exactly what the notion of travel implies: decisions taken at cross-roads, different destinations and different points of departure. The concept of path dependency implies the use of loosely coupled concepts instead of 'strong', unilateral and deterministic ones, though such concepts are not intended to rival or eclipse other more abstract explanations for the global travel of crime policies. Nor is it implied that they cannot be linked to structural theories of these processes. Explanations by 'mechanisms' and structural explanation can be complementary rather than contradictory, in particular in the case of 'modelling' mechanisms. But they should allow for the explanation of those phenomena that are often dismissed as 'exceptions' when the 'strong' concepts are used, and the global genealogy of penal practices includes as many 'exceptions' as 'fitting cases'.

Actors, mechanisms and principles

Braithwaite and Drahos (2000: 15–26) base their study of global business regulation – which strikes a common cord with many of the problems involved in the travel of crime policies – on three concepts: actors, including government agencies, organisations and networks or com-munities of actors; mechanisms as causal mechanisms which link chains of events; and principles or rationales which are standing behind a penal system and its rules, and which serve as general guidelines for actors in their decisions to adopt crime policies which are on offer in the global marketplace.[7]

Principles in the realm of crime policies are by no ways exclusively of a legal or juristic character. Beside the obvious role of law on the national level, human rights principles will certainly become more important on the global and supranational level (see Chapter 4). Pat O'Malley's (2001; see Chapter 3) analysis of the development of crime policies in Australia, which clearly deviated from what could have been expected from the endorsement of neoliberal market policies by different Australian governments, shows the powerful impact of such principles. Instead of adopting actuarial justice on a large scale and for different groups of offenders, three principles were in strong opposition to this. The principle of 'harm mimimisation' guided drug policies and the im-plementation of various measures to prevent drug abuse, to deal with drug addicts and to protect the public. The principle of 'inclusive solutions' was the backbone of policies for young people who were affected by chronic unemployment and economic and structural change. The Aboriginal population were seen as victims of a pathogenic situation, and the principle of 'cultural sensitiveness' prevented a further increase of the none the less over-representation of this group in Australian prisons (Broadhurst forthcoming).

Besides such a quite powerful instrumental use of principles, their rhetorical and symbolic use seems to be equally important in the realm of crime policies, as shown by Jones and Newburn (see Chapter 7). Edelman (1964) observes that principles are introduced to produce 'political quiescence' amongst the public. Notwithstanding a huge amount of pressure from the public and the media, the final failure to implement 'Sarah's Law' in the UK – modelled on 'Megan's Law' in the USA – shows how rhetorical and mere symbolic use of principles connect to the (non)import of crime policies. In addition, just as in the UK, 'zero tolerance' policies are only tentatively and very selectively introduced into European countries, whilst the hesitant and more or less symbolic implementation is accompanied by an excess use of rhetoric. Some symbols and rhetorical signposts actually seem to act against the transport of the related crime policies. A rhetorical 'war' on crime or drugs has never been launched in Scandinavia, Germany or Australia, and the rhetorical figure of a 'Drug Tsar' has not entered the public dialogue, while there seems to be little hesitation in the UK to import such autocratic language from one of the oldest democracies in the world.

Principles are contested between the public, politicians, the judiciary and the professionals within the criminal justice system. The discrepancy between the travel of ideas and concepts and their implementation – the 'streams of influence' and the 'level of impact' (see Chapter 7) – might be caused by such a contest of principles as became visible in the recent discussion about drug policies in the UK.

Crime polices are embedded in local and national institutional patterns, and they travel by cross-national and cross-cultural exchange. This is the reason why 'modelling' is the most important mechanism accounting for the routes and the shape they take when travelling (Karstedt 2001).[8] Other, more coercive or reciprocal mechanisms (discussed below) might play an extended role in inter-governmental co-operation or novel supranational institutions. Powerful economic interests might exert pressure in the field of private policing and private prisons, but still most of the exchange of crime policies seems to be done by modelling them.

Modelling has to be conceptualised as more than mere imitation – going beyond Tarde (1908). Modelling means 'observational learning with a symbolic content, not just the simple response mimicry implied by the term "imitation"' (Braithwaite and Drahos 2000: 580). Models are interpreted as instrumental and symbolic concepts by those who copy their content and their symbolic meaning, and the global travel of crime policies is thus achieved by 'observational learning with a symbolic content'. Modelling therefore emerges as a mechanism that is related to cultural and institutional identity, and crime policies will travel on routes which sustain cultural identity. Thus, perceptions of a shared cultural identity might explain the eager willingness of the public and politicians in the UK to adopt crime policies from the USA in comparison to Australia or other European countries. Models are adopted from the hegemonic power not because of coercion or constraint but because they come with a particular image of success. Consequently, modelling mostly takes the route from the centre to the periphery – and sometimes with disastrous consequences (Cohen 1982) – however, the development of restorative justice shows that the opposite direction might become increasingly important as a modelling process of empowerment for the powerless.

Modelling seems to be the mechanism that helps in particular to explain the variance in cultural and institutional patterns of crime policies and their trajectories amidst the global change towards 'risk societies' and neoliberal policies (see Braithwaite and Drahos 2000: 581). None the less, structural change seems to be not only a precondition for starting the process (and its timing) but in addition for successful implementation within a specific structural pattern. The quite vivid exchange of crime prevention models within the EU – notwithstanding their diversity – might be related to the (though) slow process of structural, legal and political processes of alignment.

Despite a seeming dominance of modelling, mechanisms of (economic) coercion and non-reciprocal negotiations are to be found where specific national and supranational interests are involved, mainly in the EU. Eastern European states applying for membership in the EU and to the Council of Europe have to change their criminal justice policies – in particular to abolish the death penalty – and adjust them to human rights regimes. Border policing has been one of the fields where economic pressures were exerted on the eastern European states to prohibit asylum seekers from entering the Schengen countries. Strategies of policing, including training and equipment, were exported to these states in order to prosecute offences committed in EU countries, focusing on border-crossing crimes.

Future roads for crime policies

It is a common characteristic of the crime policies that have been travelling during the last decades that they targeted 'street crime' and the other frequent types of crime mostly at the level of communities. Policies against border-crossing crimes were mostly developed at the transnational and international level. In contrast, crime policies against corruption, corporate crime and crimes of the powerful have got a late start, if they have started at all. Only in 1999 did the OECD oblige its member states to prosecute corrupt exchanges that had been committed abroad.

Obviously, crime policies that are designed to control a 'new underclass' (immigrants and foreigners) – as community crime prevention had been conceptualised in Germany (Lacey and Zedner 2000) – have mainly served as models during the last decades, while those that might control the powerful were less mobile. In addition, policies that addressed crime problems caused by extreme inequality, authoritarianism and dependency have rarely shown up on the road, notwithstanding that they are in urgent demand. It is in particular under these structural conditions that the import of crime policies can have 'malignant' (Cohen 1982) consequences, however well intended the transport is. The import of CCTV or private policing into these socio-economic environments might actually stabilise and prolong such conditions. Legal principles, in particular recognition of human rights, have played a more subdued role in the cross-national exchange of crime policies. Future travel of crime policies needs to be accompanied by human rights assessments of their implementation and impact.

Notes

1 All examples are taken from Ian Buruma's (2000) intriguing book, *Voltaire's Coconuts or Anglomania in Europe.*
2 See Anderson (1991) in particular on the adoption of British models in the colonial empire.
3 Consequently, German communities went 'model-shopping', mostly in the Netherlands and Belgium with similar political structures.
4 See Braithwaite and Drahos (2000) for a discussion of the role of NGOs in the transport of concepts, principles and ideas around the globe.
5 Concepts and institutions are vital if not defining parts of cultural patterns and, as such, they are embedded in the social structure as much as in the minds of people. It seems to be more a question of perspective on which type of pattern our analysis is focused. Given the more than 200 definitions

of culture, the culture of crime control does not need a specific one (see Melossi 2001); see Karstedt (2001) for a discussion of concepts of culture in criminology and cross-cultural research on crime and control.

6   DiMaggio and Powell (1983) define these as processes of 'isomorphism'. Their analysis suggests a slightly different perspective on the emergence of the modern prison: that it was *modelled* on the two most successful new inventions of organisations at that time, the factory and the modern army.

7   They are relying on an approach that Jon Elster (1989) advocates. He argues that events are best explained in terms of causal mechanisms that relate such events, but which are not general laws. Braithwaite and Drahos (2000: 15) state that 'mechanisms in Elster's sense are shortish causal mechanisms which are not generalizable as laws'. This clearly sets mechanisms apart from the causal chains in the over-theoretical models of penal change.

8   This might change considerably if the USA continues to exert pressure and coercion on states to change criminal procedures and penal laws against terrorism.

References

Anderson, B. (1991) *Imagined Communities. Reflections on the Spread and Origin of Nationalism* (2nd edn). London: Verso.

Braithwaite, J. (2000) 'The new regulatory state and the transformation of criminology', in D. Garland and R. Sparks (eds) *Criminology and Social Theory*. Oxford: Oxford University Press, 47–70.

Braithwaite, J. and Drahos, P. (2000) *Global Business Regulation*. Cambridge: Cambridge University Press.

Broadhurst, R. (2002) 'Crime and indigenous people', in A. Graycar (ed.) *The Cambridge Handbook of Australian Criminology*. Cambridge: Cambridge University Press.

Buruma, I. (2000) *Voltaire's Coconuts or Anglomania in Europe*. London: Phoenix.

Cohen, S. (1982) 'Western crime control models in the third world: benign or malignant?', *Research in Law, Deviance and Social Control*, 4: 85–119.

DiMaggio, P.J. and Powell, W.W. (1983) 'The iron cage revisited: institutional isomorphism and collective rationality in organizational fields', *American Sociological Review*, 48: 147–60.

Edelman, M. (1964) *The Symbolic Uses of Politics*. Urbana-Champaign, IL: University of Illinois Press.

Elster, J. (1989) *Nuts and Bolts for the Social Sciences*. Cambridge: Cambridge University Press.

Garland, D. (2001) *The Culture of Control. Crime and Social Order in Contemporary Society*. Oxford: Oxford University Press.

Karstedt, S. (2001) 'Comparing cultures, comparing crime: challenges, prospects and problems for a global criminology', *Crime, Law and Social Change*, 36: 285–308.

Karstedt, S. (2003) 'Legacies of a Culture of Inequality: The Janus-Face of Crime in Post-Communist Societies'. *Crime, Law and Social Change*, 40: 295–320.

Lacey, N. and Zedner, L. (2000) '"Community" and governance: a cultural comparison', in S. Karstedt and K.-D. Bussmann (eds) *Social Dynamics of Crime and Control*. Oxford: Hart Publishing, 157–70.

Lijphart, A. (1999) *Patterns of Democracy. Government Forms in Thirty-six Countries*. New Haven, CT, and London: Yale University Press.

Melossi, D. (2001) 'The crime of modernity: punishment, crime and migration in Italy (1863–1997)'. Paper presented at the annual meeting of the American Sociological Association, Anaheim, CA.

O'Malley, P. (1999) 'Volatile and contradictory punishment', *Theoretical Criminology*, 3: 175–96.

O'Malley, P. (2001) 'The promise of risk'. Paper given at the Department of Criminology, Keele University.

Tarde, G. (1908) *Die sozialen Gesetze. Skizze zu einer Soziologie*. Leipzig: Klinkhardt.

Chapter 3

Globalising risk? Distinguishing styles of 'neoliberal' criminal justice in Australia and the USA

Pat O'Malley

The development of risk and 'risk society' themes in current social theory has been associated in criminology with a widespread effort to identify more and more examples of risk-based justice, in more and more countries. In addition to the USA and the UK, risk has been identified as a technique in the criminal justice systems of many countries, including Canada, Australia, New Zealand, France, Germany and Italy (e.g. Castel 1991; Feeley and Simon 1992; O'Malley 1992; Hebenton and Thomas 1996; Beck 1997; Ericson and Haggerty 1998; Pratt 1998; see Melossi, Chapter 5). Perhaps reflecting Beck's (1992) view that risk is becoming a form of governmental consciousness that is global in its reach and implications, criminologists generally have been content – if often dismayed – to identify more and more examples of risk technique in the governance of crime, affecting more and more people. Consequently there has been much less emphasis on the significance of political and technical differences *among* risk technologies than on their unity as instances of risk. Yet there is surely a major gulf of form and function separating, say, the 'new vigilantism' of Megan's laws from either the therapeutic interventions of developmental crime prevention or the economically rational criminology that characterises situational crime prevention.

The partial exception to this overemphasis on risk per se has been the attention paid to the question of how technologies of risk are shaped by the political rationalities with which they are articulated. The contrast between social-liberal (welfare) and neoliberal approaches to risk, for example, has been one site for such work in criminal justice (e.g. O'Malley 1992; Rose 2000). Even this work, perhaps, is affected by a form of globalised thinking, as it is assumed that the meaning or application of 'neoliberal' is pretty well identical in nature and impact across jurisdictional and national boundaries. Yet the virulently anti-welfare stance of the US neoliberalism has little in parallel in 'neoliberal' countries such as Australia, Canada and New Zealand, where welfare apparatuses are substantially intact, if partially 'translated' into forms more compatible with economically rational sensibilities (e.g. Dean 1995).

If we attend to such differences in risk techniques and in political rationalities, then we should not expect that risk-based strategies and policies will take on substantially similar forms in all 'neoliberal' countries. Nor should we assume that variations will be of such minor nature that their 'joint' character as risk based and neoliberal will be enough to render them readily transferable among jurisdictions. In this light, I want to examine two closely linked questions. The first is why it is that 'actuarial justice', for many criminologists almost the definitive form of risk-based criminal justice, has been almost without impact in Australia. The second concerns why Australia rejected an American-style War on Drugs – a 'war' that has done much to fuel actuarial justice in the USA and that deploys actuarial techniques coercively. Instead of adopting these socially exclusionary technologies of risk, in Australia the most highly developed and visible development of risk-based governance has been a national policy of drug harm minimisation that makes a *socially integrative* strategy out of risk.

Actuarial justice in the USA

Actuarial justice has been identified as the ascendant strategy of 'risk based' criminal justice (Feeley and Simon 1992, 1994). In this form, risk-based justice is predictive and statistical, and is systematically and managerially arranged in terms of internal or system-focused criteria of efficiency (such as speed of throughput rather than reduction in recidivism rates). It also incorporates forms of knowledge and practice that reduce the interventions of justice to merely incapacitating techniques that displace punitive, reintegrative, correctional or deterrent strategies. Examples include the reappearance of curfews managing 'at risk' groups, times and places; the emergence of 'three strikes' laws that abandon proportional sentencing and individual justice in favour of formula-based sentencing according to risk; and the massive expansion of prison warehousing and of home detention as purely incapacitating measures. All these, and more, have been examined as part of the formation of knowledge and power that is actuarial justice. Accordingly, most academic research and theory – as opposed to much administrative criminology – has regarded the emergence of actuarial justice, and of risk more generally, as a blight on criminal justice (Bauman 2000; Hudson 2000; Kempf-Leonard and Peterson 2000; Miller 2001). Risk appears, explicitly or implicitly, as a negative turn that undermines the modest advances made towards a reconstructive, inclusive and reintegrative criminal justice during the middle ('welfare state') part of the twentieth century. By centring insecurity and threat, the governmental grid of risk is seen to work though negation: certain persons are defined primarily in terms of their purely negative and dangerous status as threats to others (victims), and accordingly are merely neutralised and segregated in new Gulags of incapacitation.

As is often the fate of major breakthroughs, Feeley and Simon's work on risk in criminal law and penology has been followed by a rush to identify confirming instances, and in the process the specificity of actuarial justice has become something of a casualty. Actuarial justice does not exhaust the play of risk in the field of criminal law and criminal justice, and significant distinctions among strategies of risk-based justice have tended to be overlooked. In this respect, Feeley and Simon themselves provide many insights and observations about the nature and genealogy of actuarial justice that should have merited greater caution and finer analytic investigation than they subsequently have been accorded. In the first section of this chapter I wish to return to their classic analysis and consider more closely some of their arguments. I will suggest that actuarial justice appears a categorically exclusionary strategy of risk, distinct from inclusive and restorative risk technologies and strategies such as insurance and drug harm minimisation. As such, actuarial justice is profoundly shaped by, and allied with, a tradition of political conservatism – particularly *per medium* of the political invention of the underclass as the primary problem to be governed through criminal justice.

Actuarial justice and the politics of exclusion

In their discussion of the context and shaping of actuarial justice, Feeley and Simon go to some lengths to emphasise that 'actuarial thinking represents a deeper "pre-political" thought that cannot easily be associated with conventional political labels' (1994: 190). At best, they argue, politics has some impact in shaping actuarial justice, and actuarial justice will be employed 'somewhat differently' by different political perspectives. Thus they point out that while conservatism is often associated with actuarial justice, traditionally it is associated with a deep-rooted juridical individualism that does not sit well with the statistical and categorical techniques of risk-based justice. The examples of political influence that Feeley and Simon do detect, perhaps in keeping with this sceptical stance, thus are rather indirect – the major instance being the possibility that conservative 'lock-em-up' policies created penal population pressures that facilitated the institutionalisation of actuarial techniques.

In their analysis there is thus little or no constitutive role for politics. This seems surprising at first glance, because the rise of actuarial justice historically coincides with the rise of a profoundly anti-correctional politics hostile to what Garland (1985) refers to as the 'welfare sanction'. It sought to empty prisons of social workers, reduce costs and introduce 'truth in sentencing' – but not because of promotion of a pre-political agenda of risk. Rather, it reflected a variety of reasons, including a greater acceptance of deterrence as a valid penal philosophy, a hostility to the social sciences and the helping professions, and a concern with fiscal accountability and cost effectiveness (O'Malley 1992; Rose 1996). On face value it would seem to many that such political pressures very likely contributed to the formation of tariff-based sentencing and the evacuation of correctional content from prisons, leaving them as the 'cost effective' warehouses for incapacitation. In other words, these critical elements of actuarial justice might have been an explicitly political creation.

However, the weakness of this argument, in turn, is that conservative politics has headed in other more punitive directions as well as mere warehousing, notably the current array of 'emotive and ostentatious' punishments (Pratt 2000). Likewise, we could add that neoliberalism would appear to have fostered progressive forms of rehabilitation – including the delivery of 'risk-needs' based services in prisons and the development of 'enterprising prisoner' schemes – and as this latter example suggests, in some ways mere incapacitation sits ill with the neoliberal visions of the active subject and switched-on capitalism (O'Malley 1999b). Hence, Feeley and Simon could be supported in their claim that politics are no more than a facilitating condition, rather than a major constitutive influence, in the formation of actuarial justice.

Such an argument certainly reveals weakness in the 'political' case, if by that term we mean – as do Feeley and Simon – the 'pendulum swings' to right and left of the political field. Yet it reveals an equally difficult, indeed identical, problem for their own case. That is: if the process is merely technical or pre-political why does risk take the specific shape of actuarial justice when there are many other risk-based alternatives to warehousing, such as the identification and treatment of offenders' criminogenic 'risk needs' in prison? To answer this question, we need to examine elements of the genealogy of actuarial justice proposed by Feeley and Simon.

In discussing the possible impact of the law and economics movement in this genealogy, they differentiate 'economic' thinking from 'actuarial' thinking (1994: 189). Both, they stress, emphasise the utilitarian purposes of punishment over the moral purpose. But an 'economic' approach treats the offender as a rational choice actor, whereas actuarial justice 'treats the offender as *inert*, from the point of view of influencing decision making' (1994: 189). Economic reasoning thus is associated with deterrence rather than incapacitation, and incapacitation is identified as the 'pure' actuarial response. But what is pure actuarialism? For example, if effective risk reduction is its characteristic, then risk needs and preventative interventions have been argued to be superior to incapacitation (see O'Malley 2000). If it is cost-effective risk management, isn't this an economic actuarial argument? And in any case, long-term 'empowerment' has been claimed by some as more cost effective than incapacitation (Rand Corporation 1998). In short, it is not clear on what criterion incapacitation can appear as pure or undiluted actuarialism. The point, rather, would appear to be that, as Ewald (1991: 198) observes, the technology of risk is highly abstract, so that *any* applications in an institutional setting 'are not *the* application of a technology of risk; they are always just *one* of its possible applications'.

We might also consider that it would be difficult to argue that other technologies – such as situational crime prevention – are somehow not 'actuarial' or not fundamentally risk based simply because they deploy a rational choice actor as their subject (see, e.g. Clarke 2000). This point is by no means trivial or marginal to our understanding of the character of actuarial justice. As David Garland has argued (1996, 2001), the rational choice actor is the subject of what he terms a 'criminology of the self'. This is a criminology that defines crime as 'normal' in the sense that anyone could be a criminal under the right conditions – the criminal is not a distinctive type of person. Thus, Felson and Clarke (1997) stress, for situational crime prevention 'nobody is exempt from the temptation to commit crime since human weaknesses are widespread and not confined to any one segment of the population'. Consequently, situational crime prevention and other rational choice-based approaches do not seek to exclude types or categories of persons, or sectors of the population. Rather, they seek to deter abstract and universal potential offenders by rendering the effort and risk of offending greater than the likely benefits. In this way, they converge with judicial deterrence. But they do so as Garland suggests by seeking to govern 'criminogenic situations' – that is (more generally), to focus on the risks associated with environmental conditions rather than with categories or types of person (Garland 1996).

What does this tell us about the *specific* form of risk approach taken by actuarial justice? The critical point again is made by Feeley and Simon (1994: 189) when they note that 'the rise of incapacitation and the other instruments of Actuarial Justice [are] a reflection of social forces ... [that push] a large portion of the population out of the range of normal economic signals'. In short, deterrence will not work for this social category, and thus actuarial justice is to be distinguished from situational crime prevention and related technologies of risk that focus on universal and abstract subjects. In this way Feeley and Simon see the distinction between deterrent models and actuarial justice as critical to their case. This social category is the largely black and Hispanic 'underclass', seen as permanently excluded from upward social mobility and economic integration by the effects of a global restructuring of the economy (see also Bauman 2000). Not only is deterrence imagined as unworkable for this category but reintegration and rehabilitation are also rendered irrelevant, for there is nothing to integrate them into. The heavy industrial and related economic sector that once provided for this category's employment has – as a consequence of globalisation – disappeared from the local economy. What therefore is installed is a government strategy designed quite specifically to contain this irredeemable, irremediable and dangerous 'other' population.

Looked at in this way, in line with the general tenor of Feeley and Simon's own analysis, actuarial justice emerges not as a pure form of pre-political risk management. Rather it is a specific actuarial strategy designed and assembled for a specific governmental – and in this sense, political – purpose. In contrast to the risk technologies that deploy the universal rational actor as their subject, the subjects of this strategy are neither abstract-universal nor 'normal', nor are they subject to normalisation. To these others – that are not like us and cannot become like us – the specific strategies of categorically exclusionary risk are applied.

Despite the realist dimensions of their underclass argument, equally strong is the stress Feeley and Simon place on the inventedness of this category. That is, the underclass is a governmental category originally created within a 'critical' sociology but appropriated subsequently by (largely conservative) politicians and commentators. Indeed, I would add to this argument the claim that the underclass appears as the product of a neoliberal political rationality. The same strategies of global governance that are implicated in relocating the underclass members' means of employment to the Third World – in the name of competition and efficiency – are also responsible for inventing the spectre of welfare dependency, and of welfare as generating a fiscal crisis of the state. The underclass was invented and deployed in the USA at the same time that welfare was being withdrawn as 'counterproductive and costly' – and in relation to a population that now could be defined as having become 'dependent', as having lost the will to work and the ability to make an enterprise of their lives. A governmental invention that, on the other hand, defined this population as *a victim* of global restructuring, as Bauman (2000) for example sees them, could well have rendered these people candidates for welfare inclusion and 'empowerment' rather than exclusion and incapacitation.

I find two things persuasive about this argument. First, the strategy and techniques of categorically exclusionary risk, to which actuarial justice belongs, have subsequently been applied to other categories that fall specifically under the umbrella of irremediable and dangerous otherness. Persistent violent and sexual offenders are the prime candidates. These have become subject to the array of 'Megan's laws', which in various ways notify the community of the identity of former offenders. As Simon himself subsequently has noted, the veneer of technical 'neutrality' of actuarial justice is transformed in the risk-based Megan's laws into a politics of vengeance:

> the development of modern institutions, particularly the prison, was aimed at displacing popular emotions from the centre of punishment by extending the control of state based professionals. From a spectacle of solidarity between state and the people against their common enemies, punishment became a vehicle for in-culcating habits of order suitable to a democratic society. Megan's law is a shift away from this process of modernization. Starting with its name, and with the central role given to local prosecutors in applying the risk classification, Megan's law advertises itself as a new hybrid of public and private vengeance (1998: 464).

Thus, while Megan's laws are similar in some respects to such other risk strategies as situational crime prevention, and while certainly mobilised in the name of potential victims taking 'rational' and 'reasonable' steps to protect themselves (Levi 2000), these risk strategies are distinct. They are aimed at a category of subjects who are politically and govern-mentally demonised and excluded. These people are not 'inert' – as I think Feeley and Simon mistakenly identify the subjects of actuarial justice – but 'other', and in this case, evil. Significantly, as Simon's reference to Megan's laws' movement away from modernist penology indicates, these responses are like those directed at the underclass in a key respect – they both abandon the modernist project of inclusionary reform and adopt a technology of categorical exclusion.

Actuarial justice in Australia

The second persuasive issue is that while even in Britain the term 'underclass' gained some political currency in relation to chronically unemployed youth (Reiner 1992; Hudson 2000), this did not happen in countries such as Australia and New Zealand (Pratt 2000). This was despite the existence of both youth and racial minorities eligible for the label by virtue of their chronic unemployment and high crime rates. In Australia, the early political identification of young people as being systematically exposed to chronic unemployment, and as *victims* of structural changes over which they had no control (notably under the Hawke Labour government in the 1980s), rendered the problem the responsibility of government. Inclusive solutions had to be attempted for 'our' children. The youthful unemployed were imagined as 'like us', but their *situation* was pathogenic and to be remedied. Perhaps more critically, this applies also to the Aboriginal population. Like the US 'underclass', Aboriginal people do not have substantial access to employment and retain a political profile as culturally and racially distinct from the mainstream. But in this respect they have been understood as falling victim to a pathogenic situation in the legacy of racism and colonialism, and thus they became subject to a bipartisan politics of reconciliation. Neither in word nor form has this population been subject to the exclusionary designation of underclass. Even the much trumpeted 'racism' of Pauline Hanson's 'One Nation Party' centres policies that call for assimilation of Aboriginal people rather than their exclusion.

As a result, I would suggest, actuarial justice has gained only a tenuous hold in criminal law in Australia, and much the same is true in New Zealand where similar political conditions have existed (Pratt 2000). While both Western Australia and the Northern Territory have mandatory sentencing of the 'three strikes' form, this has either been disowned or become the subject of hostile attack by all other state and federal governments, and judicatures (Roche 1999). Even the Liberal-National (conservative) federal government has attempted to buy the

Northern Territory government out of its commitment to three-strikes law, as it had become generally regarded as working a racist effect upon the Aboriginal population. And while risk-based sentencing applies to the categories of repeat sexual and violent offenders in a number of other states (e.g. Victoria and NSW, and also in New Zealand), judicial opposition has been effective in marginalising their impact (Freiberg 2000).[1] In none of these cases has statistical evidence on recidivism been prominent in justifying the strategies, although risk to the community has certainly been central, so it is not clear that these sentences are examples of actuarial justice. More important in this latter respect, where mandatory sentencing does exist, warehousing has not been the principal penological response. Thus, with respect to the Northern Territory, where mandatory sentencing has been associated with the imprisonment of many Aboriginal people, the stress is on 'culturally appropriate' interventions that provide educational and vocational courses, with specific goals of 'reducing recidivism by increasing employment prospects', reduction of alcohol and drug-related harm, developing 'restorative justice' and the development of 'partnership' programmes designed to reintegrate offenders into their communities (see http://www.ourmessage.org.au). Likewise, in the case of sex and violent offenders, whatever the emphasis on risk, treatment and therapy programmes remain critical elements of the correctional programmes set up under this umbrella (Pratt 1998).

This is not to suggest that these countries are immune to actuarial justice in the general sense of a strategy of risk-based categorical exclusion. Moral panics against particular hated categories such as paedophiles may yet see the emergence of Megan's laws and other forms of categorically exclusive actuarialism. The imprisonment of illegal migrants (refugees) in a concentration camp in the South Australian desert, although this has little to do with risk per se, certainly suggests that where existing candidates for exclusion are available, categorically excluding responses will be mobilised. But it does suggest that resort to actuarial justice and other strategies of exclusion has been substantially limited by the specific political genealogies of these countries, as distinct to that of the USA. In such settings, resort to other kinds of risk strategy (as opposed to actuarial justice itself) may still be a major characteristic of crime control and criminal justice. Crime prevention, for example, has maintained a high profile in Australia for several decades (O'Malley 2000). But the characteristic forms of risk-based intervention are those based on rational choice models of offenders, and more recently – as will shortly be discussed – programmes that deploy revised inclusive techniques and knowledges translated from the welfare social era. In general it is argued that, in the absence of a politics of the underclass, inclusive criminologies of the self, rather than categorically exclusionary criminologies of the other, have informed risk-based justice. This becomes more clear when we consider responses of the government to illicit drug consumption.

The war on drugs and harm minimisation

The US 'War on Drugs' certainly is not a risk-based *strategy* of justice, in the sense that its central rationale is risk-based governance, but it employs many risk-based or actuarial techniques (such as random drug testing). Most critically, it centres actuarial justice in its repertory of weapons, for a large proportion of those imprisoned under three strikes and related legislation are convicted on drug-related charges (Austin *et al.* 1999). This affinity between actuarial justice and a military analogy of government in no small measure lies in their shared categorically exclusionary cores. As with Megan's laws, the militarisation of drug policy shifts emphasis dramatically away from any sense of a technically neutral statistical deployment of risk. A threat is created and identified simultaneously as the source of risk and as 'other': whether this is the foreign drug producers; international traffickers from alien countries in the Third World; the drugs themselves and their addictive 'enslaving' properties; or the monstrous (and not coincidentally, frequently black and Hispanic) dealers, 'addicts' and 'abusers'. Such a moral and military agenda identifies risks with evil. The response is armed exclusion and the destruction or neutralisation of those identified with creating such risks. At the borders, the military and quasi-military forces seek to exclude the enemy, while actuarial justice excludes the enemy within. Alongside actuarial justice, risk-based techniques such as random drug testing extend the strategy of exclusion, even into the recesses of working, sporting and domestic life (O'Malley and Mugford 1992). In this sense, risk-based techniques appear to be subordinated to the broader politics of exclusion in which those testing positive are either excluded by the criminal justice system or – as Simon has suggested – appear voluntarily to have rendered themselves unfit to labour (Simon 1987).

But against the American moral War on Drugs is set the quite contrary risk-based strategy of harm minimisation (itself often a target of drug warriors; Broadhead 1991). In its Australian and New Zealand realisations, this is explicitly associated not only with specific risk *techniques,* such as drug testing and risk identification, but also with risk as a *strategy*: that is, its long-range goals and overall mode of operation are defined in terms of risks, of locating and minimising risks (e.g. HCS 1993). As with the War on Drugs, much of its character is intelligible once we recognise how and where it identifies risk. For harm minimisation the risks are multiple: health risks, risks of corruption, risks to property, risks to productivity and so on. But these risks are not understood as embedded in the nature of particular substances, or of particular categories or types of person. Rather, harm minimisation's risks are situationally pathogenic: that is, risks are created by the contexts and ways in which drugs are manufactured, supplied, used and otherwise deployed. For example, intravenous administration of drugs is linked to specific health risks; high-intensity policing in turn is identified as a risk factor because it encourages high-risk means and contexts of administration; even effective drug interdiction at the border is seen to generate risks associated with drug adulteration and price increases. Likewise, methadone maintenance programmes take a central role in harm minimisation not only because they lower health risks by stabilising opiate intake, and by reducing risks associated with intravenous administration, but also because the low price of methadone reduces the pressure to commit property crime in order to buy drugs, and because its lengthy half-life allows users to take up paid work more easily – thus having roll-on effects on crime and health risks (O'Malley 1999a). As Marsha Rosenbaum (1997) indicates, this is quite distinct from the situation in the USA, where 'by the mid 1980s methadone usage has moved essentially from medical treatment to the *containment* of addicts – just as the criminal justice system had moved from rehabilitation to containment of "the rabble"'. Thus even where seemingly identical techniques are deployed, the model of risk is distinct – the one embracing the modernist project of normalisation, the other consigning subjects to the excluded status of 'other'.

While linking such risk techniques to a framework of rational choice subjectivities is not a necessary feature of harm minimisation, in the Australian and New Zealand contexts this has become a central characteristic. Actual and potential drug users are addressed as if their drug-taking choices are, for the most part, morally neutral, but they are provided with information on the adverse risks created by drug consumption. It is then assumed they will perform the felicity calculus and many will minimise harms to themselves and others. As well as through deployment of this rational choice 'criminology of the self', illicit drug users are also 'normalised' in other, more explicit ways. Their drug taking is rendered directly comparable with licit drug taking – alcohol, tobacco and pharmaceuticals – each of which is compared unfavourably with illicit drugs in terms of aggregate health risks. They are expressly addressed as 'users' rather than as (irrational) 'addicts' or (morally corrupt) 'abusers'. And any processes that are associated with demonisation, pathologising and exclusion of users themselves are deliberately neutralised (see, generally, O'Malley 1999a). In this process, coercion likewise is minimised or displaced, as voluntary participation is strongly preferred. In consequence criminal justice is to be deployed minimally, rather than maximally as in actuarial justice, and even then primarily as a conduit to treatment or therapeutic practices rather than as a means to punishment or incapacitation.

Of course, this is not in some sense a 'perfect' arrangement. For example, harm minimisation is associated with the progressive encroachment of government of drug consumption as more and more risks are identified and measured more and more minutely. It can also be a form of government by stealth as normalisation is deployed only because it 'works', in the sense of most effectively aligning the behaviours of the users with the aims of the strategy. Particular programmes and techniques are deployed not just because in some vague sense they are 'humane', 'enlightened' or 'democratic', but because of their evaluated effectiveness in preventing initial drug use and in drawing into treatment the maximum number of illicit drug users. Thus coercion, punishment and blame are displaced explicitly because current knowledge suggests them to be counterproductive.

Risk and the politics of inclusion and exclusion

It might be convenient and even wise to end the argument here. Having demonstrated the quite contrasting realisation of risk in these two countries, the limits of the 'globalisation of risk' theses are fairly starkly illuminated. That is, one may seriously ask whether the fact that all these strategies in some ways have mobilised risk in the context of criminal justice matters very much. Their respective social impacts, technical forms and political implications are so divergent as to make this shared characteristic of risk almost trivial. As well, the rejection of these major American risk strategies in Australia, and their substitution by interventions of almost polarised form, suggest rather that local political formations and tolerances so colour risk as to dispose also of any idea that America has successfully exported a 'new penology' of exclusion and abandonment.

However, while this may be the wise course of action, it is also somewhat trite, for surely a major and unanswered question is left in its wake. How can we reconcile the US 'neoliberal' politics of exclusionary justice with the equally 'neoliberal' inclusionary justice that characterises Australian government?[2] How can both be 'neoliberal' and yet seemingly be contradictory and even incompatible? In a recent paper (O'Malley 1999b) I argue that attempts to attribute the appearance of an array of volatile and contradictory policies in contemporary criminal justice in terms of the impact of neoliberalism have been somewhat mistaken. If disciplinary boot camps, chain gangs, the death penalty, prison warehousing, enterprising prisoner schemes, restorative and reintegrative justice and a myriad of other sanctions are all neoliberal, as is claimed across the literature, then neoliberalism must be so all-encompassing as to have little political integrity and/or almost no explanatory power. Yet, despite some variation, neoliberalism is associated with fairly integrated visions of the rational choice subject, the superiority of markets to deliver efficiencies and goods, freedom of choice, a 'revised autonomy' of the enterprising self, the centrality of innovation and of enterprising individualism, the small and enabling state and so on. And it appears difficult to align such political principles of optimistic 'switched-on capitalism' with strict discipline boot camps, chain gangs, prison warehousing and the death penalty. Rather, these appear much more consistent with the doctrines of a socially authoritarian conservatism, with which neoliberalism has been allied in some contexts.

In a conservative political rationality a strong and even intrusive state is required to enforce the moral unity that is vital to social harmony, national strength and character. Duty, obedience and self-denial figure prominently. Freedom of choice, market commodification and generalised innovative individualism appear as sometimes valuable but always suspect forces, with the capacity to erode the authority of the moral order and to threaten the discipline essential to the conservative sense of social unity and purpose.

The 'New Right', influential in Britain in the Thatcher years, and largely still so in the USA, is an alliance or hybrid between neoliberalism and neoconservatism. While tensions always exist between its conservative and neoliberal elements, it is held together by agreement on broad principles, notably a preference for markets and a particular take on 'freedom of the individual'. But perhaps most especially, they are linked together by a shared opposition to the welfare state, imagined as generative of dependency, sapping of initiative and enterprise, and economically draining.

This interpretation allows for a volatile and contradictory politics of criminal justice in any state where such a hybrid predominates (for example, as mapped out by Garland 1996), as well as for considerable divergences between such jurisdictions and states. Thus, for example, it can be argued that the USA has a much stronger, and more extreme, tradition of political conservatism than is the case in Australia, and this creates two quite distinctive hybrids and thus distinct polities.

This vision of the US 'conservative neoliberalism' makes sense of the greater acceptance of categorical exclusion in the USA, and its manifestations in the moral authoritarianism of War on Drugs and social defensiveness of actuarial justice. In addition, it can make sense of the fact that the majority of the more 'emotive and ostentatious' (non-risk-based) legal sanctions discussed in the literature, such as chain gangs, the death penalty, military boot camps and mass warehousing, *remain* largely or completely characteristic of American criminal justice – and in some of these examples, particularly of the southern states (Pratt 2000).

Yet it is clear that there are other elements in such hybrid neo-liberalisms. In the Australian environment, the conservative elements are greatly moderated by the impact of a social democratic tradition (linked to chronic labour shortages, an historically strong labour movement and so on). Indeed, perhaps the current Australian polity (rather like that in New Zealand and Canada) is better thought of in terms of an alliance between neoliberalism and a social democratic politics. Thus it was Labour governments that began the push towards neoliberalism in Australia (the same was true for new Zealand). The direction taken by this neoliberal hybrid has been not so much hostility to welfare collectivism aimed at dismantling it. Rather there has been a push to render it more economically 'responsible' and accountable, more 'enterprise' based, and more compatible with discourses of the 'active subject' and enterprise (e.g. Dean 1995). Thus national health care has not been dismantled, but progressive taxation has been implemented both to make the middle classes take more of its economic burden and to push them into private sector medicine. Unemployment relief was not challenged, but linked to programmes of 'job seeking', 'lifelong learning' and the like (O'Malley 1996). As a result, I suggest, in the criminal justice arena, only in a few instances were there assaults on the provision of *correctional* services – although punishment and deterrence moved up the hierarchy of sentencing principles. Rather, corrections were made increasingly subject to evaluation. Outsourcing of services was implemented, together with some privatisation of prisons – linked to performance specifications that retain reform and retraining as central requirements. While such economic 'rationalising' has led to reductions in service provision, prison warehousing is not generally a description that could be applied to this environment.

43

In the case of harm minimisation, the impact of hybrid neoliberal and social welfare technologies is, perhaps, still more clear. Here, as we have seen, therapeutic interventions are retained as central elements of the strategy of governing illicit drug consumption, and in many cases these are provided by state institutions and much the same network of agencies that characterised welfare interventions in the mid-1980s when harm minimisation was formulated. Yet added to this is a crisply neoliberal framework in which users and potential users appear as informed choice-makers (thus neutralising visions of the welfare-dependent subject). As such, they are to be provided with information by the 'empowering' state, with the expectation that more rational activity will follow. In turn, programme evaluation and effectiveness are constant concerns, imposing some degree of 'economic responsibility', while contractual outsourcing to private and charatable agencies has replaced or supplemented state-based provision.[3]

Conclusions

Of course, a comparative analysis of this sort can never be conclusive. Other factors may well have played some role in the Australian and New Zealand rejections of the War on Drugs and the refusal of actuarial justice. The scale of the drug problem in the USA is doubtlessly larger (although not on a per capita basis) and this may have provided some impetus towards low-cost warehousing strategies, while in Australasia the smaller scale of the problem made therapeutic responses more feasible. Against this, however, we could equally see the sheer scale of the problem in the USA as one reason for *not* pursuing such a massive policy of social exclusion in the first place. That is, adopting a solution that consigns several millions of the population to imprisonment and non-custodial incapacitation would only be regarded as 'cost effective', or as an acceptable solution, in the light of precisely the style and tradition of conservative (and arguably racist) politics to which I have alluded.

Thus I would suggest that the distinction between the hybrid forms of neoliberalism in these two countries has played a key role in shaping the nature of the risk-based forms of justice that have emerged. The conservative neoliberalism of the USA provides an environment in which strategies of categorical exclusion can be directed at very large sectors of the population. The social-democratic tradition in Australia has generated distinctive responses which neoliberalism has shaped in important ways – but the hybrid form of Australian politics is far more consistent with mentalities of categorical inclusion that render actuarial justice and the War on Drugs unlikely to develop as full-blown strategies of criminal justice.

No doubt theoretical priorities and allegiances dictate whether we regard the differences between these various strategies and policies as more important than their commonality in risk. Likewise, it is – for obvious reasons – a matter of political preference that decides which of these inclusive and social-democratic, or exclusive and conservative, neoliberal modes of institutionalising risk is regarded as preferable. However, that they are distinct in major ways, and that these distinctions reflect the filtering and translating effects of national politics, seems undeniable.

Notes

1 For a 'three strikes' analogue, see also the Crimes [Serious and Repeat Offenders] Act 1992 (WA). In Victoria, s. 6A of the Sentencing Act 1991 (Vic) prescribes extended imprisonment for sex and violence offenders, as is also the case in Queensland (the Penalties and Sentences Act 1992 (Qld), s. 163), Western Australia (Sentencing Act 1995 (WA), Part 14) and Tasmania (Sentencing Act 1997 (Tas), s. 19).

2 Note that this is not exactly the same question as asking the causal question of why the two politics of justice have come to differ. Such a question might be answered in terms of major differences related to the scale of the drug problem, or the existence of large-scale and ghettoised minority populations associated with the drug industry, the influence of religious fundamentalism or the weakness of organised labour (cf. Mugford 1993). All these factors, I suspect, are highly relevant. But in the last analysis, they must all have their effects in the realm of the political in order to shape criminal justice politics, and so it is to the broader political contrast that I attend here.

3 With respect to the first point, fairly typical is this statement by the Victorian government: '[a] harm minimisation approach acknowledges that many young people will use drugs at some stage in their life, making it critical that students acquire knowledge and skills that will assist them in making informed decisions about their drug use and so minimise any harmful effects associated with that use' (DSEV 1995: 2).

References

Austin, J., Clark, J., Hardyman, P. and Henry, D. (1999) 'The impact of "three strikes and you're out"', *Punishment and Society*, 1: 131–62.

Bauman, Z. (2000) 'Social issues of law and order', *British Journal of Criminology*, 40: 205–21.

Beck, U. (1992) *Risk Society*. New York, NY: Sage.

Beck, U. (1997) *World Risk Society*. London: Polity Press.

Broadhead, R. (1991) 'Social constructions of bleach in combatting AIDS among injection drug users', *The Journal of Drug Issues*, 21: 713–37.

Castel, R. (1991) 'From dangerousness to risk,' in G. Burchell *et al.* (eds) *The Foucault Effect. Studies in Governmentality*. London: Harvester/Wheatsheaf.

Clarke, J. (2000) 'A world of difference? Globalisation and the study of social policy,' in G. Lewis *et al.* (eds) *Rethinking Social Policy*. London: Sage.

Dean, M. (1995) 'Governing the unemployed self in an active society', *Economy and Society*, 24: 559–83.

DPEC (Drug Policy Expert Committee) (2000) *Drugs: Responding to the Issues, Engaging the Community*. Melbourne: Government Printer.

DSEV (Directorate of School Education, Victoria) (1995) *Get Real. A Harm Minimisation Approach to Drug Education*. Melbourne: Directorate of School Education.

Ericson, R. and Haggerty, K. (1997) *Policing the Risk Society*. Oxford: Clarendon Press.

Ewald, F. (1991) 'Insurance and risks', in G. Burchell *et al.* (eds) *The Foucault Effect: Studies in Governmentality*. London: Harvester/Wheatsheaf.

Feeley, M. and Simon, J. (1992) 'The new penology. Notes on the emerging strategy of corrections and its implications', *Criminology*, 30(4): 449–70.

Feeley, M. and Simon, J. (1994) 'Actuarial justice. The emerging new Criminal Law', in D. Nelken (ed.) *The Futures of Criminology*. London: Sage.

Felson, M. and Clarke, R. (1997) 'The ethics of situational crime prevention', in G. Newman *et al.* (eds) *Rational Choice and Situational Crime Prevention: Theoretical Foundations*. Aldershot: Ashgate.

Freiberg, A. (2000) 'Guerrillas in our midst? Judicial responses to governing the dangerous', in M. Brown and J. Pratt (eds) *Dangerous Offenders. Punishment and Social Order*. London: Routledge.

Garland, D. (1985) *Punishment and Welfare*. London: Gower.

Garland, D. (1996) 'The limits of the sovereign state', *British Journal of Criminology*, 36(4): 445–71.

Garland, D. (2001) *The Culture of Control*. Oxford: Oxford University Press.

HCS (Victorian Government Department of Health and Community Services) (1993) *Victorian Drug Strategy: 1993–1998*. Melbourne: Health and Community Service, Promotions and Media Unit.

Hebenton, B. and Thomas, T. (1996) 'Sexual offenders in the community: reflections of problems of law, community and risk management in the USA, England and Wales', *International Journal of the Sociology of Law*, 24: 427-43.

Hudson, B. (2000) 'Punishment, rights and difference', in K. Stenson and R. Sullivan (eds) *Crime, Risk and Justice*. Cullompton: Willan.

Kempf-Leonard, K. and Peterson, E. (2000) 'Expanding realms of the new penology. The advent of actuarial justice for juveniles', *Punishment and Society*, 2: 66–96.

Kemshall, H. (1998) *Risk in Probation Practice*. Aldershot: Ashgate.

Levi, R. (2000) 'The mutuality of risk and community: the adjudication of community notification statutes', *Economy and Society*, 29: 578–601.

Miller, L. (2001) 'Looking for postmodernism in all the wrong places. Implementing a new penology', *British Journal of Criminology*, 41: 168–84.

Mugford, S. (1993) 'Social change and the control of psychotropic drugs. Risk management, harm reduction and "postmodernity"', *Drug and Alcohol Review*, 12: 369–75.

National Crime Prevention (1999a) *Pathways to Prevention*. Canberra: National Anti-crime Strategy.

National Crime Prevention (1999b) *Hanging Out. Negotiating Young People's Use of Public Space*. Canberra: National Anti-crime Strategy.

Nolan, J. (1998) *The Therapeutic State. Justifying Government at Century's End*. New York, NY: New York University Press.

O'Malley, P. (1992) 'Risk, power and crime prevention', *Economy and Society*, 21: 252–75.

O'Malley, P. (1996) 'Risk and responsibility', in A. Barry *et al*. (eds) *Foucault and Political Rationality*. London: UCL Press.

O'Malley, P. (1999a) 'Consuming risks. Harm minimisation and the government of "drug users"', in R. Smandych (ed.) *Governable Places. Readings in Governmentality and Crime Control. Advances in Criminology Series*. Aldershot: Dartmouth.

O'Malley, P. (1999b) 'Volatile and contradictory punishment', *Theoretical criminology*, 3: 175–96.

O'Malley, P. (2000) 'Risk, crime and prudentialism revisited', in K. Stenson and R. Sullivan (eds) *Risk, Crime and Justice*. Cullompton: Willan.

O'Malley, P. and Mugford, S. (1992) 'Moral technology. The political agenda of random drug testing', *Social Justice*, 18: 122–46.

Pratt, J. (1998) *Governing the Dangerous*. Sydney: Federation Press.

Pratt, J. (2000) 'Emotive and ostentatious punishment. Its decline and resurgence in modern society', *Punishment and Society*, 2: 417–41.

Rand Corporation (1998) *Diverting Children from a Life of Crime*. Washington, DC: Rand Corporation.

Reiner, R. (1992) 'Policing a postmodern society,' *Modern Law Review*, 55: 761–81.

Roche, D. (1999) 'Mandatory sentencing', in *Trends and Issues in Crime and Criminal Justice* 138. Canberra: Australian Institute of Criminology.

Rose, N. (1996) 'Governing advanced liberal democracies', in A. Barry *et al*. (eds) *Foucault and Political Reason*. London: UCL Press.

Rose, N. (2000) 'Government and control', *British Journal of Criminology*, 40: 321–39.

Rosenbaum, M. (1997) 'The de-medicalization of methadone maintenance', in P. Ericson *et al*. (eds) *Harm Reduction*. Toronto: University of Toronto Press.

Shearing, C. (1995) 'Reinventing policing. Policing as governance', in *Privatisierungstaatliche Kontrolle: Befunde, Konzepte, Tendenzen*. Baden Baden: Nomos Verlagsgesellschaft.

Simon, J. (1987) 'The emergence of a risk society: insurance, law and the state', *Socialist Review*, 95: 61–89.

Simon, J. (1998) 'Managing the monstrous. Sex offenders and the new penology', *Psychology, Public Policy and Law*, 4: 453–67.

Stanko, E. (1996) 'Warnings to women. Police advice and women's safety in Britain', *Violence against Women*, 2: 5–24.

Chapter 4

Policing, securitisation and democratisation in Europe

Ian Loader

The field of European policing

Consider the following: the movement across borders of illicit drugs ranging from contraband alcohol and tobacco to ecstasy, cocaine and heroin; expanding transnational markets in vehicles and other stolen goods; the smuggling of nuclear materials; the endeavours of economic migrants, refugees and asylum seekers from eastern Europe and beyond to enter member states of the EU; the organised trafficking of human beings by global criminal enterprises – often to work in the sex industries of Europe's cities; the circulation through the global economy of laundered money and forged currency; the persistence, in different forms, of organised political violence; and outbreaks of ethnic conflict and warfare on the EU's 'doorstep' in the Balkans. These threats whirl around our heads, threatening the security and prosperity of (western) Europe and its citizens. They are the criminogenic consequences of a world made up of flows and networks rather than boundaries and fixed points and, as such, repeatedly and decisively outstrip the capacity of any single nation-state to mount or sustain an effective response. The ability of 'sovereign' states to accomplish one of their constituent functions – the production of internal order and security – is correspondingly being eroded and undermined.

In opening with this list, couched in these terms, I am of course begging the very questions I want to raise and reflect upon in this chapter. I do so only to indicate the mix of 'public narratives' (den Boer 1994) and 'official fears' (Ruggiero 2000) that have in recent years been mobilised to justify and defend the slow and uneven, yet also discernible and significant, emergence of an enhanced policing capacity within and across Europe.[1] Centred mainly – though not exclusively – around the EU (and, as such, tied up with the unfolding development of this unique political order), this process has resulted in the dispersal across borders of the means of legitimate surveillance and violence. It has, in so doing, served to loosen the connections between police, nation and sovereign statehood that have for some 200 years been central to the making and imagining of modern European states. The key developments might best be introduced using the following – familiar – categories.

Informal professional networks

Historically, this stands as the most established mode of international police co-operation. Following unsuccessful moves to develop such co-operation in the late nineteenth century, it was eventually given institutional form, first, in the International Criminal Police Commission established in Vienna in 1923 (Deflem 2000) and then, following the Second World War, in the shape of the International Criminal Police Office – or Interpol (Anderson 1989). While this institution – which functions as a communications hub for participating national forces and as an international 'police club' – remains a player in the field of global policing, it has in recent decades been eclipsed, both by the prominent role taken by the USA in encouraging and facilitating cross-border police co-operation across the world (Nadelman 1993) and by developments in the EU. The latter – as we shall see – has greatly expanded the scope for the formation and development of transnational police networks and working cultures (Sheptycki 1998), whether in the guise of new modes of information-brokering and exchange; the control of particular zones (such as the frontier-free space created by the 1985 Schengen Agreement) and security 'hotspots' (e.g. the Channel Tunnel); or emergent co-operative arrangements between national forces and Europol liaison officers (Bigo 2000a). Mention must also to be made here of the range of steps taken under the EU's third pillar on 'justice and home affairs' to enhance co-operation between member state police forces; of the thickening of relations between western European law enforcement agencies and their counterparts in the 'post-communist' east; and, lest we forget, of the emerging intersections between state police operatives and those employed by global commercial security concerns – in respect, for instance, of the detection and detention of illegal migrants (Johnston 2000).

New modes of intergovernmental co-operation

This represents perhaps the most prominent vehicle through which cross-border policing has been advanced in recent decades, especially within the EU. Commencing in 1957 with the formation of the Trevi group (set up initially to counter terrorism, a brief that was later extended to drugs, organised crime and police training and technology), this mode of transnational policing was given further impetus with the signing (by Germany, France and the Benelux countries) of the Schengen Agreement in 1985 and a further Implementation Agreement in 1990. The latter encompassed a range of law enforcement measures designed to 'compensate' for the removal of frontier controls between signatory states, including cross-border rights of 'hot pursuit' for national police forces and the establishment of the Schengen Information System. The agreement has now been signed by all 15 EU member states except Britain and Ireland; Norway and Iceland have been granted associate status (den Boer and Wallace 2001: 498).

Modes of intergovernmental co-operation on policing-related matters received their most significant boost, however, with the signing of the Treaties of Maastricht in 1992 and Amsterdam in 1997. The former introduced a new 'third pillar' of EU competence in the field of 'justice and home affairs', thereby extending the role of – Brussels-based – officials and the intergovernmental Council of Ministers over law enforcement matters.[2] The latter ushered in a new Treaty Chapter on the 'area of freedom, security and justice'. This significantly strengthened specific EU competence over questions of visa, asylum, immigration and related matters pertaining to the free movement of persons by transferring them to the first pillar, while leaving police co-operation under the rubric of a truncated third pillar (in so doing, it incorporated the Schengen *acquis* into the new dual-pillar justice and home affairs structure – Walker 2000a: 243–4).[3] Intergovernmentalism thus remains the principal vehicle by which cross-border police co-operation is effected, whether in respect of EU responses to forms of transnational crime, or in the increasingly prominent theatre of international police 'peacekeeping'.[4]

Emergent supranational institutions

There is however one agency – though presently governed largely through intergovernmental mechanisms under the third pillar – that has acquired not insignificant cross-border powers and spheres of influence, and which clearly exhibits the potential to develop into a novel supranational police body. I am referring to the European Police Office – or Europol. Envisioned and promoted by former German Chancellor, Helmut Köhl – at a moment of 'federalist' self-confidence – as a kind of FBI for Europe, Europol was instituted by the Maastricht Treaty in 1992. After a halting first few years in which it functioned as a Drugs Unit while member governments haggled over its remit and powers, the Europol Convention was finally implemented in 1998, allowing full operationalisation to commence from 1 July 1999; a date Europol's Director Jürgen Storbeck proclaimed – in the pages of the organisation's glossy 1999 report – as 'significant for all citizens of the European Union':

> The vision of an integrated, European wide law enforcement action against international organised crime was a reality. For the first time ever, the European Union had a multi-agency law enforcement organisation with the potential to support and co-ordinate law enforcement agencies' actions to combat international organised crime (Europol *Annual Report* 1999: 4).[5]

Europol's field of formal legal competence now reaches beyond drugs to encompass illegal immigration, trafficking in human beings, stolen vehicle trafficking, money laundering, currency forgery (with especial reference to the euro), terrorism and the smuggling of nuclear materials. Its principal mode of operation – or 'core business' – lies in the 'exchange of information and intelligence' (EDU/Europol *Annual Report* 1997: 2), an activity co-ordinated through an EU-wide network of liaison officers (Bigo 2000a). In undertaking this role, Europol maintains a database of 'intelligence' on transnational crime which it deploys to provide national forces with crime analysis and 'technical expertise'. Following the landmark meeting of the EU Justice Council in Tampere, Finland in October 1999, moves are also afoot to enable the organisation to establish joint investigative teams with member state forces and to play 'a key role in supporting union-wide crime prevention, analysis and investigation' (Europol *Annual Report* 1999: 5) – a role buttressed since 2000 by the advent of a European Public Prosecutors' Office (or 'Eurojust'). Europol is also in the process of establishing closer co-operative relations with national forces in eastern Europe – particularly in Russia and with states seeking accession to the EU.[6]

   It is not my intention in this chapter to offer a detailed discussion and evaluation of this complex, always-in-motion *bricolage* of networks, processes and institutions and its connections to the wider constitutional architecture of the EU.[7] Such accounts can be found in other places (Anderson *et al.* 1995; Walker 2000a: ch. 8; 2000b; den Boer and Wallace 2001). I also want to avoid proceeding in the descriptive mode that – as Peter Manning (2000: 177) has recently pointed out – all too often (although, it should be added, understandably) characterises work on comparative and/or transnational criminal justice. Rather, my task is to attempt to *theorise* certain issues pertaining to the current trajectories and possible futures of 'European policing'. I want, in particular, to formulate lines of argument around, first, the concept of *securitisation* and, secondly, that of *democratisation*.[8] In respect of the former, my aim is to sketch a cultural sociology of policing and political identity in Europe. This entails consideration of the actors and meanings that are competing to shape the future course of European policing – the interests that are struggling over this terrain, the visions of policing that are coming to the fore or being rendered peripheral. In constructing a heuristic framework that enables better sociological sense to be made of the interplay between competing interests and meanings, I aim to situate the 'bureaucracy beyond the state' (Bigo 1994: 169) that currently prevails in determining the contours of European policing within a wider field of political and cultural possibility. In so doing, I offer an interpretative account of the elective affinity that exists between these governing interests and the tendency to articulate, and act upon, a diverse range of issues facing contemporary Europe under the sign of security – what we might term, following Wæver (1996), the *securitisation of Europe* (see also Bigo 1994, 2000b; Huysmans 2000).

In respect of the latter question, my concerns turn towards the political theory of postnational policing and focus on the problematics of authorisation and legitimation that are raised by the onset of bureaucratically dominated police processes and institutions at the European level. To what extent can it reasonably be said that European policing suffers from a series of 'democratic deficits'? What form do such 'deficits' take and how are they best remedied? What mechanisms of regulation and governance are most fitted to the task of rendering European policing more democratically responsive and legitimate? In posing these questions, and seeking to clarify what might count as plausible answers to them, I offer a schematic outline of some of the issues that must be addressed, and the criteria that might orientate us, in seeking to formulate and advance – in the policing domain – a project of postnational democracy (Curtin 1997).

Cultures of post/national policing: mapping the securitisation of Europe

> Security policy is a specific policy of mediating belonging. Discourses of danger and security practices derive their political significance from their capacity to stimulate people to contract into a political community and to ground – or contest – political authority on the basis of reifying dangers (Huysmans 2000: 757).

Policing, like all social institutions, is both 'made and imagined' (Unger 1987). It operates within societies as an ensemble of practices and technologies oriented to instrumental purposes – the production of order and security. Yet it is at the same time a cultural and symbolic form – generating and communicating social meanings about such matters as order, authority, morality, normality and subjectivity. Policing, in other words, has to be understood as *a category of thought and affect* – a 'condensing symbol' (Turner 1974) that enables individuals and groups to make sense of their past, form judgements on the present and project various possible futures. As an institution intimately concerned with the protection of the state and the security of its citizens, one that is entangled with some profound hopes, fears, fantasies and anxieties about matters such as protection/vulnerability, order/entropy and life/death, policing remains closely tied to people's sense of ontological security and collective identity, and capable of generating high, emotionally charged levels of identification among citizens. Through their presence, performance and voice, police institutions are able to evoke, affirm, reinforce or (even) undermine many of the prevailing cultural characteristics of political communities, serving, in particular, as a vehicle through which 'recognition' within such communities is claimed, accorded or denied. Policing is, in short, closely bound up with how political order and identity are represented and 'imagined' (Anderson 1991).[9]

There is, however, no single historical or cross-cultural template from which these symbolic connections can be read off. To be sure, late modern societies share a number of basic security dilemmas that policing is oriented towards and structured by. It is also true that the institutional mechanisms (democratic) states deploy to deliver and govern policing bear a number of family resemblances (Bayley 1985); and that, under globalised conditions, particular policing styles – 'zero-tolerance', 'problem-oriented policing', etc. – resonate across territorial boundaries in ways that open up 'local' practices to increased scrutiny. But none of this provides grounds for claiming that the social meanings of policing – the precise ways in which it functions as a cultural category

– are homogeneous or invariant across time and space. Rather, it seems safer to suppose that such meanings have national genealogies that vary according to how processes of state and police formation have unfolded historically; and take contemporary forms that are conditioned by, and in turn condition, the particular political cultures of which they form part. There is, indeed, plenty of comparative historical and sociological evidence to support just these suppositions (e.g. Walden 1982; Sheptycki 1999; Ellison and Smyth 2000; Emsley 2000).

How, though, do these reflections help us make sense of the connections between policing and collective identity that are – or might be – operative at the transnational level? What cultures of policing are competing, not merely for ascendancy within the field of European policing, but for the right to constitute and name the very field itself?[10] What social meanings of policing are – to adapt Raymond Williams's schema – *emergent* or assuming *dominance* within Europe? Which are being rendered *residual*, or *oppositional* (Williams 1977: ch. 8; 1981: 203–5)? How, in short, might a theoretical perspective that treats policing as a symbolic form help us to understand better certain key aspects of postnational policing and its contemporary formation?

A cultural sociology of the properties and potential trajectories of the field of European policing requires us to map (and explain relations between) the competing subnational, national and transnational agents / agencies that are – or might be – efficacious in shaping that field, and the discourses that such actors consciously or implicitly bring forth or rely upon. A threefold distinction between *professional*, *governmental* and *lay* forces and discourses is, I believe, useful here. These three containers of meaning and meaning formation are of course internally differentiated, institutionally and discursively overlapping, and unevenly articulated at subnational, national and transnational levels. The orientations to post/national policing to be located within each 'container', and the lines of divergence, convergence and hybridisation that obtain between them, clearly require filling out and refining in the light of grounded empirical inquiry. The following analytic and substantive considerations may none the less assist us in mapping the current trajectories of European policing, the values and visions that animate the field, and the alternative political possibilities that remain immanent within it.

Professional practices and cultures

Two sets of issues are brought into initial focus here. The first concerns the assemblage of institutional mechanisms that are deployed within Europe to deliver and govern policing. There are some grounds for suggesting that these vary across national boundaries and are deeply rooted in the soil of specific political cultures. Divergences between historically centralised (e.g. Sweden) and decentralised (e.g. Belgium) police systems spring to mind here, as does the contrast between 'military' (gendarmerie, carabinieri) and 'civilian' police traditions (cf. Emsley 1996, 2000). These distinctions are clearly important and remain capable of structuring police institution or capacity-building at the European level. But the sharpness and import of these institutional models may also be atrophying in the face of international policing developments. Practices of cross-national 'law enforcement shopping' are – as den Boer (1999) has recently noted – eroding the differences between national policing styles. She also argues that 'Europeanisation' is serving to strengthen central steering mechanisms in countries that hitherto possessed diverse, multi-tiered police systems, such as Belgium and the Netherlands. The post-cold war involvement of national security agencies in 'internal' policing matters may be having a similar harmonising effect.

Cognate considerations and uncertainties hold in respect of the working cultures of police organisations. The sociology of police work has amply documented the coexistence among law enforcement agents of parochialism and defensiveness (evident in tensions between ranks, functional specialisms and subnational/national police units) and a trans-force, even transnational, solidarity between officers founded on the shared structural peculiarities of the job (as witnessed in several international police associations). These conflicting tendencies stand at the European level in uneasy relation to one another. They may result, on the one hand, in modes of cross-border police co-operation in Europe being hindered, not merely by such matters as language difficulties, a lack of common working procedures and the absence of an European criminal law (Anderson *et al.* 1995: ch. 6), but also by the locally bounded cultural practices and 'Euro-police sceptical' outlooks of law enforcement agents. Such resistance is likely to be especially marked among those national policing agents/agencies who feel they are being displaced by developments at the European level (Bigo 2000a). Yet these very institutional developments may also be giving rise to new (hybrid) working practices and dispositions among officers moved by the common threat of the transnational criminal Other and possessing – as Bourdieu would say – a shared 'feel for the game'.[11] As Didier Bigo (2000a) has recently argued, Europol liaison officers are beginning to play a pivotal role here in forging the development of what he calls a 'European police mentality'. The more general thickening of police networks that is taking place under the rubric of the third pillar seems set to have similar effects (Walker 2000b: 92).[12]

Indeed, the third pillar framework now provides a vehicle through which horizontal co-operation between European police forces can be further developed, and just such a professional ideology forged. In recent years, a host of measures targeted precisely at these ends has been initiated, including the formation of an Operational Task Group of European Chief Police Officers, the advent of a European Police College and an array of dedicated justice and home affairs programmes concerned with improving police language skills, up-grading equipment and generally transferring expertise. To this one must add the specific effects of the EU 'enlargement' programme; a programme that has been couched by Europe's political elite very much in security terms, and which is witnessing (through mechanisms such as 'twinning' arrangements) the creation of closer working relations between EU member state police forces and their counterparts in countries seeking accession. None of this should occasion much surprise. Unlike other domains of EU competence (such as the social chapter, or farming and fisheries) where its role is to act at a distance to regulate market exchange, part of the *raison d'être* of the third pillar is to effect co-ordination between the public police institutions of Europe. Nor should we stand aghast at the manner is which this is currently being accomplished. In the absence of the competence (or legitimacy) that would enable European policing to proceed through explicit acts of capacity or institution-building, closer police co-operation is largely being achieved incrementally through such aforementioned acts of 'soft law' (den Boer and Wallace 2001: 511). There now exists, none the less, a powerful institutional motor driving the formation of both stronger ties between Europe's police forces and a transnational police elite oriented to forging common 'solutions' to common 'security' problems. This elite has, in turn, come to form part of an opaque, thinly accountable policy network increasingly organised around an ideology of *European* security.

Governmental institutions and discourses

Here an initial distinction needs to be made between elected political classes and permanent governing officials. With regard to the former a number of competing forces are in play. On the one hand, national politicians represent political cultures whose values and practices – with respect to matters such as citizenship (Brubaker 1992) or police governance (Loveday 1999) – condition their willingness or ability to co-ordinate security responses at a European level. They may also find themselves constrained by – or, conversely, acting as spokespersons for – national cultural sentiment that stands opposed to further integration and, in the field of policing/law enforcement especially, can be reluctant to cede control over what remains a powerful icon of legal and political sovereignty (Walker 2000b). Yet at the same time, various forces and imperatives (media campaigns, electoral competition, the perceived scale of the threat) drive political classes to act – or be seen to be acting – against matters such as illegal immigration, or money laundering, or terrorism. For politicians practically aware of the limited capacity of 'sovereign' states to act alone against these 'threats', and deeply schooled in the symbolic politics that surrounds many relevant issues, the possibility of launching crime control projects at new sites – 'unsullied by association with past failures and disappointments at the national level' (Walker 2000b: 92) – may thus have a strong allure. All in all, this works to produce some powerful political motivations for developing a European policing capacity in intergovernmental forms – forms that enable police co-operation to unfold without either a loss of national sovereignty, or close, effective forms of democratic supervision.

These various imperatives press more weakly – or, at least, more unevenly – on governmental officials tasked with the administration of law enforcement. This has the effect – as we shall see – of enabling relevant issues to be framed – away from the heat of European constitutional politics – in (technocratic) ways that are perceived to fit the 'objective' requirements of the European polity (albeit that the competing claims of intergovernmentalism and supranationalism continue to be pressed in these settings – Shore 2000: 173). Of pivotal significance here is the particular mode of governance that has come to characterise policy and polity-making in the EU, one dominated by 'middle-range officials of the Community and Member-states in combination with a variety of private and semi-public bodies' (Weiler 1999: 98). Known widely among analysts of the EU by the ugly neologism 'comitology' (Schmitter 1996: 133; Joerges and Vos 1999), this governing ethos has become especially prominent in the field of justice and home affairs. In part, this has to do with the labyrinthine committee structure established to transact intergovernmental co-operation in this policy domain – arrangements in which officials from both member state justice/interior ministries and the EU occupy a prominent, semi-permanent position. To this one must add the effects of the 'incompletely theorised' agreements (Walker 2000b: 96) that tend to characterise international treaty making, agreements that have in the justice field resulted in much important, contentious detail (in respect, say, of Europol's remit, or visa and asylum policy) being shifted to, and shaped by, the closed, self-corroborating 'committee' structure. These factors have combined to generate a field of European policing dominated and shaped by a particular, thinly accountable complex of powerful interests – what Bigo (1994: 169) terms 'a bureaucracy beyond the state'. In police co-operation as elsewhere, the EU appears to have given rise to an 'ever closer union' of governmental elites (Shore 2000: 232).

Joseph Weiler – along with a number of other academic commentators on European integration (e.g. Shore 2000: 144, 220) – has recently emphasised the managerialist dispositions of such elites, highlighting their 'belief that a rational management and regulatory solutions can be found by an employment of technocratic expertise' (Weiler 1999: 284). This contention chimes closely with that of analysts who see 'functional spillover' as the major propellant of European co-operation in matters of justice and home affairs – wherein law enforcement measures are deemed necessary to fill 'gaps' created by wider integrative processes such as the lifting of border controls (Walker 1998).[13] There are grounds for thinking, however, that this functionalist (and essentially techno-cratic) policy discourse has of late come to be *permeated* by a more substantive (and much more overtly political) disposition oriented to conceiving of Europe as a single 'internal security field' (Bigo 1994), and thus to making good its 'security deficits'. We might term this process – following Ole Wæver (1996) – the *securitisation of Europe*. It is one that entails 'framing' selected social problems (such as migration – Huysmans 2000) in ways that dramatise the threat they pose to Europe's citizens; one that couches the 'problem' at hand as one of imperatives not choices, such that new – 'tough', exclusionary, criminal-justice-centred – responses are made to seem both urgent and inevitable; one that is, as such, something other than the mere exercise of technocratic statecraft. By 'organizing social relations into security relations' (Huysmans 1998: 232), securitisation projects a very specific vision of European political order and identity.

So are the postnational policing developments set out in this chapter to be read as a sign that Europe's 'internal' and 'external' relations are now being structured by processes of securitisation (Bigo 2000b)? Is Europe today being governed *through* security (cf. Simon 1997)?[14] Such questions can be addressed along either of two dimensions, and in respect of each they are most plausibly answered by both 'yes' and 'no'. In terms of the *relative prominence of security discourse*, a negative response is called for in so far as the preponderance of policy activity within the EU is neither concerned first and foremost with security issues, nor articulated under a security banner. Governance within the European polity remains primarily oriented towards the operation of the single market and euro, and with a mix of associated regulatory matters in fields such as competition, conditions of employment and consumer rights. The discourse (and visions) of its political leaders continue to cohere in the main around the goals of economic prosperity and social cohesion (e.g. Prodi 2001). Yet, at the same time, it seems increasingly clear that, in the face of illegal migration, the international drugs trade, terrorism, armed ethnic conflict in the Balkans and cognate threats that circulate around a globalised world, security discourses are coming ever more to the forefront of European politics. It is, in this regard, of some (at least symbolic) import that two out of the three pillars of EU competence are explicitly concerned with – 'external' and 'internal' – security. It is similarly worth highlighting the degree to which the enlargement process is being nervously articulated in security terms – the incorporation of former Warsaw Pact states being seen as *both* vital to European security *and* as a potential threat to it. And we need to take note of the surge in policy activity that has taken place of late under the justice and home affairs rubric (an intensity fuelled in part by the enlargement question); a telling indicator of which is the decision of justice ministers following the 1999 Tampere Summit to embark on a work programme equivalent in scale to that which preceded the '1992' single market programme (den Boer and Wallace 2001: 517).[15] Security (and by extension policing) has, one might argue, become *central at the margins* – increasingly mobilised to protect 'Europe' from an array of external threats, increasingly implicated in constituting the meanings of both these 'threats' and the political community they are said to endanger.

In terms of the *substance of policy*, the above questions also invite both affirmative and negative responses. On the one hand, justice and home affairs policy is not merely gaining momentum, but doing so in a manner shot through with considerations of security. In part this can be seen in the event-led, 'disjointed incrementalism' that characterises EU policy-making in this field (den Boer and Wallace 2001: 514); something that seems a far cry from the formation at the European level of any kind of holistic policing or criminal justice 'system'. But it stands out most clearly in the agenda currently being advanced in relation to the treaty chapter on the area of 'freedom, security and justice'; one that is much concerned with widening and deepening police co-operation, harmonising criminal procedures, restricting asylum and other forms of migration, and combating organised crime; much less so with questions of due process, suspects' rights and democratic accountability. There is little doubt that, in these respects, 'security' triumphed at Tampere (Statewatch 1999a). Yet we must be careful not to read current developments too one-dimensionally. The EU has in also recent years taken a robust line against racial discrimination, not least in the establishment of a European Monitoring Centre on Racism and Xenophobia (Monar

2000). To this we might add the emergence – post-Maastricht – of 'European citizenship' as a field of policy activity; something that was given a significant boost at the Tampere Summit with the establishment of a panel to draft a Fundamental Convention of Human Rights covering EU institutions (de Búrca 2001). And note ought to be taken of the calls made recently by both French and German governments for Europol to be made more accountable to the European Parliament, and for its actions to be justiciable at the European Court of Justice (Jospin 2001; Schröder 2001). While some forceful 'securitising moves' are clearly being made within Europe (Buzan *et al.* 1998: 25), security is by no means the only discourse that might potentially shape the future contours of European policing.

Lay mentalities and sensibilities

By this I am referring to the structures of thought and feeling towards policing that circulate within particular European states – structures, I suggested earlier, whose substance and effects vary across different nation-states. This variance depends in part on the wider traditions of statism and state scepticism (and relations of authority more generally) that obtain across Europe (Dyson 1980; Siedentop 2000: ch. 6); and on popular sentiment towards the appropriate role of citizens, markets and government in provision of primary social goods. These, in turn, intersect closely with more specific considerations pertaining to policing, such as the place police institutions occupy in national histories, mythologies and consciousness; their involvement in forms of social and political conflict; and the narrative representations of policing that circulate in the media, whether as news or fictional drama. Taken together, these are likely to give rise to differing levels of identification with – or distance from – the police, and to specific cultural constructions of the relationship between policing and the social. Further differences are, moreover, likely to surface *within* nation-state boundaries, structured by such operative axes of social division and inequality as class, gender, ethnicity, age and region.

These lay sensibilities towards policing stand at present – in the relative absence of the kind of transnational public sphere within which a *European* consciousness towards relevant issues might take root (Schlesinger and Kevin 2000) – as the most territorially fixed component of the European policing field. This is not to say, however, that they remain analytically or politically insignificant. Attention towards them enables us, for instance, to examine which national police forms are being enacted in – or residualised by – new modes of European police delivery and governance. In so far as European policing unfolds against the backdrop of 'the cultural sub-strate of civil solidarity that developed in the context of the nation-state' (Habermas 2001: 71), one requiring police institutions to be grounded in some kind of public consent, one has also to examine the forms of subnational and national sentiment that are mobilised by political elites seeking to legitimate police co-operation beyond the state. This enables us further to identify the cultural sensibilities that have come to assume oppositional status in the light of institutional development at the European level and which thereby offer resources for an alternative politics. This seems most likely at present to take the form of movements who feel their cultural identity threatened by 'Europe' and which seek to resist further (policing) integration – what Wæver (1996) nicely terms 'nations calling states home'. But it may also, conversely, take shape as an avowedly international human rights discourse that is sharply critical of the current trajectory of European policing and security – whether in the guise of non-governmental organisations such as Amnesty, Statewatch and Helsinki Human Rights Watch, or of social movements whose opposition to neoliberal globali-sation brings them into new forms of conflict with European law enforcement agencies.

In these respects the relationship that unfolds between European elites pursuing closer police (and justice) co-operation and different strands of European 'public opinion' remains a partially open and intriguing question. At least three possibilities appear to lie before us. The first – and arguably most likely – is that the field of European policing will develop in ways that continue to *disregard* societal processes of public will-formation – whether at member state or supra-national levels. We are faced, in other words, with the prospect that security agendas will buttress and deepen the EU's already opaque, bureaucratic processes by depoliticising those issues – migration, drugs trafficking, ethnic conflict and the like – that come to be coded, and responded to, in such terms (Buzan *et al.* 1998: 23–6; Bigo 2000b). As Wæver (1996: 106) notes, security is a *social practice*. It is, as such, a way of acting that selectively problematises and makes visible social issues so as to efface the differences between them; one that lifts such issues above the realm of normal politics, severs their connections to questions of social justice, and subsumes them within a discourse of 'effectiveness' that evinces a strong tendency to trump considerations of civil liberty. Though there are signs that Europe's political elites are coming to view this way of determining the path of further integration as untenable, it is a course of action – not least in the field of justice and home affairs – that has some powerful governmental forces working to sustain it.

A second not unconnected possibility is that security rhetorics are increasingly mobilised as a vehicle for *manufacturing* a European public opinion from the 'top down'. We are confronted here – in the absence of common symbols around which postnational affiliation might more positively cohere – with the prospect of a European political identity coalescing negatively around the threats to safety and wellbeing posed to Europe's citizens by an array of dangerous Others (Bigo 2000a: 93). At a time when it is proving difficult for EU elites to legitimate the European polity among the continent's citizens, such mobilisation can have a powerful allure; and there is some suggestion, in the wake of Tampere, that European political leaders have consciously decided to use the domain of justice and home affairs as a vehicle for demonstrating the EU's 'relevance' to citizens, and building public support. As Cris Shore (2000: 63) has observed: 'the easiest way to promote a sense of European identity is to manipulate fears of Europe being invaded by enemy aliens' (cf. Huysmans 1998: 238; 2000).

Both these emergent trajectories have, it seems to me, an array of dangers associated with them – the bulk of which flow from the self-reinforcing, potentially limitless quality that characterises security discourse. Security – as a number of commentators have noted – is always more 'within us a yearning than without us a fact' (Ericson and Haggerty 1997: 99; cf. Zedner 2000); something that gives the pursuit of security – *qua* security – a powerful tendency not merely to disappoint and disenchant but also to colonise more and more domains of public policy discourse.[16] Yet, in the face of all this, alternative futures do remain open to us – futures in which European security discourses come to be more effectively *constrained* within a framework of democratic citizenship. Such a prospect remains immanent to the extent that the EU has recently begun to articulate a language of European citizenship and taken limited steps down the road of granting civil, social and political rights to EU citizens (Meehan 1993). This, in turn, has promoted movements within a still nascent European civil society to begin to mobilise against the securitisation of Europe in the name of deepening EU democracy and extending postnational citizenship (Curtin 1997: 57). There are, of course, a host of sociological questions that need to be asked about how the relationship between security and citizenship comes to be articulated within the European demos in coming years – questions that I have begun in the preceding few pages to probe. But such questions can also be recast in normative terms and pressed as an inquiry into whether European policing might offer an effective conduit for democratic politics. It is to this issue that the remainder of the chapter is devoted.

Questions of postnational democracy: the future governance of European policing

Social theory has of late been much concerned with the ways in which economic and social power is today being loosened from its territorial moorings and becoming free from effective national steering or control (e.g. Strange 1996; Castells 1997: ch. 5; Bauman 1999). Power, it is suggested, has under the globalising conditions of the present escaped from politics, shaken off the constraints of politically constituted governments, been rendered fugitive. Though originally formed to counter the security risks of a different age, the EU has in this altered context come to be represented (sometimes by these very same theorists) as a potential solution to this predicament; this polity-in-the-making being viewed both as a defensive reaction to neoliberal globalisation (Castells 1998: 318–25) and as an institutional vehicle that might yet enable – as Habermas (2001: 54) puts it – politics to 'catch up' with markets.

There is much in this assessment, at least at the level of promise and potentiality. Yet it is also arguably the case that the EU has been assembled in ways that simply recast the terms of the original problem, creating new sites and instantiations of power beyond the state that are at best dimly responsive to Europe's citizens. This has become known – among both EU 'insiders' and academic commentators alike – as the 'democratic deficit' (Beetham and Lord 1998: 26-9; Weiler 1999: ch. 8). There are, to be sure, theorists who have sought to qualify, or draw the sting from, this frequently levelled critique of EU politics. MacCormick (1999: 142-5), for instance, has powerfully defended the mix of governing styles and modes of representation that compose European constitutionalism. Others have seen in the EU's 'comitological' structure the seeds of a deliberative supranational governance (Eriksen 2000). Eric Hobsbawm (1997: 268), adopting a different tack, contends that the EU has from the outset been designedly undemocratic, and is no less – perhaps more – successful because of it. But these voices stand alongside a large body of opinion that has grown deeply concerned with the opaque, self-corroborating modes of rule one encounters in the EU, a system – described by Curtin (1997: 45) as 'a massive circus of committees operating behind closed doors and in virtual secrecy' – that exhibits some profound shortcomings as regards its democratic credentials (Weiler 1999: ch. 8). It is stretching the point, but not stretching it too far, to say that the EU represents a form of 'governance without government' (cf. Hardt and Negri 2000: 13–17).

The field of European policing both reflects this wider pattern of institutional development while, at the same time, making its own specific contribution to the overall configuration. We have already noted that under the third pillar – an arena of EU competence where 'the empowerment of the executive and of civil servants has been institutionalised particularly strongly' (Curtin 1997: 46) – arrangements for governing European police co-operation take the form of policy networks operating at some remove from direct democratic input or oversight. We are able, in addition, to highlight the secrecy and restricted information flows that attend policy formation in the justice and home affairs field (Statewatch 1999b), as well as taking cognisance of the marginal role the European Parliament plays in this domain (den Boer and Wallace 2001: 509). And we might emphasise the importance these 'deficits' assume in respect of an institutional complex possessing the means – if not a monopoly – of legitimate violence and surveillance; one that can impact significantly for better and worse on the quality of life of Europe's peoples – EU citizens and non-citizens alike. The means by which this public power and social good is allocated and made responsive to different 'publics' are clearly of some import.[17]

How then might we best respond to this situation? Is it possible to develop a policing capacity in Europe that is both effective *and* protective of democratic values and liberties? How might modes of European police co-operation be made more responsive to the public constituencies whose lives are affected by it? Can considerations of equity and justice be sustained in the face of Europe's current securitising tendencies? Plainly, these questions lie beyond the ambit of this chapter and I shall neither attempt to address them in anything approaching a definitive manner nor engage in the kind of institutional design they ultimately require (see, further, Loader 2002). My more modest aim is to accomplish two things. First, to clear a little ground by mounting a critique of two currently prevalent – and superficially appealing – responses to the EU's democratic deficits, responses which *appear* to tackle the problems of legitimation raised by the advent of postnational policing, but which both turn out to be culs-de-sac. Secondly, and in a more reconstructive vein, to examine some of the issues that must be addressed, and the criteria that might orientate us, in seeking to formulate – in the particular domain of policing – a project of postnational democracy.

The first of these 'dead-ends' is associated with the tendency – one that looms implicitly in much European security discourse – to collapse democratic legitimacy into *social legitimacy* (cf. Anderson *et al.* 1995: 267). In what might be described as a Weberian hangover (Beetham 1991: ch. 1), this latter term reduces legitimacy to the question of whether forms of cross-border police co-operation are found to be 'acceptable' to Europe's citizens. Clearly there are aspects of legitimacy that are properly addressed by such a conception. But it remains, ultimately, a discourse of effectiveness, with citizen acceptance flowing from the perceived performance of European police institutions in countering a range of criminal 'threats'. Thus understood, 'legitimacy' all too easily becomes self-confirming (Beetham 1991: 99) – amounting to not much more than law enforcement agencies responding to popular anxieties that are in part the consequence of in/securitisation projects championed by political elites, the media or police institutions themselves. This likelihood seems especially pronounced in relation to transnational crime, a terrain of 'threats' that remains experientially remote from the daily lives of most EU citizens, and where issues are often framed in accordance with the logics of a highly mediated, symbolic politics.[18] When one couples this with the paucity of institutional mechanisms through which public authorisation can be actively elicited or withdrawn, mechanisms that fall some distance short of meeting the stipulations of any coherent framework for the legitimation of power (see Beetham 1991: ch. 2; Beetham and Lord 1998), one begins to see social 'legitimacy' as sufficiently partial and reductive as not properly to warrant the nomenclature at all. The passive indifference of the many, and the impassioned – not infrequently xenophobic – demands of the noisy, or powerful few, cannot reasonably ground the democratic legitimacy of postnational policing forms.

One needs to beware, secondly, of what Neil Walker (2000a: 256–8) has termed the *national sovereignty trap*. Walker uses this term to characterise the discourse of actors who respond to the movement of legal and political power from states to the EU (and the democratic shortfalls that have accompanied this process) by striving either to claw these powers back for the nation-state, or to allow national parliaments to exercise more leverage over what is now performed at the European level. Given the fact that our received democratic lexicon – of membership, representation, participation, accountability and so forth – is saturated with presumptions concerning the sovereign primacy of states, this should hardly surprise (Schmitter 1996: 132; Eriksen and Fossum 2000: 7). But it is a trap none the less. At best, it fails to register the shifts in policing capacity that have already taken place, shifts that have significantly empowered policy networks above the level of the nation-state – it is, to this extent, a discourse that seeks to strengthen the door of a stable that the horses have long since vacated! Often, however, most obviously in the British case, this discourse functions as the barely concealed code of political and social movements that aim to undo the whole European integrationist project – in justice and home affairs as elsewhere. Addressing the democratic deficit in the place at which it arises – by strengthening European political institutions, or establishing more robust connections between national and supranational modes of governance – would strike such movements as abhorrent. Either way, this is a discourse that stands in the path of developing democratic forms properly fitted to the unique political architecture of the EU.

By way of a contribution to the furtherance of this political project, I want – in a more positive spirit – to initiate two lines of analysis. The first – which takes up and develops a point made persuasively by a number of writers on European democracy (e.g. Bellamy and Castiglione 2000) – emphasises the importance of attending closely to the *specific* institutional, political and social dynamics of the field of European policing, and of the wider polity of which it forms part. Several considerations arise here. Such specificity demands, first and foremost, that we think about designing regulatory arrangements that have some affinity with the EU's functionally variable structure of *multi-level governance* – the cap must, in other words, fit. This requires, in turn, not merely 'stretching' concepts that have been tied historically to 'the territorial logic of the state' (Eriksen and Fossum 2000: 7), nor the grafting of national institutional forms on to the political body of the EU. Rather, it necessitates some innovative thinking about the precise complex of subnational, national and supranational mechanisms best suited to the task of rendering European policing more democratically responsive – not only in respect of bounded institutions such as Europol but also when it comes to bringing under closer supervision the networks of third pillar officials and police elites that currently elude the democratic gaze.

One must recognise, secondly, that European policing is an almost entirely *informationalised* activity – a practice oriented not to the on-the-ground delivery of visible police functions such as arrest, patrol or crowd control, but towards supporting such practices through the generation, storage and dissemination of information. Some policing commentators have been inclined to conclude from this – or, more particularly, from the barriers that currently impede the efficient transaction of cross-border information-brokering – that European policing is somehow peripheral, non-operational, even largely mythical. This, in my view, is a mistake, one that fails to notice the cognate trends occurring within both national police forces in particular (Ericson and Haggerty 1997) and contemporary surveillance practices more generally (Lyon 2001); and underestimates the import of the activities that *are actually taking place* on a specifically European level. For present purposes, the *pertinent* point about such activities is that they accord European policing a low public visibility, something a postnational regulatory politics needs to take full account of.

Thirdly, and relatedly, cross-border police co-operation remains *experientially distant* from the everyday lives and outlooks of most European citizens – a practice such citizens have little *unmediated* sense of. While this of course holds in large measure in respect of police practices within European states, intra-national policing retains both a visible presence in local social relations and an orientation to dangers about which citizens often possess some personal experience or situated/local knowledge. None of this really holds at the transnational level. Here law enforcement agents operate mostly 'behind the scenes' in response to 'threats' that are either (1) obscure to lay understanding by virtue of the secrecy and technical expertise that surround them (e.g. money laundering, counterfeiting euros); or (2) apparent but rather 'placeless', operating at a distance from the lived relations of particular European localities (e.g. illegal migration, the cross-border trafficking of people, drugs or stolen goods). This, coupled with a regime of media reporting that combines routine inattention to developments in European criminal justice (den Boer and Wallace 2001: 501), with an often zealous, securitising focus on the 'dangers' posed by asylum-seeking or transnational crime, also serves to give this field of regulatory politics its particular social form.

Fourthly, one needs to address the fact that European policing is marked by a *deep asymmetry in the social distribution of its benefits and burdens*. Such asymmetries of course also obtain within national settings – policing burdens being commonly experienced by the most economically and socially disadvantaged individuals and social groups. Yet there are processes in play at this level (traffic regulation, the enforcement of soft drug laws and so on) which mean that policing remains for 'law-abiding' citizens a potentially double-edged sword, one whose burdens might periodically fall upon them (or those close to them) in ways that can make the control of police conduct an experientially pressing concern. In the field of European policing, how-ever, these benefits and burdens have been almost entirely decoupled – the policing of transnational crime being an activity directed largely *at Others* (migrants, organised criminals, drugs traffickers, etc.) on *behalf of us* (Europe's citizens). These various categories of Other are, moreover, both routinely represented as alien, marginal and dangerous, and generally lacking in cultural or political capital.

These considerations matter for a number of reasons. On the one hand, they help explain the relative absence across Europe of public demands for more democratically responsive forms of postnational policing, and the ease with which European political and police elites can secure 'legitimacy' by dramatising selected threats and indicating what is being – or 'must' be – done to repress them. Yet they also warn us of the risks that attend strategies of democratisation in this field, risks that inhere in creating institutional spaces that cement processes of securitisation by enabling voice to be given to the untutored prejudices and anxieties of European citizens vis-à-vis the threat posed by 'alien' or 'criminal' Others. It is to head off this possibility, and further the chances of European policing unfolding in a manner capable of countering tendencies towards securitisation, that my second strand of analysis is directed.

Building on recent work on the governance of plural policing in national contexts (Loader 2000), I want to suggest that we conceptualise the problem of democracy in European policing around a *principle of public justice*. In that earlier intervention, I set out the component elements of such a principle (a politics of recognition, of human rights and of allocation) and indicated how they might serve to regulate plural policing networks in ways consistent with considerations of democratic deliberation, effectiveness and equity. My task here is to demonstrate the potential value of the three constitutive moments of public justice to the task of democratising cross-border police institutions and processes, and to consider how they might be adapted to the specificities of the European policing field. Using a slight reformulation borrowed from Ulrich Preuss (1998: 148), let us briefly take each in turn.

Recognition

The politics of recognition demands that policing policy is determined by processes of public will-formation that elicit and take account of the views of all individuals and groups likely to be affected by relevant decisions. In the European field, such a politics points in the direction of creating new deliberative spaces that enable a diverse range of police audiences to contest the institutional forms and practical strategies that compose postnational policing. Opening up the 'comitology' process to a wide range of non-governmental organisations (including those representing non-EU citizens such as asylum seekers, or recipients of police interventions beyond the EU's borders) presents one obvious possibility here (Eriksen 2000). So too does the involvement on non-state actors (such as the Civil Society Forum – Curtin 1997: 57) in justice and home affairs summits, and the development of the European Parliament's role in delivering more robust forms of deliberative oversight for cross-border policing.

Rights

Concerns with questions of recognition and representation tend – quite properly – to privilege substantive outcomes that can secure the broadest levels of citizen agreement. This plainly, however, harbours certain majoritarian dangers, and to this extent needs supplementing by a politics of rights that delimits the outcomes of policy-formation processes to those that demonstrably avoid either (1) prejudicing the active rights of any individual or social group affected by the decision; or (2) being disproportionately detrimental to the other legitimate interests and aspirations of such individuals and groups. In terms of European policing, such a politics requires at least the full application of the EU's Convention of Fundamental Rights to matters of police co-operation, and, relatedly, the making of Europol's activities justiciable before the European Court of Justice. Rights-based considerations may also have a particular purchase in areas of cross-border policing (such as actions against money laundering) which are technically specialist and remote from citizens; areas where matters of due process constitute perhaps the main democratic imperative. The cultivation within the European policing complex of a human rights culture also stands as an important political priority here, not least in seeking to counterbalance dominant security agendas.

Resources

The politics of resources (or what I once – with less alliterative flair – termed allocation) is concerned with trying to ensure that all citizens are provided with a 'fair' share of available policing goods; something that requires attention both to the unwarranted 'over' (or overly invasive) policing of particular individuals or social groups, and to the inability of (disadvantaged) citizens and communities to acquire a proportionate level of such goods (cf. Johnston 1999: ch. 10). At a European level, this has two plausible levels of application. It directs attention, first of all, to the balance that is to be struck between the funds taken up by the field of justice and home affairs, and those available for other social goods delivered by the EU, something that impinges directly on the question of securitisation. Within the justice and home affairs domain itself, it signals, secondly, the importance of establishing forms of democratic input into, and oversight of, the processes that determine how governmental resources are distributed, most obviously in respect of the formulation of Europol's annual priorities. The European Parliament could, in both these respects, fruitfully be accorded a more proactive role in this field.

*

I have been able here to offer no more than a preliminary sketch of the ways in which a concept of public justice might enable the European policing field to be structured in a manner that is democratically more responsive and capable of providing an effective counterbalance to dominant securitising tendencies. The prospects of the field moving in such a direction remain however, for reasons I have touched upon, somewhat remote. There is among Europe's citizens relatively little awareness of, let alone active concern about, emergent modes of cross-border policing. In the light of this, and in the absence of effective channels of democratic supervision, Europe's political and justice elites have little trouble in either 'going on' in this field without much regard to 'public opinion' or, more proactively, in mobilizing public 'fears' about 'alien' or 'criminal' Others as a device for securing public support, or resources, or both. Herein, perhaps, are to be found the greatest – and most disquieting – temptations of securitising projects and discourses; temptations that might yet all too easily result in a European *cultural* identity being constructed negatively, in defensive opposition to an apprehended array of 'existential threats' to 'Europe' and its security (Wæver 1996; Buzan *et al*. 1998: 27).

Yet while this must stand as the dominant strand of this tale, it remains – as I have indicated – only part of the story. The EU and its democratic shortcomings have, for instance, in the aftermath of Maastricht, assumed a greater prominence in the consciousness of Europe's citizens – something with unsettling and uncertain im-plications for the EU's future development (Weiler 1999: 4). This 'polity in constant motion' also arguably exhibits a constitutional plasticity far greater than that of any of its member states; something that makes the question of capacity and institution-building both unusually prominent and more than usually 'up for grabs'. And since 1992, the EU has begun to articulate a discourse of postnational citizenship in ways that open up a space for immanent critique and an alternative democratic politics; a space around which a genuinely European civil society – and public sphere – is perhaps slowly starting to form. The further development of this political space – and with it the possibility of deepening forms of *civic* identification with common European institutions – invites us, it seems to me, to seek to infuse EU politics with a spirit of 'democratic experimentalism' (Unger 1998: 5–29). Such a project must, of course, proceed incrementally, with realistic goals, in pursuit of small gains. But it must do so in the expectation that a different, more democratic Europe remains capable of being built. It is in this – Ungerian – spirit that these reflections on the future governance of European policing are proffered.

Acknowledgements

Earlier versions of this chapter were presented as papers at the Department of Law, European University Institute, Florence; the Trento Doctoral Programme on Organised Crime, University of Bologna; the ESRC 'Future governance' programme seminar on 'How does crime policy travel?', Department of Criminology, Keele University; and the 2001 joint meetings of the Law and Society Association/Research Committee on the Sociology of Law (ISA), Central European University, Budapest. I would like to thank all those who participated in the discussions that ensued, as well as Monica den Boer, James Sheptycki and Neil Walker for their comments on the earlier text. The usual disclaimer applies.

Notes

1 These threats in fact represent but one of the motors driving the development of European policing and cannot be said to have determined the *form* of response that has emerged over the last four decades (Anderson *et al.* 1995: ch. 1). Indeed, one of the claims I want to develop in this chapter is that the 'naming' of these events is part of what is at issue in conditioning the kind of transnational policing capacity that takes shape in Europe over the coming period.

2 The third pillar is administered by an elaborate institutional structure that encompasses not only the Council of National Justice and Interior Ministers and the Committee of Permanent Representatives (Coreper), but also the Article 36 Committee (named, since 1997, after the authorising section of the Amsterdam Treaty) comprising permanent representatives from the justice and interior ministries of member states. This committee in turn has a (current) total of ten working parties, four of which deal directly with police matters (Walker 2000a: 236; den Boer and Wallace 2001: 514–15).

3 The designation 'third' pillar signifies the addition of a new field of EU competence to that of the first pillar dealing with economic integration and a second pillar concerned with common foreign and security policy. By transferring visa, asylum, etc., to the first pillar, the Treaty of Amsterdam has rendered these policy domains subject to European Commission initiative and qualified majority voting in the EU Council of Ministers, thereby reducing the power of individual member states.

4 Of particular prominence here are the involvements of EU member state police agents in dealing with the aftermath of war in the former Yugoslavia, whether in the form of 'peacekeeping' patrols, or in trying to stem migration flows into Europe through the so-called 'Balkan corridor'. Against the backdrop of the fading distinction between 'internal' and

'external' security (Anderson *et al*. 1995: ch. 5; Bigo 2000b) one should also mention the onset of the European Rapid Reaction Force, which can plausibly be viewed as a vehicle for enhancing and extending the EU's capacity to make *police* interventions beyond its borders (cf. Hardt and Negri 2000: 18–19; Statewatch 2000a; Caygill 2001). Such developments raise a host of issues – whose 'police' go where? for what purposes? upon whose authority? with what form of legitimacy? – that go to the heart of the new security constellation emerging in Europe.

5 Europol has since 1999 produced two versions of its annual report, a promotional public document (from where this quotation is taken) and a version marked 'Limite' which, though unclassified, is not routinely released to the EU institutions (Statewatch 2000b).

6 Mention ought also to be made in this context of the proposals put forward in June 2001 by German Chancellor Gerhard Schröder and French Prime Minister Lionel Jospin – in the course of their otherwise divergent schemes for the future of European integration – for the further expansion of Europol and for the establishment of a European border police, a body that would assume a visible presence (in sites such as international airports) and possess operational powers (Jospin 2001: 4; Schröder 2001: 7).

7 This restless institutional innovation is, however, a feature European policing shares with other dimensions of the wider European polity. Unlike modern European states – whose builders often took great steps to recover or invent lines of historical connection between the state and an antecedent (ethnic) nation – the EU was consciously constructed as a revolt against Europe's violent, nationalistic past – a past that has long since functioned as its Other (Wæver 1996: 122). The EU's polity-building thus appears to stand in constant fear of institutional stagnation and to seek legitimation through recourse to future-oriented myths (Shore 2000: 206).

8 This chapter aims to develop two organising thematics of my recent work on policing and security – one concerned with local/national cultures of policing (e.g. Loader 1997), the other with policing and governance (e.g. Loader 2000) – *in the direction of Europe*. In so doing, I also hope to make some small contribution to making good what Joseph Weiler (1999: 86) has recently described as 'a real dearth of ideological and cultural scrutiny' in EU studies (see, however, Shore 2000).

9 This theoretical perspective on policing and the social is set out in greater length in Loader (1997). An attempt to think through its implications for the connections between police, nation and statehood can be found in Loader and Walker (2001: 20–5).

10 I use the term 'field' here – following Bourdieu – to mean a structured space of positions within which individual and collective actors struggle for dominance; struggles whose outcome, Bourdieu maintains, depends on the distribution among such actors, and the deployment by them, of specific forms of 'capital' – economic, symbolic and cultural. A lively introduction to this and homologous terms within Bourdieu's sociology can be found in Bourdieu and Wacquant (1992).

11 This shared 'feel' seems likely to include the realisation that 'Euro-crime' offers a vehicle through which police organisations can demand – and attract – new resources, whether in the form of jobs, powers or technology.

12 We should also take cognisance here of the burgeoning role that private security companies are performing, not only – to varying degrees – within specific nation-states across Europe, but also in shaping developments transnationally (deWaard 1999). While much of the private security industry continues to comprise small to medium-sized companies operating on a local, regional or national basis, there exist a number of firms whose involvement in the production and marketing of security services is now global in its reach (Johnston 2000). As agents operating in many nation-states (but strongly rooted in none), and driven by a combination of commercial imperatives and free market dispositions, they are beginning to play an important – and very particular – role in the securitisation of Europe, not least in mushrooming security markets in the post-communist east.

13 Walker (1998, 2000b) has noted that 'federalism' has at various points provided a further imaginative resource for those seeking to develop a more robust European policy capacity, with a European police force standing – like flags, anthems, passports and other icons of nationhood – as a potent symbol of the emergent European state. Having reached a high point in the early 1990s with the formation of Europol the related elements of this federalist project seem of late to have lost some political impetus and confidence and to have become uncoupled from one another. Proposals to enhance European policing now rarely deploy this particular nation-building rhetoric (see, for instance, Jospin 2001; Schröder 2001).

14 The EU was, of course, originally conceived as a security project – one whose *raison d'être* was the pacification of interstate violence in Europe. The important exception of the Balkans notwithstanding, this goal has been largely accomplished, the great success of the European project having been to 'domesticate' relations between European states and to rule out 'anti-political' acts between them (Wæver 1996). Yet this very accomplishment has – as Weiler (1999: 257) observes – served to rob 'peace' and 'order' of their mobilising force as ideals legitimating further political integration.

15 This frenetic level of activity and policy formation has, it should be remembered, taken place in a domain where the European Commission largely lacks rights of initiative and specific legislative competence – much of it, as I have already indicated, taking the form of 'soft law'. This suggests that the distinction between intergovernmental and supranational policy-making that is so often mobilised in discussions of the EU and its futures is *not* proving decisive in this field, at least at the level of 'getting things done'. The baleful effects of intergovernmentalism on the transparency and accountability of decision-making are, of course, another matter.

16 The avoidance of these tendencies requires us to grasp more fully the paradox that the goals associated with security (order, safety, trust, etc.) can

most effectively be realised, not by the conscious, directed pursuit of 'security' policies and discourse, but – as Wæver (1998: 92) nicely has it – 'by doing other things' (see further on the 'paradoxes of security' Berki 1986: ch. 2). The example Wæver gives in this regard concerns the formation of western European states into a 'security community' in the 1950s and 1960s, a process carried out, not by thinking in terms of security/ insecurity, but by taking broader steps towards economic and political integration. The lesson he draws from this is as follows: 'For practitioners, to concentrate on non-security matters might be a sound security strategy' (1998: 71).

17 The aforementioned role that commercial security operatives are playing in processes of securitisation within Europe merely compounds these questions of distribution and accountability still further.

18 Consider in this regard the recent politics of asylum in Britain. It is likely – outside a number of specific locations – that few British citizens have ever known, met or knowingly seen, or even know anyone who has known, met or seen, an asylum seeker. As such, individuals have little situated knowledge with which to filter dominant media and political scripts about how to make sense of, and respond to, asylum; and the issue is to this extent being played out ideologically almost entirely at the level of popular imagination. The New Labour government – to its shame – has done much to fuel this imagination, little to counter it.

References

Anderson, B. (1991) *Imagined Communities: Reflections on the Origins of Nationalism* (rev. edn). London: Verso.

Anderson, M. (1989) *Policing the World: Interpol and the Politics of International Police Cooperation*. Oxford: Clarendon Press.

Anderson, M., den Boer, M., Cullen, P., Gilmore, W., Raab, C. and Walker, N. (1995) *Policing the European Union: Theory, Law and Practice*. Oxford: Clarendon Press.

Bauman, Z. (1999) *In Search of Politics*. Cambridge: Polity Press.

Bayley, D. (1985) *Patterns of Policing*. New Brunswick, NJ: Rutgers University Press.

Beetham, D. (1991) *The Legitimation of Power*. Basingstoke: Macmillan.

Beetham, D. and Lord, C. (1998) *Legitimacy and the European Union*. Harlow: Longman.

Bellamy, R. and Castiglione, D. (2000) 'The uses of democracy: reflections on the European democratic deficit', in E. Oddvar Eriksen and J. Erik Fossum (eds) *Democracy in the European Union: Integration through Deliberation?*. London: Routledge.

Berki, R.N. (1986) *Security and Society: Reflections on Law, Order and Politics*. London: Dent.

Bigo, D. (1994) 'The European internal security field: stakes and rivalries in the newly developing area of police intervention', in M. Anderson and M. den Boer (eds.) *Policing Across National Boundaries*. London: Pinter.

Bigo, D. (2000a) 'Liaison officers in Europe: new officers in the European security field', in J. Sheptycki (ed.) *Issues in Transnational Policing*. London: Routledge.

Bigo, D. (2000b) 'When two become one: internal and external securitisations in Europe', in M. Kelstrup and M. Williams (eds) *International Relations Theory and the Politics of European Integration: Power, Security and Community*. London: Routledge.

Bourdieu, P. and Wacquant, L. (1992) *An Invitation to Reflexive Sociology*. Cambridge: Polity Press.

Brubaker, R. (1992) *Citizenship and Nationhood in France and Germany*. Cambridge, MA: Harvard University Press.

Buzan, B., Wæver, O. and de Wilde, J. (1998) *Security: A New Framework for Analysis*. London: Lynne Rienner.

Castells, M. (1997) *The Information Age: Economy, Society and Culture. Vol. II. The Power of Identity*. Oxford: Blackwell.

Castells, M. (1998) *The Information Age: Economy, Society and Culture. Vol. III. End of Millennium*. Oxford: Blackwell.

Caygill, H. (2001) 'Perpetual police? Kosovo and the elision of police and military violence', *European Journal of Social Theory*, 4(1): 73–80.

Curtin, D. (1997) *Postnational Democracy: The European Union in Search of a Political Philosophy*. The Hague: Kluwer.

de Búrca, G. (2001) 'The drafting of the European Union Charter of Fundamental Rights', *European Law Review*, 26: 126–38.

Deflem, M. (2000) 'Bureaucratization and social control: historical foundations of international police cooperation', *Law and Society Review*, 34(4): 739–78.

den Boer, M. (1994) 'The quest for European policing: rhetoric and justification in a disorderly debate', in M. Anderson and M. den Boer (eds) *Policing across National Boundaries*. London: Pinter.

den Boer, M. (1999) 'Internationalization: a challenge to police organizations in Europe', in R.I. Mawby (ed.) *Policing across the World: Issues for the Twenty-first Century*. London: UCL Press.

den Boer, M. and Wallace, W. (2001) 'Justice and home affairs: integration through incrementalism?', in H. Wallace and W. Wallace (eds) *Policy-making in the European Union* (4th edn). Oxford: Oxford University Press.

deWaard, J. (1999) 'The private security industry in international perspective', *European Journal on Criminal Policy and Research*, 7(1): 143–74.

Dyson, K. (1980) *The State Tradition in Western Europe*. Oxford: Martin Robertson.

Ellison, G. and Smyth, J. (2000) *The Crowned Harp: Policing Northern Ireland*. London: Pluto.

Emsley, C. (1996) *The English Police: A Political and Social History* (2nd edn). Harlow: Longman.

Emsley, C. (2000) *Gendarmes and the State in Nineteenth-century Europe*. Oxford: Oxford University Press.

Ericson, R. and Haggerty, K. (1997) *Policing the Risk Society*. Oxford: Clarendon Press.

Eriksen, E.O. (2000) 'Deliberative supranationalism in the EU', in E.O. Eriksen and J.E. Fossum (eds) *Democracy in the European Union: Integration through Deliberation?*. London: Routledge.

Eriksen, E.O. and Fossum, J.E. (2000) 'Post-national Integration', in E.O. Eriksen and J.E. Fossum (eds) *Democracy in the European Union: Integration through Deliberation?*. London: Routledge.

Habermas, J. (2001) *The Postnational Constellation: Political Essays*. Cambridge: Polity Press.

Hardt, M. and Negri, A. (2000) *Empire*. Cambridge, MA: Harvard University Press.

Hobsbawm, E. (1997) 'An afterword: European Union at the end of the century', in J. Klausen and L. Tilly (eds) *European Integration in Social and Historical Perspective*. Oxford: Rowman & Littlefield.

Huysmans, J. (1998) 'Security! What do you mean? From concept to thick signifier', *European Journal of International Relations*, 4(2): 226–55.

Huysmans, J. (2000) 'The European Union and the securitization of migration', *Journal of Common Market Studies*, 38(5): 751–77.

Joerges, C. and Vos, E. (eds) (1999) *EU Committees: Social Regulation, Law and Politics*. Oxford: Hart Publishing.

Johnston, L. (1999) *Policing Britain: Risk, Security and Governance*. Harlow: Longman.

Johnston, L. (2000) 'Transnational private policing: the impact of commercial security', in J. Sheptycki (ed.) *Issues in Transnational Policing*. London: Routledge.

Jospin, L. (2001) *On the Future of an Enlarged Europe* (http://www.premier-ministre.gouv.fr/en).

Loader, I. (1997) 'Policing and the social: questions of symbolic power', *British Journal of Sociology*, 48(1): 1–18.

Loader, I. (2000) 'Plural policing and democratic governance', *Social and Legal Studies*, 9(3): 323–45.

Loader, I. (2002) 'Governing European policing: some problems and prospects', *Policing and Society*, 12(4): 291–305.

Loader, I. and Walker, N. (2001) 'Policing as a public good: reconstituting the connections between policing and the state', *Theoretical Criminology*, 5(1): 9–35.

Loveday, B. (1999) 'Government and accountability of the police', in R.I. Mawby (ed.) *Policing across the World: Issues for the Twenty-first Century*. London: UCL Press.

Lyon, D. (2001) *Surveillance Society: Monitoring Everyday Life*. Buckingham: Open University Press.

MacCormick, N. (1999) *Questioning Sovereignty*. Oxford: Oxford University Press.

Manning, P. (2000) 'Policing new social spaces', in J. Sheptycki (ed.) *Issues in Transnational Policing*. London: Routledge.

Meehan, E. (1993) *Citizenship and the European Community*. London: Sage.

Monar, J. (2000) 'The EU's role in the fight against racism and xenophobia: evaluation and prospects after Amsterdam and Tampere', *Liverpool Law Review*, 22: 7–20.

Nadelman, E. (1993) *Cops across Borders: The Internationalization of US Criminal Law Enforcement*. Philadelphia, PA: Pennsylvania State University Press.

Preuss, U. (1998) 'Citizenship in the European Union: a paradigm for transnational democracy?', in D. Archibugi *et al.* (eds) *Re-imagining Political Community: Studies in Cosmopolitan Democracy*. Cambridge: Polity Press.

Prodi, R. (2001) *For a Strong Europe, with a Grand Design and the Means of Action*. (http://www.europa.eu.int/comm/commissioners/prodi/paris_en.htm).

Ruggiero, V. (2000) 'Transnational crime: official and alternative fears', *International Journal of the Sociology of Law*, 28: 187–99.

Schlesinger, P. and Kevin, D. (2000) 'Can the European Union become a sphere of publics?', in E.O. Eriksen and J.E. Fossum (eds) *Democracy in the European Union: Integration through Deliberation?*. London: Routledge.

Schmitter, P. (1996) 'Imagining the future of the Euro-polity with the help of new concepts', in G. Marks *et al.* (eds) *Governance in the European Union*. London: Sage.

Schröder, G. (2001) *Responsibility for Europe* (http://www.spd.de/english/politics/partycongress/europe. html).

Sheptycki, J. (1998) 'The global cops cometh: reflections on transnationalization, knowledge work and policing subculture', *British Journal of Sociology*, 49(1): 57–74.

Sheptycki, J. (1999) 'Political culture and structures of social control: police-related scandal in the low countries in comparative perspective', *Policing and Society*, 9(1): 1–32.

Shore, C. (2000) *Building Europe: The Cultural Politics of European Integration*. London: Routledge.

Siedentop, L. (2000) *Democracy in Europe*. Harmondsworth: Penguin Books.

Simon, J. (1997) 'Governing through crime', in L. Friedman and G. Fisher (eds) *The Crime Connection: Essays in Criminal Justice*. Boulder, CO: Westview Press.

Statewatch (1999a) 'Tampere: a victory for "spin" over content?', *Statewatch Bulletin*, 9: September–October.

Statewatch (1999b) 'The story of Tampere: an undemocratic process excluding civil society', *Statewatch Bulletin*, 9: September–October.

Statewatch (2000a) 'Global "policing" role for EU', *Statewatch Bulletin*, 10: July–August.

Statewatch (2000b) 'Where now for accountability in the EU?', *Statewatch News Online* (http://www.statewatch.org/news/index.html).

Strange, S. (1996) *The Retreat of the State: The Diffusion of Power in the World Economy*. Cambridge: Cambridge University Press.

Turner, V. (1974) *Dramas, Fields and Metaphors: Symbolic Action in Human Society*. Ithica, NY: Cornell University Press.

Unger, R.M. (1987) *Social Theory: Its Situations and Tasks*. Cambridge: Cambridge University Press.

Unger, R.M. (1998) *Democracy Realized: The Progressive Alternative*. London: Verso.

Wæver, O. (1996) 'European security identities', *Journal of Common Market Studies*, 34(1): 103–32.

Wæver, O. (1998) 'Insecurity, security and asecurity in the west European non-war community', in E. Adler and M. Barnett (eds) *Security Communities*. Cambridge: Cambridge University Press.

Walden, K. (1982) *Visions of Order: The Canadian Mounties in Symbol and Myth*. Toronto: Butterworths.

Walker, N. (1998) 'European policing and the politics of regulation', in P. Cullen and W. Gilmore (eds) *Crimes sans Frontières: International and European Legal Approaches*. Edinburgh: Edinburgh University Press.

Walker, N. (2000a) *Policing in a Changing Constitutional Order*. London: Sweet & Maxwell.

Walker, N. (2000b) 'Transnational contexts', in F. Leishman *et al.* (eds) *Core Issues in Policing* (2nd edn). Harlow: Longman.

Weiler, J. (1999) *The Constitution of Europe: 'Do the New Clothes Have an Emperor' and Other Essays on European Integration*. Cambridge: Cambridge University Press.

Williams, R. (1977) *Marxism and Literature*. Oxford: Oxford University Press.

Williams, R. (1981) *Culture*. Harmondsworth: Penguin Books.

Zedner, L. (2000) 'In pursuit of security,' in T. Hope and R. Sparks (eds) *Crime, Risk and Insecurity: Law and Order in Everyday Life and Political Discourse*. London: Routledge.

Chapter 5

The cultural embeddedness of social control: Reflections on a comparison of Italian and North American cultures concerning punishment

Dario Melossi

In the field of the sociology of punishment, as in other fields of sociology, the problem of comparison is first and foremost a problem of translation. 'Translation', however, strictly speaking is impossible.[1] Conversation between different cultures is possible, but not translation from one to another (Parekh 2000). Any term, even the simplest, is embedded within a cultural context, or milieu, that gives it its meaning. If culture and even thought are inextricably linked with natural languages, as Sapir and Whorf suggested (Sapir 1933), neither language nor culture are hermetic entities. On the contrary, to get hold of a linguistic toolbox is absolutely crucial to the possibility of 'entering' into another culture: the immigrant who slowly (very slowly usually if he or she is not very young) learns a different language until such language becomes a second mother tongue has to learn at the same time to impersonate the person who is a member of the culture where that language is used. In social science, I do not think anybody has expressed the problem better than Alfred Schutz in his famous essay on 'The stranger':

> The discovery that things in his new surroundings look quite different from what he expected them to be at home is frequently the first shock to the stranger's confidence in the validity of his habitual 'thinking as usual'. Not only the picture which the stranger has brought along of the cultural pattern of the

approached group but the whole hitherto unquestioned scheme of interpretation current within the home group becomes invalidated. It cannot be used as a scheme of orientation within the new social surroundings. For the members of the approached group *their* cultural pattern fulfils the functions of such a scheme. But the approaching stranger can neither use it simply as it is nor establish a general formula of transformation between both cultural patterns permitting him, so to speak, to convert all the coordinates within one scheme of orientation into those valid within the other (1944: 503–4).

Sociologists (and others) are notorious for their tendency to invent such 'general transformation formulas'. Schutz's essay represents a radical critique of social scientists' imperialism vis-à-vis the rights of the standpoint of society's ordinary members. At the same time, such general formulas of transformation can produce important effects of cultural colonisation when they are accompanied by the simultaneous exportation of social models.

The meaning of an object represents the outcome of the communicative exchange in which that object is involved. Because such communicative exchange takes place in the midst of a complex set of communicative exchanges – what we call a 'culture', a network which is historically and spatially located in a given system of action and behaviour (Mills 1963 [1940]) – it is only within such a complex network that the object's meaning may be determined. One of the most interesting efforts at defining social control in the broadest sense sociologically is offered by those who have defined it as the ability, by given actors within a complex social system, of influencing the determination of the meanings which are typical of that system (Mead 1964 [1925]; Melossi 1990). Such determination of meaning is not separable from the act which is oriented towards the object so defined and named. Ethnomethodologists have shown that the moral characterisation of the stable features of the ordinary world, a characterisation typical of childhood, does not disappear when we become adults, and easily emerges when such stable features are somehow questioned by the appearance of unexpected or 'deviant' occurrences (Garfinkel 1967).

In the century that has recently come to an end, social theory increasingly moved towards a reaction against dualist concepts of thought and sensation, of culture and nature, of discourse and action. Pragmatism was the orientation that most clearly made of such a reaction its programmatic move (Thayer 1982; Rorty 1999). The old distinction between a 'conceptual' and a 'practical' world did not hold any longer. Mead, for instance, stated that 'the process of communication is one which is more universal than that of the universal religion or universal economic process in that it is one that serves them both' (1934: 259).[2] Discourse (or even thought) cannot be conceived in isolation from practice but is an inextricable component of social action. Discourse cannot be said simply to 'describe' what is done and acted upon. For pragmatists thought is, in a sense, a special circumstance of action, the action that cannot be completed through habit, that is faced with a difficulty or an obstacle. Sociological understanding therefore goes beyond what John L. Austin called 'doing things with words' (1962): it is not only a special kind of words, or sentences, about which we can say that we 'do' things when we use them. It is in our uttering of every word that we 'do' something in the broader perspective just mentioned. By the concept of 'embeddedness' of specific historical institutions, I therefore mean that such institutions cannot be conceived separately from the historical evolution and development of the larger setting of social action within which they have emerged – a setting constituted also through given cultural traditions.

The embeddedness of crime and punishment

All this is particularly true for analysis of that quintessential moral practice that is the attribution of criminal responsibility and punishment. Understanding of variations in penal and criminal policies across societies can only be based on recognition of the 'embedded' character of these policies. On the one hand we observe conceptualisations about how to organise the world emerging more or less at the same time in very different and very distant parts of the world – ideas such as 'the factory' or 'the prison' being very good cases in point. On the other hand the usage of identical words often obscures the degree to which they are embedded in the different history of different places, as well as being articulated through (partially) different discourses. These co-occurrences have certainly something to do with phenomena of 'translation' and 'dependency' wherein the cultural artefacts of more powerful social formations are imported into less powerful social worlds – whether these social worlds coincide or not with nation-states. To give but a few examples: the conceptualisations of the (northern Italian) positive school were not only applied mainly to southern Italian brigands (Melossi 2000b) but were also exported among southern Italian intelligentsia and later on to Latin America, where they were creatively reinterpreted in the different national settings (Del Olmo 1981; Teti 1993; Salvatore and Aguirre 1996); British criminal policies were extended and adapted to English colonies throughout the British Empire (Sumner 1982; Pratt 1992; Agozino forthcoming); North American sociology of deviance was imported into England and Europe after the early 1960s (Melossi 2000a); and southern European 'critical' criminology was again imported into Latin America starting in the 1970s.[3]

Edwin Sutherland, for one, maintained that there is a 'consistency' between the fundamental cultural values of a given society and its punitive system (1939: 348).[4] I would also add – since this is implicit in Sutherland's differential association theory – that this consistency extends to cultural values (and therefore the transmission of these values) and the prevailing types of crime. One possible way of thinking about all this could be to rely on the distinction that was advanced by Durkheim in a pioneering analysis when, writing about the 'laws of penal execution', he distinguished between a 'qualitative' and a 'quantitative' law (1969 [1900]). By 'quality' Durkheim meant the kind of penal instruments used at a specific time in a given society and by 'quantity' he meant their 'internal' variability and size. Now, as to 'quality', when we look at imprisonment in many countries, not only do we find institutions that are superficially similar but we also find that the composition of their populations is similar. The same kind of people generally inhabit prisons: inmates usually are young males, of lower-class background and often belong to racial, ethnic, cultural or national/regional minorities. The ratio of females to males, for instance, hardly strays from around 5 per cent, at least in modern times.[5] If, however, instead of the formal architecture of the prison or the internal composition of the prison population, we consider the functioning of the prison or the number of convicts, what criminologists call 'the imprisonment rate', then, from such a 'quantitative' perspective, we see wild oscillations between societies and between different historical periods. The most apparent today, for instance, is certainly the obvious disproportion between imprisonment rates in western Europe, oscillating between 50 and 100 per 100,000, and those in the USA that have now reached about 500 per 100,000. Therefore, even if the *ratio* of males to females, or of ethnic minorities, tends to be roughly the same within each prison system, if we were to compare, for instance, the *rate* of women incarcerated in the USA to those incarcerated in Italy, or the *rate* of ethnic minorities incarcerated in the USA to that of foreigners incarcerated in Italy, we would find that all the North American rates per 100,000 are much higher than the Italian ones.

This may be taken to mean that the structural types of explanation of punishment (those, in other words, which link analysis of the variations in punishment to structural variables of the kind that sociologists tend to postulate in every society – or at least in every 'developed' society – such as economic development, social stratification, type of political system, the relationship between the fiscal system and 'the state', etc.) can be used only to explain (in part) variations which are *internal* to each society (conceived of as a cultural unit) but they will be largely powerless to explain cross-cultural variations, because the latter are characterised by the unique features of a certain society in a given historical period – i.e. those features that Weber in his 'methodological' writings expressed in the concept of 'the historical individual' (1949 [1904]: 78–81).

A genealogy of punishment cannot therefore be a genealogy of punishment in general, in spite of the fact that blueprints for punitive engineering certainly are being and have been exported from society to society. Punishment is deeply embedded in the national/cultural specificity of the environment which produces it. A particularly interesting case, I believe, is the comparison of cultural traditions of punishment, as they have been developing within Protestant societies and especially in the USA – the privileged locale for Weber's analysis – and within Catholic societies in southern Europe or Latin America.[6] In this chapter I intend to compare, more specifically, the USA and Italy. These two societies would seem to place a very different emphasis on the importance of punishment, a difference that has become extraordinary in terms of imprisonment rates in the last 25 years or so, especially if one keeps in mind that international comparisons show that crime rates in the USA are not much higher than either the general European or the Italian crime rates, except for crimes of violence and especially homicides (that however contribute to a very small percentage of imprisonment[7]) (Lynch 1988; van Dijk and Mayhew 1993; Zimring and Hawkins 1997; Langan and Farrington 1998). We may want to assume, therefore, that such differences are not understandable without having recourse to modes of conceiving punishment which are rooted in the different historical backgrounds of the two cultures. It is to such different historical backgrounds that we now turn.

Democracy, the Protestant ethic and punishment

In 1844, in one of his early writings, Marx captured in a nutshell much of what later authors such as Horkheimer and Adorno (1972 [1944]) or Foucault (1977 [1975]) would elaborate:

Luther, we grant, overcame the bondage of *piety* by replacing it by the bondage of *conviction.* He shattered faith in authority because he restored the authority of faith. He turned priests into laymen because he turned laymen into priests. He freed man from outer religiosity because he made religiosity the inner man. He freed the body from chains because he enchained the heart (Marx 1975 [1844]: 182, emphases in original).

Indeed the main penitentiary institutions contrived in the USA soon after their independence, inspired by radical Protestant sectarianism (Weber 1969 [1906]), seemed to be an attempt to realise the programme exposed by Marx. The inspiring principle of the 'penitentiaries' was separation: isolation of the sinner from his fellow creatures and allowing relations only with the representatives of divine and secular authority. The model was that of penance that had first developed in the medieval monasteries of Europe only for the crimes and sins of the monks (Treiber and Steinert 1980). This system was now secularised and extended to all the members of God's flock. It thus represented a true embodiment of Protestant Reformation, especially in its more radical variants. Following Weber's famous reconstruction of this ethos (Weber 1958 [1904–5]), the main point was that the believer could not find solace in the intermediation of the Church, an intermediation that, for the rich, consisted of 'buying' their way to salvation. Such commerce had of course been one of the very bases for the accusations directed against the corrupt, power-eager and fundamentally sceptical Church of Rome, whose 'indulgences' were more a means of securing temporal power than true compassion for the weakness of the flesh. The Philadelphia inmate had no resort other than gazing at the depth of his fall in the solitary confinement of his cell. No 'pagan' delusion could save him from staring at the terrible spectacle of God's rage. No wonder that the new system soon appeared to be connected to an impressive rise in suicides – in an uncanny forewarning of a theory that the French sociologist Emile Durkheim would spell out only at the end of the century (1951 [1897]).

To the eye of the keen observer, however, it might seem incongruent that the American Republic, praised then and later as the most direct vessel to ferry peoples and intellects from the Land of the Social Contract to that of Democracy, would at the same time be the harbouring place of an institution, the prison, that however enlightenedly conceived, is usually identified with pain, suffering and oppression. In fact, it was quite a coincidence that the French aristocrat who had arrived in 1831 to write of penitentiaries would find himself not only deserting his original

85

topic (Sellin 1964) but producing instead the book, *Democracy in America* (de Tocqueville 1961 [1835–40]), which is one of the most important and lasting contributions to the theory of democracy. Could it be that the two topics had so much in common? According to American political theorist Thomas Dumm, following in Foucault's footsteps, they did, because:

> [T]he emergence of the penitentiary in the United States was a project constitutive of liberal democracy. That is, the penitentiary system formed the epistemological project of liberal democracy, creating conditions of knowledge of self and other that were to shape the political subject required for liberal and democratic values to be realised in practice. The American project, a system of self-rule, involved not only the establishment of representative government with an extensive suffrage, but also the establishment of institutions which would encourage the internalisation of liberal democratic values, the creation of individuals who would learn how to rule their selves (1987: 6).

The crucial term here is – following Foucault – self-government, or the government of the self. We could say that the American penitentiary was erected by the Founding Fathers of the nation as an imposing and monumental Gateway to the Republic. And indeed the Quaker philanthropist and reformer Benjamin Rush had described prisons as producing 'Republican machines', human beings, that is, that were supposed to turn from men who were uncivilised, or who had lost their civilisation, into good workers and citizens, able to be introduced into a conversation with their fellow men – the very prerequisite for democracy.

In similar guise, Mexican writer Octavio Paz observed, in a sharp essay comparing the USA and Mexico:

> If the different attitudes of Hispanic Catholicism and English Protestantism could be summed up in two words, I would say that the Spanish attitude is inclusive and the English exclusive. In the former, the notions of conquest and domination are bound up with ideas of conversion and assimilation; in the latter, conquest and domination imply not the conversion of the conquered but their segregation. An inclusive society, founded on the double principle of domination and conversion, is bound to be hierarchical, centralist, and respectful of the individual characteristics of each group. It believes in the strict division of classes and groups, each one

governed by special laws and statutes, but all embracing the same faith and obeying the same lord. An exclusive society is bound to cut itself off from the natives, either by physical exclusion or by extermination; at the same time, since each community of pure-minded men is isolated from other communities, it tends to treat its members as equals and to assure the autonomy and freedom of each group of believers. The origins of American democracy are religious, and in the early communities of New England that dual, contradictory tension between freedom and equality which has been the leitmotiv of the history of the United States was already present (1977: 363–4).

A major prerequisite of the Republican social contract is the identity of the parties to the contract, their basic commonality of civilisation. They were in fact to be part of a rational discourse. They could not simply be *peones* at the basis of the social pyramid, as could happen in the Catholic, authoritarian structure of the Spanish Conquest. The colonists of North America were too ambitious about the greatness and the goodness of the institutions they were building to allow uncivilised men and women to become part of them simply as labour power. Their *souls* had to be conquered. That is, they had to enter into a conversation with the other members of the American covenant. The natural consequence of such lofty ambitions therefore – as Paz observes with chilling logic –was the extermination of those whose souls (if indeed they had been endowed with one!) could not be reached, such as the native inhabitants of North America. Those who, in other words, were perceived as unable, or unwilling, to enter into an enlightened, republican, democratic dialogue.

For those lucky ones who, in spite of their being uncivilised or having lost their civilisation, were still similar enough to the members of the religious covenant to be accepted at least as potential members, it was necessary to arrange those instruments that would lead them to democracy. Of the two 'races which inhabit the territory of the United States', whose destiny deeply moved de Tocqueville in *Democracy in America* (1961 [1835–40]: 393–456), one, the Native American, was too different to be conducted through such narrow passage. The second, 'the coloured', once free, would have been instead generously exposed to the philanthropy of the new penitentiary institutions.

For a long time the 'two races' were treated in an exclusionary mode, for Native Americans to the extent of genocide. 'Indians', considered as foreign nationals (Fitzpatrick 1995), were continuously pushed west, until their land was almost completely taken over by white colonists (Takaki 1979: 80–107). As Takaki notices, citing de Tocqueville, what particularly amazed the French nobleman was 'the ability of white society to deprive the Indians of their rights and exterminate them "with singular felicity, tranquilly, legally, philanthropically ... It is impossible to destroy men with more respect for the laws of humanity" ' (1979: 81, citing de Tocqueville 1961 [1835–40]: 352–3, 364). There was no place, at the time, for Native Americans in the white men's penitentiaries, exactly because, as argued above, the penitentiary was deeply connected to an inclusionist ideology. It was intended to be the entrance into a social contract that one had voluntarily or involuntarily ignored but for which one was deemed to be at least potentially fit.

Often, an original policy of exclusion turned eventually into a policy of inclusion (through the gates of the prison). At the dawn of the Republic, however, the same exclusionist policies applied generally to all the 'black or tawny' races, a label that Benjamin Franklin (1751), for instance, applied to practically all non-English settlers (in fact the occasion of this essay by Franklin was his preoccupation with the increasing numbers of Germans in Pennsylvania (Takaki 1979: 14; Cohn-Bendit and Schmid 1994 [1993]: 96)). In 1850, though, blacks were still largely concentrated in the South as slaves. Their special status made it so that they could not be admitted to the honours of the penitentiary, their discipline 'of choice' being domestic discipline (Sellin 1976: 133–44). In fact black incarceration rates in the South in 1850 were less than half that of whites. The opposite was true in the North where, despite the small number of black men and women, their 'free' condition opened to them the gates of penitentiaries (Sabol 1989: 408–9). Already de Beaumont and de Tocqueville had noticed in their report on the penitentiary system that:

> A young society, exempt from political embarrassments, rich both by its soil and its industry, should be supposed to furnish fewer criminals than a country where the ground is disputed foot by foot, and where the cries produced by political divisions tend to increase the number of offences, because they increase misery by disturbing industry.
>
> Yet if the statistical documents, which we possess of Pennsylvania, should be applied to the rest of the Union, there are in this country more crimes committed than in France, in proportion to the population. Various causes of another nature explain this result: on the one hand, the coloured population, which forms the sixth part of the inhabitants of the United States, and which composes half of the inmates of the prisons; and on the other hand, the foreigners pouring in every year from Europe, and

who form the fifth and sometimes even the fourth part of the number of convicts (1964 [1833]: 99).

In the North, therefore, the freed coloured population and the immigrants had to go through the gateway to the Republic – prisons. This would start happening also in the South, after the Civil War, when many of the 'freed' blacks would again be reduced into servitude, this time penal servitude, through the convict lease system that flourished in the southern states after the Civil War, the clients of which were largely blacks (Sellin 1976: 409). By 1870 in the South, the black incarceration rate was triple that of whites and almost 15 times what had been the case 20 years before, before the Civil War and their 'liberation' (Sabol 1989: 408). However, the disproportionality rate in the South remained lower than in the North (Sabol 1989: 409) because in the North it accompanied the process of migration of blacks from the rural South to northern cities such as Chicago.

In the Protestant New England mould of American culture – a mould which still has a firm grip over the essentials of American culture – there is no place for the fuzzy, authoritarian and deeply conservative indulgence of Catholicism. Right or wrong, white or black, who is (or is perceived to be) on the wrong side of the law shall be punished. But, alas, like with everything else in society, who breaks the law and is powerful (economically, politically, ethnically, racially, culturally, by virtue of sex and so on and so forth) can afford a full use of the 'guarantees' that a developed legal system provides them with. For the others, tough luck. All in all, this policy, however weak on the side of social justice, is 'useful' because an economic system based on competition cannot work without punishments and rewards. Those at the bottom of the social pyramid are perceived as being tempted to break the law more often: less to lose and more to gain. Isn't it therefore only fair that the law pays more attention to their behaviour? As, once again, de Beaumont and de Tocqueville went on:

If we should deduct from the total number of crimes, those committed by Negroes and foreigners, we should undoubtedly find that the white American population commits less crimes than ours. But proceeding thus, we should fall into another error; in fact, to separate the Negroes from the whole population of the United States, would be equal to deducting the poorer classes of the community with us [in France], that *is* to say, *those who commit the crimes* (1964 [1833]: 99, emphasis added).

Such original propensity to punish 'those who commit the crimes', deeply rooted in the premises of American beliefs, has not abated until today. On the contrary, as we saw earlier, US imprisonment rates started rising at a very fast speed during the 1970s climbing up from about 100 per 100,000 to almost 500 per 100,000, giving rise to what we could very well call the US 'great confinement' of the end of the twentieth century (Beckett 1997; Chambliss 1999; Chaiken 2000).

'Scandal of indulgences' in Rome

In Italy, on the other hand, imprisonment rates, especially since the 1950s (Melossi 1998), have oscillated between 50 and 90 per 100,000 inhabitants, with almost insignificant numbers for minors. According to Massimo Pavarini this was accomplished through a very mild and generous application of criminal law at the individual level, and a regular recourse to clemency acts at the collective level (1994: 50). The attempts at launching 'law and order' campaigns in Italy generally speaking have not produced great results for those 'moral entrepreneurs' who were their proponents, the only exceptions being the more politically motivated campaigns, like those against terrorism, organised crime and corruption. In other words, the soft authoritarian paternalism, which has traditionally been the style of choice of Italian elites, has not known a rhetoric of strong penal repression[8] in the same way that it has not generally known a rhetoric of self-government, the opposite of what has been happening in North America.

If we go back to the comparison outlined by Paz, one could claim that, in Italian history – a history strongly defined, especially *politically* by the presence of the Papacy – there has been a tendency to frame religion within a rigid dualism of shepherds and sheep, a sacerdotal caste separated from the rest of the believers. At the moral and legal level, one of the results of this Catholicism Italian-style has been the tendency to be very tolerant, *de facto* if not *de jure,* on moral or social issues, but very rigorous instead against any open challenge to religious and political hierarchies (and therefore also against any open challenge to the Church's teaching on moral issues; the deviant practices that are not openly advocated may instead be tolerated, and the sinner absolved).

In this we may also find a remote cause for the fact that the only law-and-order campaigns that have had some following in Italy have been those carrying a somewhat political profile.[9] The long series of affairs that have punctuated Italian public life, which have been uncovered since 1989 and have also had the effect of bringing down the Christian

Democrat Party, can be explained essentially by the interlacing of crime and politics, namely, the political system and corruption in the North (Della Porta and Vannucci 1999) and the political system and organised crime (*Mafia*) in the South (Stille 1995). In relation to some of these events, Giulio Andreotti, the Christian Democrat leader who was at the time the most powerful man in Italy and who subsequently had to face trial for charges of conspiracy with leading figures from organised crime,[10] in commenting in Parliament about a series of Mafia-related murders in the South, perhaps unwittingly following the precepts of a 'critical' strand of criminology, asked 'not to amplify the cases of violence' (Melossi 1994: 212–14).[11] By saying this, Andreotti was appealing to a culture of indulgence that is often presented in Italy as a manifestation of tolerance. This was nothing particularly new in Italian history. According to analyses by Southern Question writers (*meridion-alisti*), at least since Italian unification in 1861, Roman central governments have shown a very ambiguous behaviour towards organised crime in the South (Putnam 1993; Teti 1993). Gramsci, for instance, wrote that '[p]opular "subversivism" correlates with "sub-versivism" at the top, i.e. with the fact of there never having existed a "rule of law", but only a politics characterised by absolute power and by cliques around individuals or groups' (1971 [1929–35]: 275). The presence in the South of a network of power of which organised crime has been an integral part was functional to the reproduction of conditions of backwardness and political control in those regions, in order to balance the more advanced, and less easily controllable, 'demographic composition' of the North (Gramsci 1971 [1929–35]: 279–318). These authors pointed, in other words, to a very good example of what more recently Foucault has suggested in that very interesting yet often forgotten section of *Discipline and Punish,* where the 'failure' of the prison is 'explained' in terms of its role in transforming potentially dangerous *illegalities* into a much more (politically) useful *delinquency* (1977 [1975]: 257–92). In sum, there has traditionally been, in the Italian cultural tradition, a sort of 'soft' authoritarianism linked to low levels of penal repression, which is the opposite of a democratic rhetoric in North America which goes together with very high levels of penal repression.

Is religious tradition the explanation for the different propensity to punish?

Or so it would seem. It would be quite tempting to conclude that the current very large imprisonment differential between a country characterised by a radical Protestant tradition such as the USA and a country characterised by a homogeneous Catholic tradition such as Italy has to be looked for in the different religious roots of their respective cultures. Such roots would explain the rigorous attitude of severity in one and the indulgent laissez-faire attitude of the other, according to stereotypical images that go at least as far back as Luther's polemic against the sins of Rome.

If one bothers, however, to look at available data, things do not seem to be all that simple. On the one hand, René van Swaaningen (1997: 20–3), for one, has pointed out that Holland has had both a strong Calvinist background and a strong tradition of tolerance. Even more importantly, however, if we examine the long historical development of imprisonment rates in Italy and the USA, matters become much more complicated. Let us consider Figure 5.1, where Italian and US imprisonment data are superimposed. As we can see, American imprisonment rates have been higher than Italian imprisonment rates only since the early 1950s,[12] and the difference appears really huge only after the 1970s, in the period we have called the North American 'great confinement'. Now, were religion the explaining factor, would it not be reasonable to assume that, in secularising societies, as the USA and Italy are both deemed to be, the influence of religion should have become less and less relevant? If this were the case, however, and if our hypothesis of an 'elective affinity' between Protestantism and stern punishment were true, then the imprisonment rates of Italy and the USA should show a behaviour

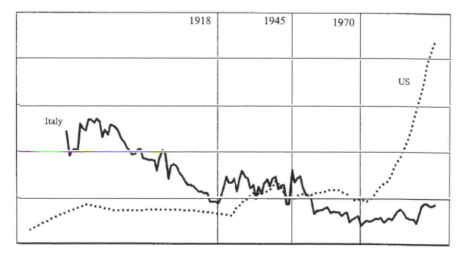

Figure 5.1   Number of inmates per 100,000 inhabitants in Italy and the USA.[14]

exactly the opposite of the one we can see in the figure. American imprisonment rates should have been declining in the long run and Italian imprisonment rates should have been increasing in the long run.[13]

The theoretical point which is raised by this question is the one, I believe, about the role of what we call 'culture'. Instead of thinking of culture as one of the many 'forces' or 'variables' that 'shape' associated life, we may want to think of it as a sort of repertoire of motives (Burke 1969 [1950]), which, as far as religious vocabularies are concerned, are specific to given religious traditions, within each of which it is possible to modulate motives both of severity and of forgiveness. For instance, in his reconstruction of 'the search for alternatives' to imprisonment, David Cayley (1998) reminds us that many caring and forgiving alternatives are currently being shaped in North America by the action of deeply motivated Christian believers from a number of Protestant denominations. And Applegate and others, in a recent article (2000), found that Protestant Christian orientations in the USA may be linked *both* to fundamentalist/punitive motives *and* to compassionate/ rehabilitative ones. I concur therefore with the position taken in a paper by Joachim Savelsberg (1999), where he outlined the importance of what he calls 'foundational cultures', especially religion, in explaining different punitive attitudes and practices between the USA and Germany. In his view, based on a landmark article by Ann Swidler (1986), Catholic and/or Protestant discourses on religion would not be 'determinants' of punitive attitudes but resources available within a cultural 'toolkit'. Swidler's argument cannot be taken to mean, I believe, that cultural repertoires are ready to be picked up within a kind of huge cultural shopping mall. A Catholic tradition of authoritarian paternalism is not the same thing as a Calvinist obsession with legislating morality. Likewise, a Protestant attitude of 'forgiveness' is not the same thing as Catholic 'indulgence'. Specific 'vocabularies of punitive motive' (Melossi 1985) will be selected, in accordance with historically situated settings of action, among available cultural traditions. These are often also the result of a cross-cultural activity of exchange and 'translation' – if, by translation, we mean the process of active reinterpretation outlined at the beginning of this chapter.

All this does, however, beg the question of 'causal' explanation. Available cultural traditions are comprised within a rather limited historical horizon which is the horizon marked by the setting of social action given at a specific time. If there is indeed what Weber used to call an 'elective affinity' (Howe 1978) between given types of ethos of punishment and specific religious orientations, the prevalence of severity or forgiveness will probably result from the interplay of what we called at the beginning of this chapter 'qualitative' and 'quantitative' dimensions of punishment. There is a historical specificity of the behaviour of the two rates, in other words, that should be kept in mind, especially in relation to the variables that have been traditionally associated with changing imprisonment rates. For instance, in the case of Italy, I have found evidence of the impact on imprisonment of economic change (Melossi 1985), of crime and especially serious crime, homicide (Melossi 1995, 1997, 1998 1999), and of migratory movements (Melossi 2001). More generally, Rusche and Kirchheimer's hypothesis of a relationship between the social and economic structure, and particularly the labour market, and imprisonment, has also found ample evidence especially in the USA (for a summary of research, see Chiricos and DeLone 1992). Furthermore, Jacobs and Helms (1996) have also shown, for the USA, the influence of prevailing political orientations.[15]

Focusing on Figure 5.1, we could divide the whole period into four subperiods: before the First World War, between the end of the First World War and the Second World War, between the end of the Second World War and 1970, and from 1970 until the present. Let us briefly consider these four periods in turn.[16] During the period before the First World War, we can observe an early stage – during which both the USA and Italy were being forged from the union of various composing states[17] – characterised by an effort by the two young nations to 'build' a prison system as part of a modern political and legal order. Under these conditions, which lasted until about the 1870s, imprisonment rates were destined to grow, but this would happen under extremely different conditions in the two countries. While, as de Tocqueville stated, the USA was characterised by 'a natural equality of condition' that especially meant an equal possibility of access to the land (for 'the white race'), in Italy, and especially southern Italy, characteristic processes of expulsion of peasants from the countryside were starting to take place that pushed them increasingly towards emigration, while in the North the living conditions of the working class started slowly to turn for the better. In Italy, very high imprisonment rates during the first two decades after the Unification in 1861 were then followed by a second stage, characterised by a continuous declining trend, common to all of Europe in the period, linked to a now fully fledged emigration but also and especially to the improvement of social conditions (Sutherland 1956 [1934]). In the USA at the same time imprisonment rates were quite stable and low (even if, as we have seen, these were very low for whites and already characteristically many times higher for those who could not take advantage of the 'natural equality of conditions', i.e. the Afro-American population).

The period between the two wars was dominated, in both countries, by the 1930s worldwide depression that put a stop to the liberalism and progressivism of the early decades of the century and called for harsher penal policies even if, especially in the USA, the general political progressivism of the New Deal made sure that the huge economic hardships never translated into a comparable rise in imprisonment rates (Jankovic 1977). On the contrary, in Italy the somewhat limited economic impact of the Depression on penal policies was exacerbated by the authoritarian political management of the Fascist regime that, as in contemporary National Socialist Germany, made the fight against crime an essential part of its political agenda.

Matters became even more entangled after the Second World War: on the one hand in the USA the well-being of the period did not really translate into a decline of the imprisonment rates (so that, towards the early 1970s, Al Blumstein and colleagues could write of a homeostatic, self-regulating, basically stable imprisonment system (Blumstein *et al.* 1977)) while, on the other hand, Italy experienced a most decisive fall in its imprisonment rates that around 1970 were among the lowest in the world. The early 1970s represented a turning point for both countries: the 'crisis decades' ensued (Hobsbawm 1994), and 1960s liberalism started to be rejected. While, however, this happened with a real vengeance in the USA, bringing the imprisonment rates of the country to unparalleled heights, in Italy this simply meant a very slow, oscillating tendency to a moderate increase.

The decisive diverging trends after 1945 suggest one last considera-tion. A few years ago, Dane Archer and Rosemary Gartner, basing themselves on extensive cross-national data, proposed a 'brutalisation' theory of crime, according to which 'exemplary' actions by govern-ments, such as the meting out of capital punishment and engaging in wars, would have the effect of presenting their citizens with the message that violence is indeed a way by which differences and conflicts can be resolved, thereby legitimising it. Governments would then act as tried and true 'moral entrepreneurs' and such 'official' forms of legitimisation would then translate into higher rates of violent crime, murder, etc. (Archer and Gartner 1984). Along the same lines, one could then hypothesise that the political institutions of those countries that have found the use of violence and state power 'rewarding' would be much more inclined to recommend the use of violence and stern power, and therefore also severe punishment, than those which have found it 'punishing'. The USA, which exited victoriously from the Second World War and as the only superpower from the confrontation with the Soviet Union at the end of the so-called 'Cold War', would be an example of the former situation; Italy and Germany, for both of which the strong governments of the 1920s and 1930s and then those governments' engagement in war produced disastrous results, would be good examples of the latter case. Certainly, it is a rather common observation in Italy that the experience of Fascism powerfully contributed to a lack of confidence in government and 'the state' after the Second World War (Pavarini 1994: 50–3). There is no doubt at the same time that such a feeling would articulate quite nicely with the 'indulgentist' tradition that, as we have seen, has its roots in a long Italian history and found its logical interpreters in a Catholic party such as the Christian Democrats – a party that held uninterrupted political power exactly for the time of the so-called 'Cold War'.[18] On the contrary, the positive rewards that the USA have seized from the use of violence and power in international relations, engaging in a new war every few years in the course of the twentieth century, would articulate quite nicely with the stern rigour of the most radical varieties of Protestantism. It would also be consistent with the fact that in a small and peaceful country such as Holland, Calvinism has traditionally shown its more tolerant attitude, as Van Swaaningen observed. The personal memories and reflections of the Dutch criminologist, Louk Hulsman, a leading 'abolitionist' thinker, may very well be applied not only to the case of Holland but also more generally to the situation in western European countries after the experience of the horrors of war, dictatorship, military occupation and concentration camps:

> There were quite a lot of people involved in making crime policy and doing things in that field who had war experience and some like me who had also had the experience of being imprisoned. I had seen as a kid how unreliable an official system is. I had seen how most of the people in Holland after the German occupation cooperated with the Germans. I had also been arrested by the Dutch police for resistance, and I had seen that you can't trust them. That naturally has an influence, and there were several other people in the Ministry of Justice with comparable experiences (interview in Cayley 1998: 17).

Likewise, the political culture of a country like Italy – where one of its presidents (from 1978 to 1985), Alessandro Pertini, was just the most famous among the many Italian politicians who had known long periods of imprisonment under Fascism – was highly unlikely to express sympathies for imprisonment and stern punishment.

The cultural embeddedness of discourse on penality, whether in the direction of punitiveness or in that of indulgence and forgiveness, is therefore confirmed by analysis but in a way which appears different from any cultural determinism (that would merely substitute a new determinism for the old 'structural' one). There seems to be indeed an elective affinity between social, economic and political relationships and conditions, and the way in which cultural manifestations have found their roots within religious traditions in various societies and periods. However, such affinity, rather than functioning through rigid ties and linkages, reminds one of the ways in which human beings and especially their intellectual and political elites, responding to change, select motives within available repertoires, rhetoric or 'cultural tool-boxes'. These are, to be sure, *limited* repertoires. As already mentioned, the rigour of radical Protestantism is different from Catholic paternalism, while at the same time the experience of evangelic forgiveness is not the same as a 'Roman' tradition of indulgence. These choices are there to be made nevertheless. A mutual relation of feedback exists between given historical conditions and choices within cultural vocabularies. Once again, also in relation to punishment, we have come to face a conundrum that has been central to social sciences at least since their inception.

Acknowledgements

I would like to thank Tony Jefferson, David Nelken, Joachim Savelsberg, Maximo Sozzo, Colin Sumner, Patrizia Violi and the anonymous reviewers of *Theoretical Criminology* for having read and commented upon previous versions of this chapter, even if of course the whole responsibility for its contents is mine only. I would also like to thank Tommaso Gennari for technical help.

Notes

1 I develop this more fully in Melossi (2000a).
2 One can notice *en passant* that such a standpoint implies a severe blow to that dualism of systems of action and meaning that is still present in Marx's distinction of structure and superstructure, in spite of those pages in the section on Feuerbach of *The German Ideology* (Marx and Engels 1970

[1845–6]: 39–95) where Marx seemed at times to anticipate pragmatist positions.

3 These remarks about exchanges between Italy and Latin America were the matter of a number of fruitful conversations with Maximo Sozzo.

4 Sutherland in turn had probably been inspired by Georg Rusche's manuscript (that was to become Rusche and Kirchheimer 1969 [1939]) of which he was one of the first North American readers (Melossi 1980).

5 Long-term historical analyses of data on women in prison show quite a different picture (Feeley and Little 1991).

6 On Italy, see Melossi (1981 [1977]: 63–95); on Latin America, see the collection edited by Salvatore and Aguirre (1996).

7 I was able to show, however, that at least in the Italian case the statistical association between the murder rate and the imprisonment rate is much stronger than what would simply be the result of the number of incarcerations triggered by murder charges (Melossi 1995, 1997, 1998, 1999). In other words, in statistical terms – and whatever the cause of that – one murder is associated with many more incarcerations than the very few that are a direct legal consequence of the murder.

8 This does not mean that politically motivated *military* repression or violence has not often happened in Italian history.

9 At least until the appearance of immigration in the 1980s but that is another story (see Melossi 2001)!

10 He was then acquitted.

11 About these events, see Alexander Stille's very careful reconstruction (1995).

12 However, in comparing the two curves, one should keep in mind that the US data are somewhat underestimated because we were unable to locate jail data over such a long period.

13 The 'secularisation' theme, however, should be considered with much caution in the case of the USA. The USA is among the most religious societies in the world, in terms of the penetration of religious ideology within their culture, even in the course of the twentieth century (Putnam 2000: 65–79), to the point that 'one systematic study of the history of religious observance in America estimates that the rate of formal religious adherence grew steadily from 17 percent in 1776 to 62 percent in 1980' (Putnam 2000: 65).

14 Italian data are my elaboration of data assembled by the official governmental institute of statistics in Rome (ISTAT). They go from 1863 to 1997 and are equal to the sum of inmates in all adult prison institutions. US data go from 1850 to 1997 and are equal to the sum of inmates in state and federal prisons. They are based on an update of the data originally collected and elaborated by Margaret Cahalan (1979) (the line between 1850 and 1925 is a linear interpolation based on the years for which we have data, that is 1850, 1860, 1870, 1880, 1890, 1904, 1910 and 1923).

15 I had previously argued for using the concept of 'political business cycle' in this connection (Melossi 1985).

16 See what follows in terms of changing 'representations' of criminals in Melossi (2000b).
17 Italy became a unified country only in 1861; for the USA, an important state like California joined the Union only in 1850 (see Berk *et al.* (1981) for the quantitative development of the California penal system).
18 Developments in Germany have been somewhat similar (Graham 1990; Savelsberg 1999).

References

Agozino, B. (forthcoming) *Counter Colonial Criminology: A Critique of Imperialist Reason.*

Applegate, B.K., Cullen, F.T., Fisher, B.S. and Vander Ven, T. (2000) 'Forgiveness and fundamentalism: reconsidering the relationship between correctional attitudes and religion', *Criminology*, 38: 719–54.

Archer, D. and Gartner, R. (1984) *Violence and Crime in Cross-national Perspective.* New Haven, CT: Yale University Press.

Austin, J.L. (1962) *How to Do Things with Words.* Cambridge, MA: Harvard University Press.

Beckett, K. (1997) *Making Crime Pay: Law and Order in Contemporary American Politics.* New York: Oxford University Press.

Berk, R.A., Rauma, D., Messinger, S.L. and Cooley, T.F. (1981) 'A test of the stability of punishment hypothesis: the case of California, 1851–1970', *American Sociological Review*, 46: 805–29.

Blumstein, A., Cohen, J. and Nagin, D. (1977) 'The dynamics of a homeostatic punishment process', *Journal of Criminal Law and Criminology*, 67: 317–34.

Burke, K. (1969[1950]) *A Rhetoric of Motives.* Berkeley, CA: University of California Press.

Cahalan, M. (1979) 'Trends in incarceration in the United States since 1880', *Crime and Delinquency*, 25: 9–41.

Cayley, D. (1998) *The Expanding Prison.* Cleveland, OH: Pilgrim Press.

Chaiken, J.M. (2000) 'Crunching numbers: crime and incarceration at the end of the millennium', *National Institute of Justice Journal*, January: 10–17.

Chambliss, W.J. (1999) *Power, Politics, and Crime.* Boulder, CO: Westview Press.

Chiricos, T.G. and DeLone, M.A. (1992) 'Labor surplus and punishment: a review and assessment of theory and evidence', *Social Problems*, 39: 421–46.

Cohn-Bendit, D. and Schmid, T. (1994) *Patria babilonia. La sfida della democrazia multiculturale.* Rome: Theoria.

De Beaumont, G. and de Tocqueville, A. (1964) *On the Penitentiary System of the United States and its Application in France.* Philadelphia, PA: Carey, Lea & Blanchard.

Della Porta, D. and Vannucci, A. (1999) *Corrupt Exchanges.* New York, NY: Aldine de Gruyter.

Del Olmo, R. (1981) *América Latina y su Criminología.* Mexico City: Siglo Veintiuno Editores.

De Tocqueville, A. (1961[1835–40]) *Democracy in America.* New York, NY: Schocken.

Dumm, T.L. (1987) *Democracy and Punishment: Disciplinary Origins of the United States.* Madison, WI: The University of Wisconsin Press.

Durkheim, E. (1951 [1897]) *Suicide.* Glencoe, IL: Free Press.

Durkheim, E. (1969 [1900]) 'Two laws of penal evolution', *Cincinnati Law Review* 38: 32–60.

Feeley, M.M. and Little, D.L. (1991) 'The vanishing female: the decline of women in the criminal process, 1687–1912', *Law and Society Review 25:* 719–57.

Fitzpatrick, P. (1995) 'The constitution of the excluded – Indians and others', in I. Loveland (ed.) *A Special Relationship? American Influences on Public Law in the United Kingdom.* Oxford: Clarendon Press, 191–212.

Foucault, M. (1977 [1975]) *Discipline and Punish.* New York, NY: Pantheon.

Franklin, B. (1751) 'Observations concerning the increase of mankind and the peopling of our countries', in *The Papers of Benjamin Franklin. Vol. 4.* New Haven, CT: Yale University Press.

Garfinkel, H. (1967) *Studies in Ethnomethodology.* Englewood Cliffs, NJ: Prentice Hall.

Graham, J. (1990) 'Decarceration in the Federal Republic of Germany', *British Journal of Criminology*, 30: 150–70.

Gramsci, A. (1971 [1929–35]) *Selections from the Prison Notebooks.* New York, NY: International Publishers.

Hobsbawm, E. (1994) *The Short Twentieth Century 1914–1991.* London: Abacus.

Horkheimer, M. and Adorno, T.W. (1972 [1944]) *Dialectic of Enlightenment.* New York, NY: Herder & Herder.

Howe, R.H. (1978) 'Max Weber's elective affinities: sociology within the bounds of pure reason', *American Journal of Sociology*, 84: 366–85.

Jacobs, D. and Helms. R.E. (1996) 'Toward a political model of incarceration: A time-series examination of multiple explanations for prison admission rates', *American Journal of Sociology* 102: 323–57.

Jankovic, I. (1977) 'Labor market and imprisonment', *Crime and Social Justice.* 8: 17–31.

Langan, P.A. and Farrington, D.P. (1998) *Crime and Justice in the United States and in England and Wales, 1981–96.* Washington, DC: Bureau of Justice Statistics.

Lynch, J.P. (1988) 'A comparison of prison use in England, Canada, West Germany, and the United States: a limited test of the punitive hypothesis', *Journal of Criminal Law and Criminology*, 79: 180–217.

Marx, K. (1975[1844]) 'Contribution to the critique of Hegel's philosophy of law. Introduction', in K. Marx and F. Engels, *Collected Works. Vol. 3.* London: Lawrence & Wishart, 175–87.

Marx, K. and Engels, F. (1970[1845–6]) *The German Ideology.* New York, NY: International Publishers.

Mead, George Herbert (1934) *Mind, Self, and Society*. Chicago, IL: University of Chicago Press.

Mead, G.H. (1964 [1925]) 'The genesis of the self and social control', in G.H. Mead, *Selected Writings*. Indianapolis, IN: Bobbs-Merrill, 267–93.

Melossi, D. (1980) 'Georg Rusche: a biographical Essay', *Crime and Social Justice*, 14: 51–63.

Melossi, D. (1981[1977]) 'Prison and labour in Europe and Italy during the formation of the capitalist mode of production', in D. Melossi and M. Pavarini, *The Prison and the Factory*. London: Macmillan, 9–95.

Melossi, D. (1985) 'Punishment and social action: changing vocabularies of punitive motive within a political business cycle', *Current Perspectives in Social Theory*, 6: 169–97.

Melossi, D. (1990) *The State of Social Control: A Sociological Study of Concepts of State and Social Control in the Making of Democracy*. Cambridge: Polity Press.

Melossi, D. (1994) 'The "economy" of illegalities: normal crimes, elites, and social control in comparative analysis', in D. Nelken (ed.) *The Futures of Criminology*. London: Sage, 202–19.

Melossi, D. (1995) 'The effect of economic circumstances on the criminal justice system', in *Crime and Economy*. Strasbourg: Council of Europe Publishing, 73–96.

Melossi, D. (1997) 'Moral panic Italian style: murders, economy and imprisonment in Italy, 1863–1994'. Paper presented at the annual meeting of the American Society of Criminology, San Diego.

Melossi, D. (1998) 'Omicidi, economia e tassi di incarcerazione in Italia dall'unità ad oggi', *Polis*, 12: 415–35.

Melossi, D. (1999) 'Murders, economy and imprisonment rates in Italy from unification to the present day'. Paper presented at the annual meeting of the American Sociological Association, Chicago.

Melossi, D. (2000a) 'Translating social control: reflections on the comparison of Italian and North-American cultures concerning social control, with a few consequences for a "Critical" Criminology', in S. Karstedt and K.D. Bussmann (eds) *Social Dynamics of Crime and Control*. Oxford: Hart Publishing, 143–51.

Melossi, D. (2000b) 'Changing representations of the criminal', *British Journal of Criminology*, 40: 296–320.

Melossi, D. (2001) 'The crime of modernity: punishment, crime and migration in Italy (1863–1997)'. Paper presented at the annual meeting of the American Sociological Association, Anaheim, CA.

Mills, C.W. (1963[1940]) 'Situated actions and vocabularies of motive', in *Power, Politics and People*. New York, NY: Oxford University Press, 439–52.

Parekh, B.C. (2000) *Rethinking Multiculturalism: Cultural Diversity and Political Theory*. Basingstoke: Macmillan.

Pavarini, M. (1994) 'The new penology and politics in crisis: the Italian case', *British Journal of Criminology*, 34: 49–61.

Paz, O. (1977) 'Mexico and the United States', in *The Labyrinth of Solitude*. London: Penguin Books, 355–76.

Pratt, J. (1992) *Punishment in a Perfect Society: The New Zealand Penal System 1840–1939*. Wellington: Victoria University Press.

Putnam, R.D. (1993) *Making Democracy Work*. Princeton, NJ: Princeton University Press.

Putnam, R.D. (2000) *Bowling Alone*. New York, NY: Simon & Schuster.

Rorty, R. (1999) *Philosophy and Social Hope*. London: Penguin Books.

Rusche, G. and Kirchheimer, O. (1968[1939]) *Punishment and Social Structure*. New York, NY: Russell & Russell.

Sabol, W.J. (1989) 'Racially disproportionate prison population in the United States', *Contemporary Crises*, 13: 405–32.

Salvatore, R.D. and Aguirre, C. (eds) (1996) *The Birth of the Penitentiary in Latin America: Essays on Criminology, Prison Reform, and Social Control, 1830–1940*. Austin, TX: University of Texas Press.

Sapir, E. (1933) 'Language', in *Encyclopaedia of the Social Sciences. vol. 9*. New York, NY: Macmillan, 155–68.

Savelsberg, J.J. (1999) 'Cultures of punishment: USA – Germany'. Paper presented at the annual meeting of the American Society of Criminology, Toronto.

Schutz, A. (1944) 'The stranger: an essay in social psychology', *American Journal of Sociology*, 499–507.

Sellin, J.T. (1964) 'Tocqueville and Beaumont and prison reform in France', in G. de Beaumont and A. de Tocqueville, *On the Penitentiary System of the United States and its Application in France*. Philadelphia, PA: Carey, Lea & Blanchard, xv–xl.

Sellin, J.T. (1976) *Slavery and the Penal System*. New York, NY: Elsevier.

Stille, A. (1995) *Excellent Cadavers*. London: Vintage.

Sumner, C. (1982) *Crime, Justice and Underdevelopment*. London: Heinemann.

Sutherland, E.H. (1939) *Principles of Criminology*. Philadelphia, PA: Lippincott.

Sutherland, E.H. (1956[1934]) 'The decreasing prison population of England', in A. Cohen *et al.* (eds) *The Sutherland Papers*. Bloomington, IN: Indiana University Press, 200–26.

Swidler, A. (1986) 'Culture in action: symbols and strategies', *American Sociological Review*, 51: 273–86.

Takaki, R. (1979) *Iron Cages: Race and Culture in 19th-century America*. New York, NY: Knopf.

Teti, V. (ed.) (1993) *La Razza Maledetta*. Rome: Manifestolibri.

Thayer, H.S. (1982) *Pragmatism: The Classic Writings*. Indianapolis, IN: Hackett.

Treiber, H. and Steinert, H. (1980) *Die Fabrikation des Zuverlaessigen Menschen*. Munich: Moos.

Van Dijk, J.J.M. and Mayhew, P. (1993) 'Criminal victimisation in the industrialised world: key findings of the 1989 and 1992 International Crime Surveys', in A. Alvazzi del Frate *et al.* (eds) *Understanding Crime: Experiences of Crime and Crime Control*, Rome: UNICRI, 1–49.

Van Swaaningen, R. (1997) *Critical Criminology: Visions from Europe.* London: Sage.

Weber, M. (1949 [1904]) ' "Objectivity" in social sciences and social policy', in *The Methodology of the Social Sciences.* New York, NY: Free Press, 49–112.

Weber, M. (1958[1904–5]) *The Protestant Ethic and the Spirit of Capitalism.* New York, NY: Scribner's.

Weber, M. (1969[1906]) 'The Protestant sects and the spirit of capitalism', in H.H. Gerth and C. Wright Mills (eds) *From Max Weber: Essays in Sociology,* New York, NY: Oxford University Press, 302–22.

Zimring, F.E. and Hawkins, G. (1997) *Crime is not the Problem: Lethal Violence in America.* New York, NY: Oxford University Press.

Chapter 6

Controlling measures: the repackaging of common-sense opposition to women's imprisonment in England and Canada

Pat Carlen

Introduction

Despite the publication of many official and semi-official reports criticising the increased use of imprisonment as a punishment for law-breaking women, and deploring inappropriate regimes in women's prisons, the number of females held in custody in England continues to increase. Equally depressingly, reports from Canada about the fate of recent reforms in the federal prisons for women there are making British anti-prison campaigners think twice about some of the new pro-grammes currently being implemented in the women's institutions in the UK. Indeed, many people, after reading about some of the unexpected outcomes of the Canadian experience (Hannah-Moffat and Shaw 2000; Hannah Moffat 2001), may conclude that in relation to prison reform, 'nothing works'. Pessimists, moreover, may also conclude that this is inevitably so because of the seeming power of the state to incorporate all reformist discourse into the administrative machinery of the prison. One reading of what follows might suggest that that is my argument in this chapter. Such a reading would be unfortunate.

In what follows it will certainly be contended that there are neces-sarily limits to prison reform and that these limits – hereinafter termed 'carceral clawback' (Carlen 2002a) – logically inhere both in the involuntary nature of a subject's imprisonment and in the logical necessity of keeping a prisoner *in prison* (for a slightly different argument, see Hannah-Moffat 2002). But the argument will distinguish between logical and political necessity and, in assuming that carceral clawback is a *logical* necessity, will not assume that, like the sentence of the court, it is a fairly direct outcome of the state's 'power to punish'. For the state's power to continue to punish by imprisonment, though formally vested in the criminal law, is, in the neoliberal state, politically dependent upon the maintenance of the popular legitimacy of prison as an institution which *should* and *can* keep people in custody. The conditions under which that legitimacy can be maintained, however, vary between jurisdictions and according to specific mixes of cultural and political conditions. This chapter will examine recent attempts to introduce innovative reforms in women's imprisonment in Canada and England with the aim of assessing both the extent to which carceral clawback is a necessary feature of imprisonment, and the different cultural and political conditions which facilitate carceral clawback taking the form it does.

In outline, the argument is as follows:

1 Despite the appearance of reform in the regimes of the English women's prisons, a carceral clawback is already underway – made necessary by the prison's continuing need for legitimacy and, in part, made possible by some of the constitutive common-sense elements of recent anti-prison discourses about women's imprisonment in England.

2 The main similarity between the Canadian and English experiences of female prison reform is exemplified by an analysis which claims that most of the cosmetically new policies currently reinvigorating the power of carceral clawback in the English women's prisons have been powered by the common-sense ideologies of optimistic campaigners (and prison-illiterate therapeutic experts) who have failed to remember (or who never have realised) that prison is for punishment by incarceration; and whose subsequent common-sense campaigning principles and strategies have been insufficiently theorised to protect them against incorporation into prison administrative discourses wherein the necessity of carceral clawback (and its constant discursive renewal) is taken for granted; furthermore, that this ideological incorporation of reformist into administrative discourses is similar to that which occurred in Canada and which was first identified and analysed by Hannah-Moffatt (2001).

3 The main difference between the ways in which carceral clawback has occurred in Canada and England as an institutional (as opposed to an ideological) configuration is that in Canada clawback occurred via an institutional and self-exclusion of the most prison-knowledgeable campaigning groups, whereas in England it is proceeding via finan-cially coerced, inclusionary controlling measures which are presently

making imperialistic bids for greater control of ontological knowledge about the causes of crime and the causes of desistance from crime, together with epistemological claims about the only ways in which that knowledge can be obtained – and, for good measure, guaranteed via official accreditation.

4 The need for accreditation of prison programmes in England converts the programme priorities of the supplying agencies from a professional concern about the therapeutic needs of the client into a functionalist concern about the survival of the organisational contract with the Prison Service; and that the new measures thereby being brought into play are such that the language of auditable reform is able to paper over the cracks in the legitimacy of women's imprisonment without the threat to the status quo ever being realised and, ironically, with its critics disarmed by the language of reform – unrealised.

The chapter is structured as follows. First, the Canadian experience of attempted reform of the Federal Prison System for women is outlined and its unexpected outcomes identified; secondly, the formal logic of carceral clawback is explicated; thirdly, the differences between common-sense and theoretical discourse are briefly described and their relationships in the construction of recent official discourse on women's imprisonment metaphorically analysed; fourthly, some of the sub-stantive transformations of theoretical discourses into common-sense discourses which powered a new official discourse on women's prisons in England are described and located in their sustaining and converging ideologies in anti-prison, pro-prison and extra-prison discourses; and, lastly, the implications of the analyses and arguments are discussed.

The Canadian experience

In 1990 a report by the Task Force on Federally Sentenced Women, entitled *Creating Choices*, resulted in a raft of reforms which involved the design of a new 'supportive' women-centred model of punishment which would 'empower women', create 'meaningful choices', reinforce notions of 'respect and dignity', and respond to the unique experiences and context of women prisoners in Canada (Hannah-Moffat 2001: 4).

Since then, five new prisons have been built to replace the old Prison for Women, and the government has committed itself politically and financially to reforms which have also been supported by campaigners, many of whom were initially implicated in the implementation of the *Creating Choices* recommendations. Now, 'Over ten years have passed since the project began and yet ... many argue that little about the regime has changed and that few lessons have been learned' (Hannah-Moffat 2001: 4). Moreover, after she has painstakingly traced out the complex of ever-fragmenting and exponentially multiplying histories that helped constitute the present regime of federally sentenced women in Canada, Kelly Hannah-Moffat (2001: 18) concludes that 'The governance of women by women can be as problematic as the governance of women by men, especially when the relations among the "keepers" and the "kept" are shaped by the institutional dynamics of imprisonment '.

In the next section it will be argued that the formal and necessary institutional dynamics emanating from the prison's essential coerciveness and, *by definition*, imperative of total physical security, must always claw back the power apparently abdicated by the prison and vested in prisoners through such notions as 'prisoner choice' and 'empowerment'; but that how that clawback is achieved will vary according to the culture and political conditions in which the prison operates. One of the most favoured methods both in politics and discourse is exclusion; though if self-exclusion can be provoked (again, either politically or discursively) the legitimacy of the ensuing exclusion is more forcefully secured.

In Canada, as is presently happening in England, many groups and campaigners with long experience of women's imprisonment were (in effect, though not formally) simply excluded from the reform implementation process. While continuing to disarm criticism by adhering to the language of reform, once the implementation process was under way, Corrections Service Canada subverted the more radical elements of reform by seeking 'the advice of outside "experts" with limited experience in Canadian women's corrections' (Hannah-Moffat 2001: 146); until, in June 1992, the lead campaigning group, the Canadian Association of Elizabeth Fry Societies, excluded themselves from the implementation process in protest at the way in which the vision of *Creating Choices* had been interpreted and operationalised (Hayman 2000: 47; Hannah-Moffat 2001: 146).

The main ideological ploy of the Canadian government when challenged about the non-implementation of the 'empowerment' vision of *Creating Choices* was, according to Hannah-Moffat, to centralise the notion of personal 'responsibility' and argue that women have to *choose* to be empowered and that those who do not so choose thereby demonstrate that they are 'unempowerable' and, by definition, self-excluded from the prison's remit to 'empower' (Hannah-Moffat 2001: 173)! However, Hannah-Moffat also argues that the campaigning discourses which had talked about empowering women had, in part, facilitated such a discursive move because, in operating with a unitary category 'women', they had failed to recognise that women's needs vary according to race, class and their different socio-biographies (2001: 191; cf. Carlen 1988, 1994). They had also overlooked the fact that, by definition, prison is involuntary punishment by containment in secure surroundings and that 'choices' in such a context must always be severely circumscribed by institutional demands. For surely if a prisoner had a 'choice', she would walk out the door and the prison would be no more?

The logic of carceral clawback

Prison is for punishment. It has other functions, but the only characteristic sentenced prisoners have in common is that they have been convicted of a crime for which the sentence of the court was punishment, either by a term of immediate imprisonment or by one of those 'alternatives' to custody which are backed up by the explicit threat of incarceration for non-compliance with sentencing conditions. Like all other 'others', therefore, alternatives to imprisonment are predicated upon the continued existence of the binary partner – in this case, the prison itself.

Yet although prison is the most compelling symbol of the state's power to punish, it is also a politically dangerous symbol. The power to punish by imprisonment is not static and its legitimacy has to be constantly renewed in a political struggle wherein each side (for the purposes of this chapter, pro and anti-prison ideologists) empowers the other at the moment of triumph of its own rhetoric. Indeed, it is partly because of the alternate triumphant insistence of both prison and prison-reformist claims that prison clawback takes the form it does.

Since the inception of penal incarceration, the punitive function of the prison has been occluded by governmental, professional or reformist claims that prisons – especially women's prisons – are, or could be, for something other than punishment: psychological readjustment, training in parenting, drugs rehabilitation, general education or whatever else might provide a legitimating rationale for locking up not only women who commit very serious crimes but (when there is nowhere else to contain them – for example, family, the reformatory or the factory) also those who commit very minor ones.

Why do such myths about the possibilities of a benign prison persist and multiply? First, because imprisonment so nearly violates so many human rights and is so painful that democratic governments need continually to relegitimate its systematic and almost exclusive use against certain classes and categories of law-breakers for quite minor crimes (and especially nowadays when the promise of the state to reduce crime via its criminal justice apparatus has signally failed – Garland 1996, 2001); secondly, because the prison business is still (as it was during the early days of psychiatry) an opulent shareholder in, and consumer of, the modernistic fashioning, retailing and consumption of new therapies and 'psy' sciences; and, thirdly, because advocates of penal reform, becoming disillusioned by repeated failures of governments to reduce prison populations, have (though usually with ambivalence and in fear of co-optation) reluctantly (but repeatedly) accepted the invitation of prison administrations to help shape prison regimes designed to reduce both the pain and the damaging effects of imprisonment. The undertheorised nature of their reform attempts (in terms of the failure of the reformers to take seriously the nature of imprisonment and the way it might affect reform outcomes), together with the deliberate appeal to populist common sense of their tactical rhetoric, have facilitated the incorporation of some key feminist concepts (for example, resistance to victim status, personal responsibility) into an official discourse on reform of the women's prisons and a presently vibrant carceral clawback (e.g. in England the opening of two new private prisons for women) which is far removed from the spirit of the reforming agendas of most anti-prison campaigners, many feminists and many prison personnel too.

Common sense, theory and official discourse

To make sense, all discourse has to exclude certain versions of reality and privilege others. The main difference between theoretical discourse and common-sense discourse is that, while the former has, by definition, to explicate and defend the ontological and epistemological assumptions and concepts of its knowledge claims, the meanings and referents of *common*-sense have, ironically, an infinite plasticity. As they are represented as being the consensual and natural constructions of reality held by all sane and respectable persons, they also appear at any one time to be both unchanging and at one with their conditions of existence. Consequently, the power of common sense inheres in its ability constantly to adapt to challenging discourses at the same time as calling into question the credibility and/or probity of the challengers. Common-sense discourses only have to be defended when challenged by a theoretical discourse which forces them to lay bare their ideological underpinnings, ambiguities and, in institutional and political terms, their choice of epistemological masters.

Some of the most sophisticated common-sense discourse is, as one might expect, official discourse – i.e. the discourse which justifies the governmental pursuit of one course of action, programme or policy rather than another.

In *Official Discourse*, Burton and Carlen (1979) used the metaphor of the 'other' taken from psychoanalysis (Lacan 1975; Freud 1976) to describe how, when it is confronted by competing theories or pedagogies, official discourse has to erase the 'other' from the mirror of its own desire/imperative.

In the case of women's imprisonment in England at the dawn of the twenty-first century, the official imperative was to face a challenge to the legitimacy of disproportionately imprisoning poorer and ethnic minority women for relatively minor crimes. Through the closing off of any alternative discourses about the extra-discursive conditions shaping women's imprisonment, an in-house prison service discourse had to be created, a 'prison-speak' which, by appearing to mirror many discursive elements of the critical discourse against women's imprisonment, could also absorb and neutralise the threat. Indeed, for the state or the prison (as for the oppressed) it is in the analytic resistance to the exercise of power by theoretical or political opponents that the strongest ideological weapons for its own continuance are to be found (Foucault 1978).

Even at the end of twentieth century, neither of the main political parties in England was prepared to contest populist conceptions of the necessity and efficacy of imprisonment as the symbolic centrepiece of a punitive (if ineffective, in terms of crime reduction) criminal justice system. The only opposition to the increased use of imprisonment came from anti-prison theorists, the long-term campaigning organisations such as Women in Prison, the Howard League, the Prison Reform Trust and NACRO, together with the Prison Inspectorate and some of the more enlightened among the judiciary and Prison Service personnel. By the mid-1990s, the strongest case for prison reductionism was being presented in relation to women's imprisonment. Women criminals were not seen as posing the same risks to the general public as men and, moreover, their claims to special treatment as mothers were receiving sympathetic publicity. To meet the threat of this ideologically obstructive Other, the Prison Service set up a Women's Policy Group to ensure that women prisoners' interests and different needs were in future taken seriously (in effect, authoritatively defined and circumscribed) by the service itself. In other words, the Prison Service wanted to reassert ownership of a part of the prison population that it was constantly being accused of neglecting.

At the same time, many in the campaigning organisations were questioning the utility of their own 'outsider' and often abstract critiques of women's imprisonment and modifying them to appeal to the common sense of a public which might be prepared to sympathise at least with women prisoners who had suffered abuse, or with children of prisoners damaged by their mothers' imprisonment. They were met halfway by the Prison Service's new Women's Policy Group (WPG) which, in an attempt to diffuse the mounting criticism, went out of its way to consult with a range of campaigning, statutory and voluntary organisations (see Lowthian (2002) for a detailed analysis of the work of the WPG).

The anti-prison campaigners were caught off-guard. Dispirited by their previous lack of success in reducing the female prison population (during the 1990s it had doubled), many abandoned the theoretical critique of the legitimacy of imprisoning non-violent women for minor crimes, and instead packaged their criticisms in the language of common sense with a populist (and official) appeal, content merely to argue, for instance, that it was important to treat women prisoners well because they were mothers and guardians of the next generation; that women in prison would be less likely to commit crime if they received some kind of therapy in prison; and that women prisoners had been treated as victims by too many writers on women and crime when in fact there were many strong women in prison who would be even stronger if their custodial sentence could be made into a much more positive experience, etc. The dominant message was that women in prison should resist the 'deterministic' victimhood conferred upon them by critics of penal welfare; they should take responsibility for their lives by recognising their own needs; they should engage in activities that might enable them to be crime free in the future; and they should have the opportunity to convert their period of imprisonment into a positive period wherein they might recuperate from the problems they had suffered outside prison, etc. This insistence on responsibility and resistance to being a passive victim meshed very well with some elements in the rhetoric of welfare critics such Charles Murray (1990) and even with some elements in the arguments of left-realist criminologists (see, for example, Young 1986) who, like some anti-prison campaigners and feminists, were anxious to have their views on crime taken seriously by a New Labour government.

Meanwhile, in the reports on women's imprisonment, less and less mention was made of class or racism, until in 2000 the Wedderburn

Report (based on the investigations of people chosen for their establishment credentials and, in the main, their lack of 'contamination' through previous knowledge of women's prisons) marked the beginning of the new millennium by managing not to mention class and racism in the criminal justice system at all! Confusingly, the language of 'class' and 'racism' had been replaced by the New Labour 'speak' of 'social exclusion' – which, in terms of imprisonment must, literally, either be circular or oxymoronic.

Thus, by the beginning of the twenty-first century, and with the aid of its own new ideological machinery in the guise of the Women's Policy Group, the Prison Service had regrouped and put its own gloss upon the common-sense (i.e. neutered-theoretical) arguments contained in reports such as those by Wedderburn (2000) and NACRO (2001). In consultation meetings between the Prison Service and 'others', the challenge to the legitimacy of imprisoning disproportionate numbers of 'excluded' (i.e. working-class and ethnic minority) women was common-sensically transformed (and theoretically neutralised) within the new orthodoxy about the efficacy of prison programmes in addressing social problems such as drug usage, sexual abuse and housing (to name but a few) from within the prison and, overall, the whole process illustrated once more the point that Burton and Carlen made in 1979 that

> official discourse on law and order confronts legitimation deficits and seeks discursively to redeem them by denial of their material genesis. Such denial establishes an absence in the discourse. This absence, the Other, is the silence of a world constituted by social relations the reality of which cannot be appropriated by a mode of normative argument which speaks to and from its own self-image (p. 138).

At the time of writing the newly forged self-image of the women's prison system in the early twenty-first century in England is of a system legitimated by its provision of programmes, treatments and therapies, the underlying justifications for which mesh well with common-sense rhetoric of some feminist criminologists and some anti-prison cam-paigners about the needs to devictimise and 'empower' women in prison. Moreover, many of the new programmes received the blessing (at a price) of the organisations which had previously put forward the radical critiques whose common-sense appeal had been partly responsible for the reforms taking the new forms they had. At the moment of official recognition of the utility of certain elements of those critiques to a new official discourse on women's crime and women's imprisonment, their theoretical sting had been drawn because 'The ideological metonymies of official discourse are directed not only to the destruction of their real conditions of existence, but also, through denial of those conditions of existence, to their partial and surreptitious reproduction. To this extent, official discourse is always directed at discursive closure' (Burton and Carlen 1979: 138). In other words, because of the increase in populist punitiveness that had occurred as a result of the heightened awareness of criminal risk coinciding with a political, media and electoral demand for more and harsher custodial punishment, critical discourses presenting a threat to carceral increase had to be silenced or, at least, neutralised. The most threatening critical discourse at the end of the 1990s was in relation to the multiple jeopardy which women prisoners suffered as law-breakers, women and members of ethnic minority groups. Via the newly instituted Women's Policy Group alliances were forged with campaigning or non-statutory organisations and, in the Prison Service's revamping of its regimes for females, it began to appear as if much of the radical critique of women's imprisonment was being taken on board. Not so. When previous critics abandoned, modified or discursively adjusted their critiques of sentencing and prison policies, so that they might join as credible partners in common-sense policy-making with the Prison Service's Women's Policy Group, prison clawback was strengthened. Any further talk of the class and ethnic minority-biased conditions of existence of the female prison population was now discursively erased as being 'unhelpful' and 'irrelevant'. Within the new official policy discourse of prison programming for self-governance, class and gender analyses were in future to be considered 'unspeakable': first, because theories which argued that class and gender discrimination played any part in explaining women's criminal careers were lacking in 'evidence'; and, more importantly, because not being 'evidence-based' any 'programmes' based on such theories were definitely non-fundable! I will now examine in more detail just how it was that a radical critique of prison legitimacy based on structural analyses of class, racism and gender discrimination produced the constitutive elements of a carceral clawback characterised by psy-technologies and programmes which, after abstracting women prisoners from their concomitantly recognised and denied structural conditions of existence outside prison, relocated and isolated them within psychological needs-based therapies for the governance of the self within prison.

How theoretical critique empowered contemporary official discourse on women's prisons in England

It has already been argued that, by the mid-1990s, the British penal system was suffering a minor legitimacy crisis in relation to women's imprisonment, a crisis made worse by a growing popular awareness that women prisoners were more likely to be suffering from multiple problems of material deprivation than male prisoners and less likely than males to be 'career' or 'dangerous' criminals; additionally, that as they were more likely than men to have dependent children for whom they were the main carers, their children at home could be expected to suffer all kinds of mental, emotional and psychological damage as a result of their mothers' imprisonment. Yet, at the same time, there was a growth in punitiveness towards single mothers and an increasing number of sentencers who argued that if women wanted equality with men they should equally expect to receive equality of punishment with men when they broke the law. There was no way that an official discourse (always dependent upon common sense for its coherence in contradiction) could construct a populist argument around the complex notion of substantive rather than formal equality (see Heidensohn 1986). None the less, and as always, the constitutive threads of a new official discourse were there waiting to be metonymised from discourses contesting both the frequency and the nature of women's imprisonment. It did not take long to stitch them together in a new form – though still according to the old strategy of erasing from the new official discourse all reference to the material conditions of existence (i.e. poverty, racism and sexism) of a majority of female prisoners, and replacing it with an 'imaginary' realignment of signifiers (in this case the literal words and slogans of the prison critics) and signifieds – i.e. differently contextualised meanings of those very same words. Displaced from their original theoretical or campaigning contexts, words such as 'responsibility', 'victim', 'need', 'citizenship', 'risk', 'rehabilitation', and 'choice' now took on very different meanings and referents. Moreover, they were destined to have entirely different effects from those envisaged by their radical authors. Other words, such as class and racism were, as we have already seen, omitted altogether.

Newly to contextualise the language taken from the discourses of the anti-prison campaigners and feminists, the criminological archives of a previous era were raided, and words like 'criminogenic' and 'criminal career' were dug out and put to new uses. While some critics were quick to point out that in many cases research commissioned by the Prison

Service's Women's Policy Group was attempting to reinvent the wheel, other critics were more concerned that the new wheel was already careering in a penologically conservative direction. In other words, when the Women's Policy Group commissioned research into women's criminal careers, the purpose was more to investigate the psychological needs that prison therapists could claim to address within custodial programmes than investigation and address of the tangle of social deprivations that so many female prisoners suffer outside prison. The main transformations in female prison reform discourse lay in the following areas.

From 'prison works' (Conservative Home Secretary Michael Howard) to 'prison doesn't work, but we'll make it work' (Labour Home Secretary Jack Straw)

The thrust of much anti-prison campaigning in the early 1990s was directed at refuting a Conservative Home Secretary's justification for increases in the prison population – the claim that 'prison works' in terms of reducing crime. In an address to the Howard League soon after the New Labour government came to power, the new Home Secretary amended that claim to 'prison doesn't work, but we will make it work'. The repairing gell, we learnt, was to be found in the magic of 'programming' (see Kendall 2002). This move towards 'programming' could also claim to meet another objection to women's imprisonment: that the women most vulnerable to imprisonment were also those with multiple social problems and deprivations. 'Agreed', said Prison Speak: 'Therefore we must develop programmes to address those needs, and this can be done better in prison than in the community where the resources are just not available.' But the needs addressed turned out to be only those which could be represented as related to 'criminogenic' behaviour – i.e. needs rooted in the women rather than in their social circumstances.

From the demand for prison accountability to the insistence on prisoner accountability

During the 1980s one recurring demand of reformers had been that prisons should be 'accountable', that structures should be put in place to safeguard prisoners' rights (Maguire *et al.* 1985) and that a charter of minimum prison standards should be published and made enforceable by the courts. By the 1990s the concept of 'accountability' was well embedded in prison ideology, but the emphasis now was on the 'accountability' of the prisoner – not only for her own behaviour but, via prisoner compacts and the Incentives and Earned Privileges Scheme, for the standard of her prison conditions and access to prison 'privileges' too.

The *coup* for official discourse inhered in the 'contractual' nature of the Incentives and Earned Privileges Scheme; it appealed to a liberal common sense (e.g. about individual freedom and self-governance) and a feminist common-sense insistence that women take responsibility for their own lives and not be seen as victims. As David Garland (2001) points out, contractual modes of governance appeal strongly to the middle classes because, in mimicking traditional middle-class forms of self-governance, they appear to be both 'obvious', and 'natural'. To give women in prison the opportunity to choose to govern their own lives may be an oxymoron, but if we add in the imaginary of the discursive desire of anti-prison campaigners that women prisoners should have equal opportunities with all other women, in other words, *as if they were not in prison*, it becomes unassailable 'common sense'.

From female prisoner resistance to class, gender and penal victimisation, and from oppression to responsibilisation

One of the transformations in discourse about women's imprisonment which has already been well documented (see Hannah-Moffat and Shaw 2000; Hannah-Moffat 2001) is that which, in my opinion, has its roots in feminist discourses which balked at representations of female law-breakers in the criminal justice system as being solely victims of class or racist discrimination and, instead, insisted that they should also be represented as survivors with an agency capable of resisting the various forms of oppression to which, it was usually admitted, they had indeed been subject. At its extreme, this argument was also put forward as an organising principle to explain the experiences of women in prison (see Bosworth 1999). But although none of the 'insistence on resistance' brigade actually denied that a majority of women prisoners had been subjected to various forms of oppression outside prison, many of them, especially if they held to a totally untheorised view of what prison actually entails – that is, punishment in the form of involuntary but secure custody – tended to underplay those aspects of custodial power which are necessarily activated and enhanced by prisoner resistance – in other words, the disciplinary and security mechanisms.

Thus, within the women's prisons, a number of programmes were developed which, far from addressing the roots of women's oppression outside prison (and, incidentally, outside their own, or any one individual's sphere of direct influence), focused instead on the prisoners' attitudes to their criminal behaviour – on the rather simplistic grounds that changing how prisoners thought (within the prison) about their behaviour (outside the prison) would reduce their law-breaking behaviour upon release. Thus it was that a progressive feminist exhortation – that oppressed women should take charge of their own lives and act to resist oppression – was transformed into a 'responsibilisation' of prisoners which (through silencing all reference to structural constraints) implied that not only were they solely responsible for their own behavioural choices but also for the conditions in which those choices were made (see O'Malley 1992, 1996; Garland 1996, 2001; Hannah-Moffat 2001). Unlike the prison governor quoted below, many who helped to frame these programmes just did not take note of the prison's controlling imperative. Prison staff, on the other hand, take it for granted that the demands of prison security and the demands of therapeutic practice are inevitably antagonistic: 'We have the institutional dilemma of saying to women, "Be assertive, be confident". And as soon as they begin to exercise that assertiveness, staff say, "Whoa. This is a prison. Get back there" '(male prison governor cited in Carlen 1998: 89; cf. Hannah-Moffat 2001: 18).

The translation of 'risk as dangerousness' into 'risk as need'

In the 1980s and early 1990s, a number of campaigners against the imprisonment of minor female offenders had argued that women should only be imprisoned if they posed such a serious risk to public safety that a custodial sentence had to be imposed on the ground of protection of the public. In the 1990s, however, 'risk' came to be translated into 'risk of committing another crime' and, especially in the case of women, 'risk to oneself'. Women with the greatest social needs were also seen as being those most 'at risk' of being in criminal trouble again in the future. As this new interpretation of risk took hold, prison could be justified on two related grounds: if a woman's needs were such that she was at increased risk of committing crime in the future she should go to prison because, being needy, she posed a risk; and by going to prison she could have her needs addressed and the risk diminished. Needless to say, the needs to be addressed in prison were psychological needs relating to the adjustment of how the woman viewed her criminal behaviour rather than the material needs that, according to the anti-prison campaigners had, in part, created the conditions conducive to many women's law-breaking behaviour in the first place.

Holism and partnership operationalised as centralism

One of the key features of late modern neoliberal states, according to Garland (1996), is the displacing of responsibility for crime control from the state to the citizen. Given that the criminal justice system can no longer make good its claim to deliver order and security via policing, the courts and the prisons, citizens have been subjected to a responsibilisation strategy whereby responsible citizens are expected to help themselves in these matters, for instance, via increased private security, insurance and a reliance upon other private organisations with whom the state may or not claim to be 'in partnership'. In England, the Prison Service has certainly invited voluntary and other statutory organisations to join 'in partnership' in the design and running of many prison programmes and, because this has often been done under the ideological signs of 'interagency' or 'co-ordination', anti-prison campaigners at first applauded the approach as being 'holistic'. Once again, their approval was premature. A recurring criticism directed at services for female offenders during the last decade related to the fragmented nature of service delivery. It was argued that too often provision by one agency undermined that of another and that although women in prison often required a great deal of specialist help, the expertise was not available within the prison and, furthermore, that although the relevant provision could be made by specialist agencies, the Prison Service did not make as much use of specialist agencies as it could. A third argument related to the need for 'one stop' provision – of information and all other types of service – so that ex-prisoners with children and/or a paucity of resources could easily identify and access their own specific mix of appropriate rehabilitative services. Proponents of these arguments (who included this author – see Carlen 1998) confidently believed that a holistic approach would lead to more and more 'community' organisations going into prisons with a greater variety of approaches to prisoners' 'needs' being practised. The reverse happened. Harnessing the perennial campaigning rhetoric about the desirability of higher standards in prison provision to a justification for a new accreditation process, one designed to authorise and recognise (for funding purposes) only those programmes deemed by the accreditors to address offending behaviour, the Prison Service fashioned a new machinery for the three-fold centralisation of penological knowledge: causes of criminal behaviour were located in individual offenders; the best way to remedy these criminogenic tendencies was by cognitive behavioural technique; and the best way to gain knowledge of anything penological whatsoever – success of therapeutic programmes, quality of prison and prison–officer performance – was to measure it.[1]

From symbolic interaction to the construction of a new official criminology of women in prison

In the discourse of official knowledge there is a happy conjunction between necessity and desire. To be coherent, all discourse necessarily has to exclude certain statements and include others; to maintain its legitimacy, all official discourse desires to exclude oppositional knowledge of certain material conditions and replace it with an alternative worldview.

Most of the academic books and campaigning and semi-official reports of the last decades of the twentieth century implicitly challenged the legitimacy of continuing to imprison women with such appalling histories of poverty and abuse as characterised by the socio-biographies of a majority of women in prison. Having in part met the challenge to legitimacy by claiming that the justification for imprisoning such women was that their needs would be met by the new prison regimes and programmes, official assurance had to be made doubly sure: first, by discrediting the knowledge claims of those who argued that in-prison programmes run by psychologists would hardly address the poverty-stricken circumstances to which so many prisoners would return upon release; and, secondly, by making sure that all those running the new programmes held to an ontology and epistemology of women's crime which would further bolster the legitimacy of imprisoning them.

The basic ontology of the New Official Criminology of Women in Prison is contained in a remarkably clever document entitled *The Government's Strategy for Women Offenders* (Home Office 2000). In it, the arguments which had been put forward by some qualitative researchers that women committed crime because it appeared to them that they had few legitimate options (see Carlen 1988) were turned on their head. Implicitly allowing the symbolic-interactionist claim (and, incidentally, justification for qualitative, as opposed to quantitative, research) that their ways of seeing the world shape people's actions, the solution of the New Official Criminology for Women in Prison is simple. Change their *beliefs* about the world; the problem is in their heads, not in their social circumstances:

> The characteristics of women prisoners suggest that experiences such as poverty, abuse and drug addiction lead some women to *believe* that their options are limited. Many offending behaviour programmes are designed to help offenders see there are always positive choices open to them that do not involve crime. At the same time, across Government, we are tackling the aspects of social

exclusion that make some women *believe* their options are limited (Home Office 2000: 7, emphasis added).

This approach also justified the commissioning of new research into women's criminogenic needs, the only research to be welcomed in future being that which produces 'research evidence on effective ways to tackle women's re-offending' (Home Office 2000: 23). As the only programmes authorised for tackling women's offending behaviour are those which have been officially 'accredited', it seems that official discourse on women's imprisonment has indeed momentarily triumphed – by shoving the unofficial 'other' explanations of women's crime right out of the frame (especially the research funding frame!) – though not, of course, out of the archive.

Conclusion

I began this chapter by stating that I would not be arguing that prison reform is impossible because of some functionalist loop-back between the supposed 'needs' of the state and the forms that social change can take. Nor have I. In one sense, I have been more positivistic than that: I have argued that logically the prison necessarily has to engage in a carceral clawback whenever its being as a prison is threatened by prisoner emancipation – of mind or body.

However, for the state, the political problem is the management of penal legitimacy. Comparison of the ways in which the legitimation deficit in women's imprisonment has recently been handled in Canada and England suggests that in both jurisdictions the main discursive strategies involved a separation of reformist discourses from their extra-discursive referents, and that this process was made easier in Canada because of the institutional and self-exclusion of the main reforming group; whereas in England the process was facilitated by the abandonment by campaigning anti-prison critics of a coherent (and watchful) theoretical approach to female prison reform so that they might more easily enjoy a 'common-sense' 'partnership' with the Prison Service in order to 'get something done'. Something was done; and oppositional discourses supposed to be championing a reduction in the women's prison population unwittingly helped fashion a new policy discourse on women and crime, an official discourse which will justify more and more women being locked up in the future – so that their 'criminogenic needs can be met' – not somehow, but legitimately!

Acknowledgement

This chapter was first presented as a paper at a symposium entitled 'How crime policy travels' at Keele University Department of Criminology in June 2001. The author acknowledges with gratitude all comments made by participants, and especially those by Richard Sparks. The author also thanks Kelly Hannah-Moffatt for her useful written comments, and the ESRC for funding (Award L216 25 2033) under the Future of Governance Programme.

Note

1   In a private communication, Kelly Hannah-Moffat has pointed out that because the ideology of 'holism' has been applied to medicine which treats 'the whole person', it can also be made an excuse 'for increasingly invasive penal probing. It means that every part of a woman's life is fair game for intervention … not just that part related to the crime'.

References

Bosworth, M. (1999) *Engendering Resistance: Agency and Power in Women's Prisons*. Aldershot: Dartmouth.
Burton, F. and Carlen, P. (1979) *Official Discourse*. London: Routledge & Kegan Paul.
Carlen, P. (1988) *Women, Crime and Poverty*. Buckingham: Open University Press.
Carlen, P. (1994) 'Why study women's imprisonment? Or anyone else's?' in *British Journal of Criminology*, 34 (special issue): 131–140.
Carlen, P. (1998) *Sledgehammer: Women's Imprisonment at the Millennium*. London: Macmillan.
Carlen, P. (2002a) 'Carceral clawback: the case of women's imprisonment in Canada' *Punishment and Society*, 4(1): 115–21.
Carlen, P. (ed.) (2002b) *Women and Punishment: The Struggle for Justice*. Cullompton: Willan.
Foucault, M. (1978). 'Politics and the study of discourse', *Ideology and Consciousness*, Spring (3).
Freud, S. (1976) *The Interpretation of Dreams*. Harmondsworth: Penguin Books.
Garland, D. (1996) 'The limits of the sovereign state: strategies of crime control in contemporary society', *British Journal of Criminology*, 36(4): 445–71.
Garland, D. (2001) *The Culture of Control: Crime and Social Order in Contemporary Society*. Oxford: Oxford University Press.
Hannah-Moffat, K. (2001) *Punishment in Disguise: Penal Governance and Federal Imprisonment of Women in Canada*. Toronto: University of Toronto Press.

Hannah-Moffat, K. (2002) 'Creating choices: reflecting on the choices', in P. Carlen (ed.) *Women and Punishment: The Struggle for Justice*. Collumpton: Willan.

Hannah-Moffat, K. and Shaw, M. (2000) 'Thinking about cognitive skills? Think again!', *Criminal Justice Matters*, Spring (39): 8–9.

Hayman, S. (2000) 'Prison reform and incorporation: lessons from Britain and Canada', in H. Kelly-Moffat and M. Shaw (eds) *An Ideal Prison: Critical Essays on Women's Imprisonment in Canada*. Halifax: Fernwood.

Heidensohn, F. (1986) 'Models of justice: Portia or Persephone? Some thoughts on equality, fairness and gender in the field of criminal justice', *International Journal of the Sociology of Law*, 14.

Home Office (2000) *The Government's Strategy for Women Offenders*. London: Home Office.

Kendall, K. (2002) 'Time to think again about cognitive-behavioural programmes', in P. Carlen (ed.) *Women and Punishment: The Struggle for Justice*. Cullompton: Willan.

Lacan, J. (1975) *The Language of the Self*. New York, NY: Delta.

Lacan, J. (1977) *Ecrits*. London: Tavistock.

Lowthian, J. (2002) 'Women's prisons in England: barriers to reform', in P. Carlen (ed.) *Women and Punishment: The Struggle for Justice*. Cullompton: Willan.

Maguire, M., Vagg, J. and Morgan, R. (1985) *Accountability and Prisons*. London: Tavistock.

Murray, C. (1990) *The Emerging British Underclass*. London: Institute of Economic Affairs.

NACRO (2001) *Women Beyond Bars*. London: NACRO.

O'Malley, P. (1992) 'Risk, power and crime prevention', *Economy and Society*, 21: 252–75.

O'Malley, P. (1996) 'Post-Keynesian policing', *Economy and Society*, 25(2): 137–55.

Power, M. (1997) *Audit Society*. Oxford: Oxford University Press.

Wedderburn Report (2000) *Justice for Women: The Need for Reform*. London: Prison Reform Trust.

Young, J. (1986) 'The failure of criminology: the need for a radical realism' in R. Matthews and J. Young, (eds) *Confronting Crime*. London: Sage.

Chapter 7

The convergence of US and UK crime control policy: exploring substance and process

Trevor Jones and Tim Newburn

Introduction

A number of writers have commented on what appears to be a growing convergence between criminal justice and penal policies in different nation-states. In particular, attention has been drawn to the emergence of 'US-style' criminal justice policies in other industrial democracies (Christie 2000; Nellis 2000; Newburn 2002; Garland 2001; Jones and Newburn 2002a). Such studies have focused on developments such as 'zero tolerance' policing strategies, privatisation within criminal justice and penal systems, harsher sentencing policies and expanding rates of imprisonment. It is suggested that these phenomena are increasingly 'global' in character, and in this sense reflect wider concerns about 'globalisation' processes that increasingly lead nation-states to adopt similar economic, social and cultural policies (Robertson 1992; Bernstein and Cashore 2000).

The apparent convergence of crime control policy has been explained in different ways. Some criminologists focus upon the structural and cultural conditions that shape policy-making in different countries (Christie 2000; Garland 2000, 2001). In this view, fundamental shifts in economic and social structures and changes in cultural sensibilities have led political actors to adopt similar forms of penal response. Such accounts, while not being crudely deterministic, place relatively less weight upon the role of political agency. By contrast, other authors have adopted a different level of analysis, and highlighted the growth of policy imitation and policy transfer between jurisdictions. The focus of these arguments, although not always explicit, is upon the purposive actions and decisions of key actors in the policy process (see Nellis 2000; Jones and Newburn 2002a). The different emphases of these two broad approaches are, of course, ultimately irreconcilable in so far as they relate to the 'unavoidable tension between broad generalization and the specification of empirical particulars' (Garland 2001: vi). However, the central argument of this chapter is that both approaches have much to gain from a more detailed empirical consideration of both the substance of policy and the processes through which it comes about.

The chapter is divided into four main sections. The first outlines in more detail the respective strengths and limitations of 'structural-cultural' and 'agency-led' approaches to explaining penal policy convergence. The second section explores the concept of 'policy' and, in particular, the distinct dimensions of 'substance' and 'process'. The third examines the substantive dimensions of policy in the three particular areas of interest, and in particular explores the distinction between the more symbolic aspects and 'concrete' manifestations of policy. The fourth examines policy processes in the three specific examples of 'policy convergence' between the USA and UK.

Explaining penal policy convergence

Growing similarity between the penal policies of industrialised countries has been a central theme within much recent comparative work in criminology. Nils Christie (2000) has argued that the explosion of US prison populations over the past 30 years is now being mirrored in increased incarceration rates in many other nations. Christie relates these developments to a number of structural factors, including changes in capitalist societies that have produced a greater 'supply' of criminal acts due to weakened informal social controls and a greater tendency to 'criminalise' incidents by reporting them to the authorities. At the same time, a more generalised sense of insecurity (which finds its roots in structural and cultural developments in capitalist societies) has helped to fuel public demand for harsher punishments. A key factor behind penal expansionism is the commodification of crime control in capitalist societies, as witnessed by the burgeoning international commercial corrections market. Christie argues that, during recent decades, penal policy in many industrialised countries has been increasingly shaped by the 'prison-industrial complex', a transnational alliance of commercial interests that profit from expansionist penal policies. Christie also refers to the importance of national political cultures and differences in political institutions (for example, the relative influence of public and expert opinion) in mediating some of the 'global' trends he describes, but does not analyse these in great detail. The key focus of the argument is the impact of broader economic and social forces upon developments in penal policy.

These arguments are echoed in the work of David Garland (2000, 2001) who has suggested that a common 'culture of control' is emerging in both the UK and USA. This work concentrates primarily upon convergence and similarity in patterns of penal problems and policies between the two countries.[1] There are, according to Garland, striking similarities both in the nature of the problems faced by policy actors, and the style and substance of the responses adopted. He argues that a key factor behind these similarities concerns shifts of social structures and cultural configurations within late modern capitalist societies. Garland notes that in both the USA and UK, two kinds of contrasting strategy have been introduced. First, policy-makers have recognised the limitations of the state in delivering crime control and have implemented pragmatic 'adaptive' strategies. These include managerialist reforms to criminal justice systems, privatisation and contracting-out, diversion and the active 'responsibilisation' of non-state organisations and individuals. The second type of strategy has, conversely, involved the promotion of policies of 'denial' and symbolic assertions of the state's sovereignty in crime control. This has involved governments engaging in 'acting out' behaviour in the form of tough law enforcement and sentencing policies overlaid with a strident punitive rhetoric. The object of such policies is primarily expressive – 'to denounce the crime and reassure the public' (2001: 133) – rather than instrumental (in terms of aiming to reduce levels of crime).

The key to understanding policy convergence lies, therefore, in identifying and analysing more fundamental developments in capitalist societies. Garland does not argue that a kind of cultural and structural determinism is active in shaping crime control policy in the UK and USA. As he states, '[p]olitics and policy always involve choice and decision-making and the possibility of acting otherwise' (2001: 139). However, given the nature of this broad 'generalising' study, Garland inevitably avoids becoming embroiled in the empirical detail of particular cases and therefore does not focus upon the specifics of political processes. Although it is accepted that a degree of conscious emulation and policy transfer has occurred, it is suggested that the political choices involved here are themselves a function of more fundamental shifts in social structures and cultural sensibilities.

Another body of writing also emphasises the convergence of crime control policy in the USA and the UK. However, a different level of explanation for such developments is presented. In contrast to the 'structural-cultural' arguments outlined above, they suggest a more direct form of policy influence being exerted over the UK by the USA. There is a view, although not always framed explicitly, that the field of British social policy in general (including crime control policy) has become increasingly 'Americanised' in recent years. Such arguments often suggest a rather straightforward exertion of American influence, which manifests itself via deliberate policy transfers from the USA and the conscious emulation of US policy innovations by UK policy-makers. Commentators have highlighted perceived US influences over the introduction of 'workfare' type schemes into the UK labour market, and other reforms brought in both by New Labour and its Conservative predecessors (Dolowitz *et al.* 1999; King and Wickham-Jones 1999). These themes are also visible within the field of crime control. Several authors have suggested that there is an increasing incidence of 'policy transfer' from the USA to other western industrialised countries. For example, Nellis (2000: 115) argues that 'a process of policy transfer indisputably took place' with regard to the emergence of electronic monitoring of offenders in the UK. Others have related policy transfers in the field of commercial corrections to the activities of multinational corporations (Lilly and Knepper 1992). In general, recent commentary has placed American influences as central to many significant developments in crime control policy that have occurred under the Blair-led Labour governments (Downes 2001; Faulkner 2001). Crime control policy under New Labour, it is often suggested shows distinct signs of Democratic Party influence (Rutherford 2000; Jones and Newburn 2002a). All these approaches tend to focus primarily upon the role of political choice and decision-making. They are concerned with political agency – the strategic decisions and actions taken by key policy actors. The deeper structural and cultural factors that may shape such actions and decisions are rarely discussed in any detail, other than some broad references to cultural and linguistic similarities between the UK and USA.

We argue here that detailed empirical examinations of penal policy-making in different countries have much to offer both these broad approaches to understanding policy convergence. The structural-cultural approach has identified important social and cultural conditions that provide the broader context for policy-making, and have plausibly argued that changes in these wider conditions have made certain policy responses more probable. Such approaches have provided important analysis of some of the deeper structural/cultural changes that are being experienced across many societies. They have also made some extremely plausible suggestions about their impact upon penal policy responses. However, the precise ways in which these broader conditions have worked to shape the perceptions and decisions of key actors in the policy process have yet to be identified. 'Economic forces', 'social structures' and 'cultural sensibilities' do not lobby for penal innovations, frame legislation, pass sentences or vote in elections; people do (Hudson 1996). We still need to shed light upon the *intervening processes* via which these deeper structures and cultural forces come to shape key political decisions. The 'agency led' approach could potentially provide the further evidence that is required here. In this way, 'sweeping accounts of the big picture can be adjusted and revised by more focused case studies that add empirical specificity and local detail' (Garland 2001: vi). However, to date few studies have provided detailed evidence about how penal policy comes to be the way it is. Although plausible claims have been made about the sources of influence over policy outcomes, these are rarely based upon systematic empirical analysis of the process of policy formulation. Too often, transfer or emulation is assumed in a straightforward way from similarities in policy responses in different jurisdictions.

This can be related to two factors. First, criminologists to date have tended to take the notion of 'policy' for granted in so far as their empirical research has concentrated on its impacts rather than its origins. Secondly, political scientists, while having a more sophisticated notion of what policy is and what are the processes via which it comes about, have tended to focus upon areas other than crime control.[2] Taking the first of these points, there have been a few empirical studies of criminal justice policy-making conducted by criminologists (Rock 1990; Jones *et al.* 1994; Windlesham 1998). However, these studies did not really explore the idea of 'policy transfer' from other countries and in general do not draw on the existing body of political science literature on policy-making. There have also been influential studies of the interests and ideologies involved in the politics of crime control (Bottoms 1995; Downes and Morgan 1997). However, we still know remarkably little about how and why criminal justice policy changes, particularly in the UK. To develop the second point, political scientists have produced a huge body of work about the policy-making process in the policy arenas of health, education, agriculture, economic policy and environmental regulation. They have explored the resources of, and relationships between, key players in the policy process, and have explored the main strategies adopted by key policy actors and the impact of such factors on policy outcomes. They also have analysed the development of 'policy networks' in different policy domains, and the impact of such networks on policy decisions (Atkinson and Coleman 1992). In recent years, there have been studies by political scientists exploring the idea of 'policy transfer' between different jurisdictions (Dolowitz and Marsh 2000). However, there remains a paucity of empirical studies of policy formulation in the arena of crime control. A precondition for such studies, however, is a more sophisticated understanding of the concept of 'policy'.

Policy dimensions

Public policy is a complex, multifaceted concept. We here draw a particular distinction between two dimensions of 'policy' – those concerned with 'substance' and 'process', respectively. First, policy can be considered substantively at a number of different 'levels'. These range from ideas and rhetoric to more concrete manifestations such as specific policy instruments and practices. Secondly, it is important to emphasise that policy-making is a process involving a number of analytically distinct elements.

Policy levels

At any one point in time 'policy' may be broken down into a number of substantive 'levels'. Authors such as Bernstein and Cashmore (2000) have argued that empirical studies need to focus upon formal policy decisions such as statutes, regulations and statements, because these manifestations of policy capture the 'actual choices of government'. However, others have suggested that such definitions underplay the complex multilayered nature of public policy. For example, Bennett (1991) identifies a number of distinct elements of policy, including policy content (statutes, administrative rules and regulations), policy instruments (institutional tools to achieve goals such as regulatory, administrative, judicial tools) and policy style (overall nature of process – consensual, confrontational or incremental). Similarly, Dolowitz and Marsh (2000) outline various different elements of policy, including policy goals, content, instruments, programmes, institutions, ideologies, ideas and attitudes. In particular, a broad distinction may be drawn between *policy styles, symbols and rhetoric* and the more concrete and formalised manifestations of policy in terms of *policy content and instruments*.

Process

There is a large body of work within political science that has analysed policy-making by dividing it up into distinct stages, and undertaking detailed examinations of each (Easton 1965). In such approaches, policy is seen as arising from a distinct set of problem-solving processes: problem definition, formulation of alternative solutions and considerations of implications of alternatives to experimentation with the preferred choice. While recognising the analytical importance of identifying such stages, a number of authors have pointed out that such an approach runs the risk of implying a rather mechanistic model of the policy-making process (Hill 1997). Policy-making in practice rarely looks like the textbook discussions of the 'policy cycle', and the process is rarely as rational and sequential as analytical models seem to imply (Nelson 1996). The content of policies is not determined only by the decision-making stage but is negotiated continuously in the problem definition, legislation, regulation and court decisions, and again in the decisions made by practitioners and 'street-level' bureaucrats.

One model that seeks to 'deconstruct' the policy process while paying due regard to its apparently somewhat anarchic character is that developed by Kingdon (1995). He suggests that public policy-making can be seen as a linked set of stages including agenda-setting, alternative specification, authoritative choice and implementation (1995: 2). However, he emphasises that policy-making does not proceed in a neat set of temporal sequences. Rather, it is helpful to identify three distinct 'process streams' that operate fairly independently of one another:

1   The problem stream (the process of generation of 'problems' requiring attention by policy-makers).
2   The policy stream (the generation of policy ideas and proposals).
3   The political stream (developments in the 'public mood', key interest group support, etc.).

Kingdon suggests that these distinct streams, although independent for much of the time, converge at critical periods whereby 'solutions become joined to problems, and both of them are joined to favourable political forces' (1995: 20). From time to time, 'policy windows' (opportunities for promoting certain proposals or conceptions of a problem) are opened by developments in the political stream, or the emergence of particularly compelling problems. Such windows provide an opportunity for what Kingdon calls 'policy entrepreneurs' whose 'defining characteristic, much as in the case of a business entrepreneur, is their willingness to invest their resources – time, energy, reputation, and sometimes money – in the hope of future return' (1995: 122). Policy entrepreneurs both push their 'pet' proposals and problems, and link problems and proposed solutions to the political stream. The success of policy entrepreneurs depends upon their ability to respond quickly to these 'windows' of opportunity, before other 'solutions' become favoured. Although a good part of this is down to the skill of the policy entrepreneur, crucially, there is also a substantial element of luck involved. In sum, a significant development in policy is most likely when problems, policy proposals and politics are linked together into a clear package.

The dimensions of penal policy convergence

This approach has important implications for the way that we attempt to understand policy convergence. As noted earlier, it is possible to identify a significant number of penal policies in the UK over recent years that resemble similar developments in the USA. It is clear these arise from the interaction of structural and cultural forces and the decisions of key actors. However, in order to reflect on the nature and causes of the apparent convergence of penal policy between the USA and UK, it is helpful to focus upon the different dimensions of policy change in particular cases. This shows that below the surface of broad similarity there may be important differences of substance, and/or significant differences in the processes by which change came about. By way of illustration, we focus below on the substance and process of policy change in three ostensibly 'US-style' penal policy developments in the UK: 'zero-tolerance' policing, contracting out prisons to the private sector, and sex offender registration policies. In doing so, we begin to trace important differences within the overall appearance of similarity. Such differences help us to shed light on the real nature and causes of convergence, and the respective roles of structure and agency in policy formation.

The symbol and substance of policy

In each of the three specific areas explored in this chapter it appears, at least on the surface, that very similar policies had been adopted in the USA and the UK. Moreover, in each of these cases the chronology of the policy changes in question made it seem possible that they represented examples of US influence on UK crime control policy. However, a closer analysis of the substantive dimension of policy in each area (in terms of 'policy content' and rhetoric) shows considerable divergence between the US and UK experience. More particularly, it is in connection with 'policy styles, symbols and rhetoric' that convergence is clearer.

Zero-tolerance policing

The term 'zero-tolerance policing' (ZTP) has been associated with a wide range of different policing strategies and practices with the result that 'definitive conceptual definitions have remained elusive' (Innes 1999: 397). However, the term has come to be closely associated with the policing policies adopted in New York following the election of Mayor Rudolph Guiliani, and his appointment of police commissioner William Bratton in 1993.[3] Central to the resonance of this term in popular debate was the view that signficant falls in crime in New York City during 1990s were the result, at least in part, of 'zero tolerance' policing (although this has been strongly contested; see Greene 1999). Leaving aside debates about terminology and impact, it is possible to identify a number of specific policing policies and practices that have come to be associated with ZTP. Most specifically, inspired by Wilson and Kelling's (1982) 'broken windows' thesis, the term has been associated with a vigorous enforcement-oriented approach towards incivilities and disorder in local areas. The broken windows thesis suggests that neighbourhood disorders lead to a vicious circle of decline in local areas and encourage more serious crime in a number of ways. In particular, the neighbourhood disorder may result in the erosion of informal community controls, greater fear of crime and less willingness for law-abiding people to use public space. By controlling disorderly behaviour, it was felt that a real impact both on quality of life and on serious crime rates could be achieved. Within New York, ZTP came to be associated with a range of specific developments, including the use of civil law to crack down on low-level disorder, aggressive enforcement policies in which arrest and prosecution were prioritised, the introduction of crime mapping and targeted policing, and significantly increased police numbers and visibility. These developments were key features of the policing reforms introduced in New York City during the 1990s,[4] with the police being encouraged strongly to target behaviours such as public begging, low-level incivilities, public drunkenness and urination, fare dodging and, most famously of all, 'squeegeeing'(Bratton 1998).

Within mainstream policing in the UK there have been a small number of experiments with so-called 'zero-tolerance policing'. In 1996, the Metropolitan Police introduced Operation Zero Tolerance which ran for six weeks in the King's Cross area of London. This involved high-visibility policing and a vigorous enforcement-oriented campaign to 'clean up' the area by focusing as much on minor infractions and incivilities as on major crimes. However, this was a rather short-term and localised initiative compared to the changes in policing practices that were introduced across New York. In Scotland at around the same time, Strathclyde Police introduced the 'Spotlight Initiative' involving a vigorous policing approach to minor crime and disorder, which the media associated with 'zero tolerance', although this was strongly denied by the chief constable of the force (Orr 1998). In the UK, ZTP has been most closely associated with Cleveland Constabulary and, in particular, the policing initiatives introduced in Middlesbrough and Hartlepool by Detective Superintendent Ray Mallon. From April 1994, a policy of 'confident policing' of minor crime and disorder was introduced in the Hartlepool division under Mallon (Dennis and Mallon 1998). Sharp falls in recorded crime figures over the following two years brought Mallon national attention, and the media nickname 'Robocop'.[5]

When we focus upon the 'policy content' of ZTP, although it appears to have been associated with a concrete set of policing practices in New York City, in the UK experiments in 'zero tolerance' were much more limited. This is true in the geographic sense (small localised initiatives), in the temporal sense (relatively short-term experiments) and in terms of content (more limited changes in actual policing practice). By contrast, the terminology of 'zero tolerance' became widespread, not so much within the field of policing but more so within wider political rhetoric and discourse. To the extent that anything crossed the Atlantic it was terminology, ideas and ideologies rather than practices and policies. The phrase 'zero tolerance' proved to be particular popular with politicians, and remains so today. Following his visit to New York in July 1995, Jack Straw made public references to the 'aggressive begging of winos and addicts' and the 'squeegee merchants who wait at large road junctions to force on reticent motorists their windscreen cleaning service' (cited in Newburn 1998). Echoing his Shadow Home Secretary, Tony Blair made a major, and controversial, speech in January 1997 in which he stated his support for the idea of 'zero tolerance' ('Clear beggars from streets, say Blair', *The Times*: 7 January 1997). In fact as early as December 1995, Tony Blair had signalled his willingness to use the term in a much broader manner to signify a more general 'style' in which New Labour would operate given the opportunity. In launching proposals for improving educational standards, he promised to 'sweep away the second rate and tackle head-on the half-baked and the ineffective', adding: 'There will be zero tolerance of failure from any government I lead' ('Teachers savage Blair school plan', *Guardian*: 6 December 1995). The same message eventually found its way into the Labour Party election manifesto in 1997. It was at this stage that zero-tolerance rhetoric from politicians really took off. Whereas there had been occasional sightings prior to this, particularly around major speeches by Blair and Straw, in the run-up to the 1997 general election and in parliamentary debates during the six months afterwards, there were regular reappearances of 'zero tolerance'. The terminology of 'zero tolerance' has declined in visibility in the past couple of years, though occasionally politicians (Ann Widdecombe at the 2000 Conservative Party conference) and, less frequently, senior police officers (during the May Day riots in 2001, for example) still make use of it.

One of the very clear lessons learnt by the New Democrats, subsequently passed on to New Labour, was the power and importance of symbolic politics; of using a phrase or an action to convey something more powerful and significant. As two influential New Labour archi-tects put it in the early 1990s, 'the lessons which the British left can learn [from the US] are not so much about *content* – although there is valuable intellectual exchange already underway – as about *process*' (Hewitt and Gould 1993: 47). They might have gone on to note that in addition to learning lessons about process, they learnt at least as much about 'style'. From the rebranding of the party, through the adoption of a new form of political language (Fairclough 2000) and the use of 'spin' and 'sound bite', New Labour consciously adopted much from the New Democrats. However, so far as 'zero tolerance' is concerned, there is little evidence of the transfer of formal policies – instruments or practices. Rather the term, the symbol, was utilised, primarily by politicians, to embody particular attributes and a political style. In this manner 'zero tolerance', like other terms such as 'three strikes and you're out', and even the broader metaphor of the 'war on crime', serves a primarily symbolic function. It diverts attention from 'causes' of crime, and from alternative 'policies'; it has the potential to reaffirm faith in the criminal justice system and possibly even rational policy-making. It acts as what Murray Edelman (1971: 135) calls a 'condensation symbol', merging 'diverse anxieties and emotions with a shared expectation about the time, the place, and the action that will evoke common support and a common perception of the enemy'.

Much of the policy transfer literature examines the extent to which practices and policies are copied, more or less faithfully, from one jurisdiction to another. The example of zero tolerance illustrates the possibility that the degree of accuracy in 'successful' transfer varies depending on the nature of the 'policy'. Where programmes of action are concerned – the transfer of 'welfare to work' policy, for example – it may be that a certain degree of fidelity is important. By contrast, in the area of ideas, such as zero tolerance, we might argue that it is the ability to be flexible in copying concepts and ideas that allows them to survive. A term such as zero tolerance may shift from jurisdiction to jurisdiction, but its meanings will almost certainly vary with context. Yet the concept may retain its plausibility irrespective of the faithfulness of the copy in existence. In fact, in practice, ZTP has barely been copied at all in the UK. More than this, there has been considerable cultural resistance to the idea of ZTP – a form of policing that runs counter in many respects to the dominant model of policing developed and adopted in mainland Britain since the early 1980s. In this respect at least the cultures of crime control in the USA and the UK would appear to differ. At this point, however, we should note that it is by no means the case that there has been universal adoption of ZTP styles in the USA (Harcourt 2001; Taylor 2001). Again, it is important to recognise not only that there exist important differences between the USA and the UK but also that within the USA there is considerable variation in cultures of control.

Prison privatisation[6]

The involvement of the private sector in the building and running of prisons has been a notable policy development in recent decades in both the USA and the UK (as well as some other countries such as Australia; see Harding 1997). In the USA (and in particular, southern and western states), a window of opportunity opened for the commercial prisons sector during the early 1980s. This was related to a number of factors, including expanding prison populations with attendant problems of overcrowding, federal court rulings requiring state governments to improve prison conditions, tighter budgetary controls on state spending and an ideological climate supportive of privatisation (Ryan and Ward 1989). Nevertheless, it was widely felt that prison privatisation in the USA would remain rather limited in scope. By the end of the decade, one academic commentator noted that 'there is considerable opposition nationwide to privatization of adult mainstream [prison] populations' (Weiss 1989: 31). The position changed remarkably quickly, and the first half of the 1990s saw a significant expansion in the private corrections sector (Mattera and Khan 2001). By 1993 there were over 50 privately contracted prisons. This number rose to 78 by mid-1994, 92 by the end of 1995 and 152 by mid-2001. Particular groups of southern and western states were major contributors to this overall figure. By contrast, other parts of the USA remained largely untouched by privatisation, so that by the mid 1990s a significant number of states still had no privately run prisons at all (Ryan 1996).[7] The late 1990s, however, saw a substantial slowing in the growth of private corrections. This was associated with an increase in 'bad news' stories about commercially run prisons in local and national media, and effective campaigning at the state level by prison reform groups, penal reform organisations and public sector trade unions (Sentencing Project 2002). This led a number of state governments to bring private prisons back under public control, or cancel the introduction of new private prison contracts (Mattera and Khan 2001). However, recent years have seen the Federal Government become an increasingly important customer for private prison corporations.

In the UK, privatisation of mainstream correctional institutions followed some years behind the USA. Within the UK, the possibility of 'contracting out' first entered the penal policy agenda during the mid-1980s, but by the end of that decade it still appeared that 'in the immediate future, the private sector's role in prison management in Britain [was] likely to be marginal at most' (Rutherford 1990: 62). This situation was soon to change. The Criminal Justice Act 1991 contained a provision allowing the management of any prison, not just remand centres, to be contracted out to any agency the Home Secretary considered appropriate. In April 1992 Group 4 Security won the contract to manage a new purpose-built institution for remand prisoners, the Wolds, and a second prison, Blakenhurst, opened in 1993 under the management of UK Detention Services (linked to the Corrections Corporation of America). Privatisation has gathered pace since that time with a dozen prisons now being privately managed. Although in opposition, the Labour Party strongly opposed the contracting out of prisons but, following the 1997 election, the party's position changed rapidly. In 1998, the Home Secretary announced that from that time, all new prisons in England and Wales would be privately constructed and put out to tender (Cavadino and Dignan 2002).

It was in relation to the privatisation of prisons that there was most evidence of policy transfer from the USA to the UK in terms of substantive manifestations of policy content and instruments. It is clear that prison privatisation occurred first in the USA and followed later in the UK. Key policy entrepreneurs in the genesis of the policy in the UK all explicitly used US developments as exemplars to promote similar policies on this side of the Atlantic. Finally, US-based corporations were centrally involved in the actual implementation stages of the policy in the UK. It was not surprising, therefore, that the 'substance' of policy, in terms of the requirement for legislative change and the administrative instruments of private contracting, displayed strong similarities in the two countries. However, it is possible to point to an important difference in terms of the symbolic element of the policy. At a key turning point for the UK development of the policy, during 1990, prison privatisation took on a symbolic element that does not seem to have been present to the same extent in the southern states of the USA where commercial prisons first developed. In these parts of the USA, the policy arose in the USA primarily as a pragmatic response to legal requirements on overcrowding, and difficulties in raising sufficient capital expenditure in the public sector. Although the UK was experiencing similar economic pressures, they were arguably not a primary contributory factor in policy development. In fact, during the late 1980s, the prison population was actually falling and consequently there were fewer pragmatic pressures towards commercial involvement. The policy of the UK had an avowedly symbolic dimension that can be seen in a number of ways. First, prison privatisation was both perceived as, and presented as, an 'ideological bridgehead'. Secondly, the decision to incorporate a clause in the Criminal Justice Act 1991 that would open the way to experiment with a privately managed remand centre was primarily driven by the symbolic need to appear radical. It was 'a symbol as well as an experiment' (Windlesham 1993: 307). For Margaret Thatcher, the decision symbolised her independence, her radical nature and her belief that her government should be perceived as a 'conviction government' (Jenkins 1987: 183). Despite this, because of the close similarity in policy content and instruments, of the three policy areas discussed in this chapter, the privatisation of prisons comes the closest to fitting into the 'convergence' model. Even here, however, examining policy development and transfer suggests the existence of potentially important differences as well as significant similarities.

Sex offender registration

In both the USA and the UK, recent years have seen heightened public concerns about sex offenders and, in particular, the risks posed by paedophiles in the community. In the USA, the introduction of sex offender registration laws began in California in 1947, and other states progressively followed suit, so that by the late 1990s all 50 states had passed such legislation (Earl-Hubbard 1996). Of these, 20 restrict access to information on sex offender registers to law enforcement and related authorities. However, others allow broader access, ranging from criminal records checks for agencies in some, to full public access and community notification schemes in others. The origins of full-scale notification schemes in the USA date back to the late 1980s. The first public notification law, the Community Protection Act, was passed in Washington State in 1990 following a number of serious crimes involving sex offenders. In 1989 an 11-year-old boy, Jacob Wetterling, was abducted and assaulted resulting eventually in the passage of Minnesota's Sex Offender Registration Act. The Wetterling Foundation, set up in the aftermath of the abduction, campaigned at both state and federal level for legislative action. In 1994 Congress enacted the Jacob

Wetterling Crimes against Children and Sex Offender Registration Act. A major turning point occurred that same year, with the sexual assault and murder of 7-year-old Megan Kanka in New Jersey in 1994. The assailant, who had recently moved to live in the same street, was, unbeknown to the residents of the local community, a twice-convicted paedophile. At the time of the assault he was sharing a house with two other sex offenders. A host of states subsequently enacted sex offender registration laws, many with community notification provisions. In 1996, an amendment to federal legislation (the Jacob Wetterling Act) was passed making community notification mandatory in all states. In practice, the requirement has been implemented in variable form across the USA. In some states the names, addresses and photographs of violent sex offenders have been posted on the Internet by the police. Others have seemingly failed to set up notification schemes at all and a number have faced constitutional challenges to the provisions they had made (Windlesham 1998).

In the UK during the 1990s, growing public and political concerns about sex offenders led to the introduction of a number of legislative provisions designed to manage sexual offenders in the community. The first of these, the Sex Offenders Act 1997, established the Sex Offenders Register. However, it was generally accepted that the names and addresses of the people on the register should remain confidential, and disclosed by the police only on a 'need to know' basis to other agencies involved in the management of risk. In partnership with the Probation Service, the Act required the police to undertake a risk assessment of every offender who registers and, where risk levels were deemed sufficiently high, a plan was to be drawn up to 'manage' the risk. This would, where appropriate, involve the sharing of information and tasks with other agencies (Maguire *et al.* 2001). Decisions about whether or not information should be disclosed more broadly, for example to other organisations or to the public in general, were to be made by the police on a case-by-case basis.

Though community notification schemes have enjoyed a far from uncontroversial history in the USA, and considerable doubts exist as to the benefits to be derived from such schemes (Finn 1997), a number of developments have heightened media and public support for more widespread disclosure of information about sex offenders in the UK. The abduction and murder of an 8-year-old girl, Sarah Payne, from a Sussex village in July 2000, and the anxious period that followed before her body was eventually found, provided momentum for a campaign for the introduction of what, before long, became known as 'Sarah's law'. The campaign, using Sarah's parents as figureheads, was 'managed' by

The Mirror and the *News of the World* newspapers. For a short period the *News of the World* undertook what it called a 'naming and shaming' campaign, printing pictures of convicted sex offenders.[8] Criticism from government, and from the police and probation service, particularly in response to a series of outbreaks of vigilantism against alleged paedophiles, led the paper to stop printing the photographs after just a few weeks. However, the overall campaign retained momentum and the bereaved parents met with Paul Boateng, junior minister in the Home Office at the time, to discuss the introduction of community notification. They emerged from the meeting saying that it had been agreed that the public would get some access to the sex offenders' register and that they had 'been assured there will be a Sarah's law' (*Guardian:* 13 September 2000). Quite what had been promised, if anything, is somewhat unclear. However, on advice from the police and probation services that were alarmed at the likely consequences of community notification, the Home Secretary very quickly announced that he did not support such proposals, but that he would be putting the police and probation services under a new statutory duty to set up risk assessment and monitoring programmes for violent and sex offenders released into the community. Sarah's Payne's mother said she and her husband were 'quite pleased that we have managed to get 60 percent of Sarah's law and [we] will carry on the campaign to get 100 percent' (*Guardian*: 16 September 2000).

Looking at the concrete manifestations of policy, there were clearly some basic similarities in so far as statutory registration schemes of varying types were introduced in both countries. However, here the comparison becomes even more complex, because of the great variation in the nature of schemes across the USA and, in particular, the different approaches to public notification. Under the Sex Offenders Act 1997, people convicted of most forms of sexual offence are required to register their name and address with the local police within 14 days of conviction/caution, or within 14 days of moving house. However, as outlined earlier, the Act gave no guidance to the police concerning the issue of disclosure of such information, and local practitioners and criminal justice professionals have so far successfully resisted campaigns for the kind of public access that exists in many American states (Kemshall 2001).

In this regard the example of paedophile notification schemes is perhaps instructive. As outlined above, the circumstances that led to campaigns for public notification schemes were remarkably similar in both the USA and the UK. Both arose from the brutal abduction and murder of a young child and involved vigorous press campaigns. In the

UK, it certainly seemed for a time that the transfer of a particular form of legislation, US Megan's Laws, might occur. In the event, at least to date, the introduction of a 'Sarah's law' has been resisted. Moreover, this policy area provides another area where symbolic politics diverges considerably from the substance of policy. Politicians from both major parties in the UK have been keenly aware of the strong public feelings on this issue, and have used rhetoric and symbolism to imply support for stronger measures regarding notification, at the same time as bowing to the professional judgement and influence of criminal justice prac- titioners. This could be seen, for example, during the passage of the Sex Offenders Act 1997. The overall tone of the senior government spokes- people during the press campaign (and indeed during the 1997 election campaign) has suggested support for public notification. Yet at no point have senior government figures actually suggested anything other than minor reforms, and no minister has explicitly stated support for general public notification. Thus, while the symbolic elements of 'policy rhetoric' and 'style' appear to have been remarkably similar on both sides of the Atlantic, the degree to which this rhetoric has been played out in concrete changes in policy has been strikingly different. This appears to be due, in large part, to the resistance of key players in the penal policy 'network' to public notification schemes. The fact of this resistance, and the form it took, again speaks to at least a degree of difference between the extant cultures of control on the two sides of the Atlantic. It also shows how institutional and political differences can mediate the practical impact of populist campaigns. Furthermore, it reinforces the importance of considering the role of agency in the development of policy. This is one very clear area in which forms of resistance to the importation of an Americanised crime control strategy were active and, at least at the time of writing, successful.

The process of policy convergence

Zero-tolerance policing

There is at the very least a surface attraction to the idea that 'zero tolerance' is a clear example of 'Americanised' influences within the UK crime control arena. The term appears to have its roots in the USA. It was only later that such a notion developed any currency in the UK. In most cases when the term has been used in the UK clear links have been made to New York City as an exemplar of what could be achieved. Secondly, these links were given form by the connections between policy entrepreneurs on both sides of the Atlantic. For a period in the mid-1990s

New York was all but besieged by British policy tourists arriving to learn the lessons of the policing 'miracle' there. Similarly, zero-tolerance proselytisers like Bill Bratton and his one-time deputy, Jack Maple, made several visits to the UK to spread the word. They were aided and abetted in this work by two major, and linked, neoliberal think-tanks, the Manhattan Institute and the Institute for Economic Affairs.

However, the picture is considerably more complicated than this. As suggested above, the term 'zero tolerance' has a longer history than its most recent association with the policing of New York City would imply. Its origins – at least in the crime control arena – appear to lie in the Reaganite 'War on Drugs' in the 1980s. The White House, under pressure to be seen to be responding to the emerging crack epidemic, adopted what it referred to as a 'zero tolerance' approach to drugs and sought to create a 'drug-free America' by the year 2000. In the early 1990s – by which time the term had long since stopped being associated with federal drugs policy – it reappeared in both Canada and subsequently in Scotland in connection with campaigns against male violence against women. It is in that connection that the term 'zero tolerance' was most frequently been used in the UK during the 1990s. It is only more recently that the term has become associated with a particular style of policing. Turning to Kindgon's (1995) model, preliminary analysis of the different streams of problems, policies and politics suggests some significant differences between the process of policy change regarding 'zero-tolerance policing' that begin to help explain some of the substantive differences outlined earlier.

In New York the 'problems', according to the key actors, were essentially threefold. First, the city was beset by a quite extraordinary murder rate. Though homicides had declined during the first half of the 1980s, in the second half of the decade it rose to an all-time high (2,262 in 1990) before beginning the dramatic decline recorded during the course of the last decade (Karmen 2000). Secondly, and relatedly, the city had during the 1980s been in the grip of a 'crack epidemic' (Bowling 1999). Thirdly, at least as argued by those responsible for policing New York in the 1990s, a general sense of disorderliness in the city was given vivid illustration by what was perceived to be the increasingly commonplace activities of aggressive panhandling, fare dodging and 'squeegeeing' (Bratton 1998). None of the above could be said to characterise the UK generally, or any of its cities in particular. There had been no particularly spectacular rise in the murder rate in the UK or, say, in London. Secondly, despite fears to the contrary, crack use in the UK never reached anything approximating 'epidemic' proportions. Finally, despite the fact that British politicians occasionally latched on to terms such as 'squeegeeing', there was little evidence of widespread public concern about disorderliness and civic breakdown on the scale evident in New York.

By contrast, in the UK, the 'problem' was essentially a *political* one: there was a cross-party search for punitive policies, and particularly rhetoric, that could be used to convince an electorate to cast their vote for those who could be trusted to be toughest on crime. This is not to say that the 'political' stream was not important in New York. The adoption of 'zero tolerance' tactics and terminology was closely linked to the careers of Mayor Giuliani and his first commissioner, Bill Bratton. Another key difference within the 'political' streams between New York City and policing in the UK concerns the relatively high degree of autonomy of senior police officers in deciding policing policy. In New York City (as in many other parts of the USA), the police chief is clearly a political appointment of, and subordinate to, the mayor. By contrast, although the professional autonomy of chief constables has become increasingly constrained by the directions of politicians in recent years, the level of political influence remains some way off that exercised in many US cities. In addition to this, the nature of the relationship between the 'political' and 'problem' streams differed on both sides of the Atlantic. This becomes clearer if we focus on the 'policy stream'. In New York 'zero tolerance' or 'quality of life' policing was associated with an identifiable set of policies. Though there was talk of such strategies being imported from the USA, in reality not only was there little evidence that such policing policies were adopted in the UK but there were also very clear historical and political reasons why there was in fact considerable resistance to such approaches to policing.

In the early 1980s the civil disturbances that occurred in Brixton in south London had been sparked by an aggressive policing operation, Swamp 81, which shared many characteristics with what we might think of as 'zero-tolerance policing'. The aftermath of the riots led not only to the Scarman Inquiry and report but also to some rethinking of policing in mainland Britain. A consensus emerged within British policing that the tactics that had been employed in Brixton were in all but the most extreme cases likely to be counterproductive, leading to the alienation of the local community at best and to violent confrontation at worst. Consequently, at the time talk of 'zero tolerance' reached British shores in the mid-1990s most senior police officers were against the use of the tactics associated with such an approach (see, for example, Pollard 1998). Though there have been one or two minor and conspicuous exceptions, police forces in Britain have rejected both the terminology and the practices associated with zero tolerance. As noted earlier, this is also true for much of the USA where the New York policing example has not been widely copied.

Thus, while on the surface a plausible argument can be made that 'zero-tolerance policing' is another example of policy convergence in US and UK crime control, as we have seen above, the substantive policy outcomes (within policing) demonstrated considerable differences. This clearly relates to differences in the nature of the relationships between the various 'streams' of influence on the two sides of the Atlantic. More particularly, the strategies adopted by the New York Police Department which, rightly or wrongly, have come to be associated with the term 'zero tolerance' have not been visible in other than very minor experiments in mainstream British policing. Though points of convergence can no doubt be found, a number of by now historically long-standing points of departure continue to exist in the policing systems of the USA and the UK (Jones and Newburn 2002b).

Prison privatisation

In some ways, the parallel histories of prison privatisation in the USA and UK might be presented as a straightforward case of policy convergence related to common structural and cultural influences. For example, US states and the countries of the UK are common law jurisdictions with a more limited view of the state in contrast with the continental European view of the state as an integrative symbol. Both the USA and the UK were profoundly influenced by the rise of the neoliberal right, and their respective national administrations and leaders also shared much in terms of political ideology. Within these broader structural and cultural constraints, however, the role of political agency and the conscious transfer of ideas were crucial. In recent times, private prisons emerged first in the USA, and thus provided exemplars upon which UK 'policy entrepreneurs' and other supporters of privatisation could draw. During the mid-1980s, Peter Young of the Adam Smith Institute actively promoted US private prisons as examples of good practice (Young 1987). At a later stage, members of the House of Commons Home Affairs Committee visited a number of privately managed correctional institutions in the USA. Leading members of the committee subsequently used this experience as the basis for recommending that the government experiment with a privately contracted remand centre (Home Affairs Committee 1987). In addition, a number of US corrections corporations were actively involved both in lobbying for the policy change and in the initial bidding for contracts in the UK (in partnership with UK construction companies). Since this time, these firms have provided a direct form of US influence into the implementation stage of the policy.

An analysis of the process of policy change in each country drawing upon Kingdon's model highlights important differences between the two countries. Crucially, the trajectory followed in the USA differed in several important ways from that in the UK. In particular, the permutations in the streams of problems, policies and politics were far from identical. In the USA, the key 'problem' confronting policy-makers in many states was the substantial growth of prison populations and the threat of litigation against overcrowded prison systems. The 'policy stream' included a range of theoretical alternatives, including the reduction of prison populations via changes in sentencing policy, or the building of new prisons. Private involvement in the building and running of prisons provided an opportunity for states to address overcrowding, without having to provide the capital investment 'up front' for a new prison-building programme. There are important contrasts here with the UK. The UK too faced the problem of an expanding prison population and consequent overcrowding during the 1980s. However, prison privatisation was at the time seen as politically unthinkable, even in Conservative circles. The policy stream did include an explicit advocacy of prison privatisation during the 1980s, found not least in the work of the Adam Smith Institute (ASI) and, later, the reports of the House of Commons Home Affairs Select Committee. The key policy entrepreneurs in this regard were Peter Young of the ASI and the leading members of the Home Affairs Committee at the time, Sir John Wheeler and Sir Edward Gardner. However, despite their best efforts, it initially appeared that the privatisation of prisons was considered a step too far, even for a radical Conservative government. What changed? At noted above, it appears that the eventual U-turn was related not to instrumental concerns about costs and overcrowding but more to expressive concerns and the need to make a 'grand gesture' about the radicalism of the government. The decision was taken by the Prime Minister, as Windlesham (1993: 421–2) notes, 'because of her conviction of the need for radical reform outside the prevailing consensus; not for any reasons of penological principle or administrative practice'. In Kingdon's (1995) terms, the 'solution' (privatisation) was in each case attached to slightly differing problems and, at least as importantly, the process by which attachment was brought about involved different political processes and 'windows'.

Sex offender registration

In relation to policy convergence, and possible policy transfer, this is a particularly interesting case. On the surface it would appear that there were ostensibly similar circumstances in the UK to those that led to the adoption of full-scale notification schemes in the USA. In both the high-profile cases of Megan Kanka in the USA and Sarah Payne in the UK, there was a 'projected, politicised victim' (Garland 2001: 143). There was apparent public support and certainly vigorous media campaigning. In addition, at least some senior politicians were keen to be seen to be sympathetic to the bereaved campaigners. Yet, despite the fact that the 'problem streams' were remarkably similar on both sides of the Atlantic, the legislation wasn't forthcoming. Why? To continue with Kingdon's (1995) terms, it appears that although the policy stream in the UK was quickly filled by a proposal largely imported from the USA, the political stream in the UK had a very different make-up from that in the USA. Put a different way, it appears that certain important forms of 'political' resistance came into play. What was absent in the UK was the support of the Probation Service and, crucially, the support of the police for the introduction of US-style notification schemes. Given their position as key opinion-formers in the area of crime control, the police can, and in this case undoubtedly did, exercise a decisive influence on both the public handling of this issue and, at least as importantly, how cabinet ministers felt able to respond. Importantly, the networks of influence in penal policy-making in the UK were such that there was sufficient resistance to what otherwise was a very powerful lobby in favour of such a scheme.

Conclusion

In this chapter we have explored some aspects of the apparent convergence of crime control policies and cultures in the USA and the UK. At the outset we suggested that it was possible to identify two broad approaches to the analysis of such convergence. The first, and most influential, is a structural-cultural approach that focuses on the deep cultural, political and social changes taking placed in advanced democracies or 'late modern' societies. The second, by contrast, places human agency closer to the centre of the account that is offered. This approach focuses more closely on the details of policy development and political influence and moves from these to the broader issues of emergent social routines and cultural sensibilities. In this chapter we have acknowledged the importance of broad structural and cultural changes to an understanding of policy convergence but, within this, have argued that it is useful to 'reinsert' a closer study of the role of political actors into the narrative. Doing so, we suggest, is revealing in a number of ways. First, by reinserting agency in this way a fuller picture of the processes of cultural formation and reproduction is produced. Secondly, doing so enables a better understanding of the specific nature of 'convergence' between the cultures of control in the USA and the UK. Finally, and linked to this, such an approach illustrates the limits of convergence. That is, it also highlights the continuing existence of dissimilarity and difference. Simultaneously, therefore, it is possible both to acknowledge the existence of elements of cultural convergence in crime control while drawing attention to important divergences both within and between particular nation-states. In this connection Tonry (1999, 2001) has recently noted what he sees as striking differences in substantive penal policy interventions between countries with different historical and cultural traditions. As he argues: 'The world increasingly may be a global community … but explanations of penal policy remain curiously local' (2001: 518).

David Garland (1990) has argued that penal policy is the outcome of 'a large number of conflicting forces', and it is ultimately impossible to identify and analyse the full range of 'swarming circumstances' that work to shape penal developments. In this he is undoubtedly correct. However, we would argue that it none the less remains the case that more detailed empirical studies of the concrete changes that are occurring, and the processes that lead to change, can significantly add to our knowledge and understanding of the determinants of penal policy. It is only via detailed empirical work that we can begin to map out the reflexive relationships between local, national and global influences that come to shape penal policy. In developing this argument we argued that it was important not to treat the term 'policy' unproblematically. Indeed, the study of (the limits of) policy convergence is enhanced by examining what we suggest are the two major dimensions of policy: the *substance of policy* and the *policy process.*

Applying this approach to three specific areas of policy change, and possible policy convergence, we suggested first of all that an important distinction exists between policy content and instruments on the one hand and policy styles, symbols and rhetoric on the other (see Edelman 1971; Bennett 1991; Tonry 2001). In relation to the three areas of policy change considered in this chapter it was clear not only that differences existed in the processes that led to policy change but also in connection with the balance between the substantive and symbolic elements of policy. Even our brief analysis suggested that at least in two of the three areas under consideration convergence has occurred more at the level of symbols than practices. We then suggested that these differences are related to the fact that the 'streams' of influence in each case differed both between policy areas and between nation-states. That is, even in the one area where there was a significant level of similarity in policy 'outcome' (prison privatisation) the nature of, and relationships between, the political, policy and problem streams differed. In the case of sex offender registration and paedophile notification schemes, for example, such differences were significant in the different policy outcomes that are visible in the USA and UK. In saying this we recognise that the observations we might make might differ, possibly markedly, if different 'policies' were under discussion. None the less, it is our contention that an approach that examines both the policy process and policy levels allows a more nuanced picture of policy convergence, and its limits, to be developed.

Acknowledgements

This chapter is an edited version of a previous paper (Jones, T. and Newburn, T. (2002) 'Policy convergence and crime control in the USA and UK: streams of influence and levels of impact', published in a special issue of the journal *Criminal Justice* 2(2)). It arises from a research project entitled 'International influences on UK crime control and penal policy in the 1990s', funded by the Economic and Social Research Council as part of their Future Governance Research Programme (Grant L216 25 2035). We are grateful to Stephen Nathan and to the participants in the Keele colloquium for advice and support.

Notes

1   It is important to note that this argument does not reject the existence of important dissimilarities between the two jurisdictions. Indeed, such dissimilarities are an inevitable finding of more detailed empirical studies of particular policy areas. However, by adopting a more general level of analysis, Garland argues that it is possible to identify and explore some of the broader factors that structure the field of crime control in both the USA, and the UK. The primary emphasis remains, therefore, on similarity and convergence.

2   This argument is slightly less applicable to the USA where there have been some important studies of crime control policy-making undertaken by political scientists. However, even in the USA, given the centrality of the issue of crime within public and political debate, the apparent lack of interest of political scientists in studying crime policy is quite remarkable.

3   In fact, the term 'zero tolerance' was rarely used by the key players in New York who preferred terms such as 'quality of life' or 'order maintenance' policing.

4   In fact this was just one part of a package of wider reforms, including a major reorganisation of the NYPD so that accountability was devolved to local area commanders, the introduction of a comprehensive analysis of local area crime and disorder figures, and a range of strategies to deal with particular kinds of crime.

5   Following a disciplinary investigation, Mallon subsequently left the Cleveland force and was later elected Mayor of Middlesbrough.

6   Michael Tonry (2001: 532) has recently argued that the privatisation of prisons should not be viewed as a penal policy but, rather, as 'a mechanism for implementing penal policy'. This is not a position with which we agree. While 'privatisation' in the field of corrections is indeed a delivery mechanism, the fact that it is not value-neutral but has penological consequences (potentially, at least, the expansion of the penal estate itself) makes it also, in our view, a penal policy.

7   In fact, a small number of states had legislation expressly forbidding such developments.

8   The *News of the World* carried the phrase 'For Sarah' on its front-page masthead every Sunday for many months after.

References

Atkinson, M. and Coleman, W. (1992) 'Policy networks, policy communities and problems of governance', *Governance*, 5(2): 154–80.

Bennett, C. (1991) 'What is policy convergence and what causes it?', *British Journal of Political Science*, 21: 215–33.

Bernstein, S. and Cashore, B. (2000) 'Globalization, four paths of internationalization and domestic policy change: the case of ecoforestry in British Columbia, Canada', *Canadian Journal of Political Science*, 33(1): 67–99.

Bottoms, A. (1995) 'The philosophy and politics of punishment and sentencing', in C. Clark and R. Morgan (eds) *The Politics of Sentencing Reform*. Oxford: Oxford University Press.

Bowling, B. (1999) 'The rise and fall of New York murder: zero tolerance or crack's decline?', *British Journal of Criminology*, 39(4): 531–54.

Bratton, W. (1998) *Turnaround: How America's Top Cop Reversed the Crime Epidemic*. New York, NY: Random House.

Cavadino, M. and Dignan, J. (2002) *The Penal System: An Introduction* (3rd edn). London: Sage.

Christie, N. (2000) *Crime Control as Industry* (3rd edn). London: Routledge.

Deacon, A. (1999) 'Learning from the US? The influence of American ideas upon "New Labour" thinking on welfare reform', *Policy and Politics*, 28(1): 5–18.

Dennis, N. and Mallon, R. (1998) Confident policing in Hartlepool, in N. Dennis (ed.) *Zero Tolerance: Policing a Free Society* (2nd edn). London: Institute for Economic Affairs.

Dolowitz, D., Greenwold, S. and Marsh, D. (1999) 'Policy transfer: something old, something new, something borrowed, but why red, white and blue?', *Parliamentary Affairs,* 52(4): 719–30.

Dolowitz, D. and Marsh, D. (2000) 'Learning from abroad: the role of policy transfer in contemporary policy-making', *Governance,* 13: 5–24.

Downes, D. (1993) *Contrasts in Tolerance: Post-war Penal Policy in the Netherlands and England and Wales.* Oxford: Clarendon Press.

Downes, D. (2001) 'The macho penal economy: mass incarceration in the US: a European perspective', *Punishment and Society,* (1): 61–80.

Downes, D. and Morgan, R. (1997) 'Dumping the "Hostages to fortune"? The politics of law and order in post-war Britain', in M. Maguire *et al.* (eds) *The Oxford Handbook of Criminology.* Oxford: Oxford University Press.

Earl-Hubbard, M. (1996) 'Child-sex offender registration laws', *Northwestern University Law Review,* 90(2): 788–62.

Easton, D. (1965) *A Systems Analysis of Political Life.* Chicago, IL: University of Chicago Press.

Edelman, M. (1971) *Politics as Symbolic Action.* Chicago, IL: University of Illinois Press.

Fairclough, N. (2000) *New Labour, New Language?* London: Routledge.

Faulkner, D. (2001) *Crime, State and Citizen: A Field Full of Folk,* Winchester: Waterside Press.

Feigenbaum, H., Henig, J. and Hamnett, C. (1999) *Shrinking the State: The Political Underpinnings of Privatization.* Cambridge: Cambridge University Press.

Finn, (1997) *Sex Offender Community Notification.* Washington DC: National Institute of Justice.

Garland, D. (1990) *Punishment and Modern Society.* Oxford: Oxford University Press.

Garland, D. (2000) 'The culture of high crime societies: some preconditions of recent "Law and order" policies', *British Journal of Criminology,* 40: 347–75.

Garland, D. (2001) *The Culture of Control: Crime and Social Order in Contemporary Society.* Oxford: Oxford University Press.

Greene, J. (1999) 'Zero-Tolerance: a case study of police policies and practices in New York City', *Crime and Delinquency,* 45(2): 171–87.

Harcourt, B. (2001) *Illusion of Order.* Cambridge, MA: Harvard University Press.

Harding, R.W. (1997) *Private Prisons and Public Accountability.* New Brunswick, NJ: Transaction Books.

Hewitt, P. and Gould, P. (1993) 'Lessons from America: learning from success – Labour and Clinton's New Democrats', *Renewal,* 1(1): 45–51.

Hill, M. (1997) *The Policy Process in the Modern State* (3rd edn). London: Prentice Hall/HarvesterWheatsheaf.

Home Affairs Committee (1987) *Contract Provision of Prisons.* London: HMSO.

Hudson, B. (1996) *Understanding Justice: An Introduction to Ideas, Perspectives and Controversies in Modern Penal Theory*. Buckingham: Open University Press.

Innes, M. (1999) ' "An iron fist in an iron glove?" The zero tolerance policing debate', *Howard Journal*, 38(4): 397–410.

James, A.L., Bottomley, A.K., Liebling, A. and Clare, E. (1997) *Privatizing Prisons: Rhetoric and Reality*. London: Sage.

Jenkins, P. (1987) *Mrs Thatcher's Revolution: The Ending of the Socialist Era*. London: Pan Books.

Jones, T. and Newburn, T. (2002a) 'Learning from Uncle Sam? Understanding US influences over UK crime control policy', *Governance* (in press).

Jones, T. and Newburn, T. (2002b) 'The transformation of policing? Understanding current trends in policing systems', *British Journal of Criminology* (in press).

Jones, T., Newburn, T. and Smith, D.J. (1994) *Democracy and Policing*. London: Policy Studies Institute.

Karmen, A. (2000) *New York Murder Mystery: The True Story behind the Crime Crash of the 1990s*. New York, NY: New York University Press.

Kemshall, H. (2001) *Risk Assessment and the Management of Known Sexual and Violent Offenders: A Review of Current Issues. Briefing Note, Police Research Series Paper* 140. London: Home Office.

King, D. and Wickham-Jones, M. (1999) 'From Clinton to Blair: the Democratic (Party) origins of welfare to work', *The Political Quarterly*, 70(1): 62–74.

Kingdon, J. (1995) *Agendas, Alternatives and Public Policies* (2nd edn). New York, NY: HarperCollins.

Leigh, A., Read, T. and Tilley, N. (1998) *Brit Pop II: Problem-oriented Policing in Practice. Police Research Series Paper 93*. London: Policing and Reducing Crime Unit, Home Office.

Lilly, J.R. and Knepper, P. (1992) 'An international perspective on the privatization of corrections', *Howard Journal*, 31(3): 174–91.

Maguire, M., Kemshall, H., Noaks, L. and Wincup, E. (2001) *Risk Management of Sexual and Violent Offenders: The Work of Public Protection Panels. Police Research Series Paper* 139. London: Home Office.

Mattera, P. and Khan, M. (2001) *Jail Breaks: Economic Development Subsidies Given to Private Prisons*. Washington, DC: Good Jobs First.

McLaughlin, E. and Muncie, J., (2001) *The Sage Dictionary of Criminology*. London: Sage.

Nellis, M. (2000) 'Law and order: the electronic monitoring of offenders', in D. Dolowitz (ed.) *Policy Transfer and British Social Policy*. Buckingham: Open University Press.

Nelson, B. (1996) 'Public Policy and Administration: An Overview', in R. Goodin and H.D. Kingeman (eds) *A New Handbook of Political Science*. Oxford: Oxford University Press.

Newburn, T. (1998) 'Tackling Youth Crime, Reforming Youth Justice: The Origins and Nature of New Labour Policy', *Policy Studies*, 19(3–4): 199–212.

Newburn, T. (2002) Atlantic Crossings: Policy Transfer and Crime Control in America and Britain, *Punishment and Society*, 4(2): 165–94.

Orr, J. (1998) 'Strathclyde's Spotlight initiative', in N. Dennis (ed.) *Zero Tolerance: Policing a Free Society* (2nd edn). London: Institute for Economic Affairs.

Pells, R. (1997) *Not Like Us: How Europeans have Loved, Hated and Transformed American Culture since World War II*. New York, NY: Basic Books.

Pollard, C. (1998) 'Zero tolerance: short-term fix, long-term liability?', in N. Dennis (ed.) *Zero Tolerance: Policing a Free Society* (2nd edn). London: Institute for Economic Affairs.

Ritzer, G. (1993) *The McDonaldization of Society: An Investigation into the Changing Character of Contemporary Social Life*. Newbury Park, CA: Pine Forge Press.

Robertson, R. (1992) *Globalization: Social Theory and Global Culture*. London: Sage.

Rock, P. (1990) *Helping Victims of Crime: The Home Office and the Rise of Victim Support in England and Wales*. Oxford: Clarendon Press.

Rollins, R. (ed.) (1989) *The Americanization of the Global Village: Essays in Popular Culture*. Bowling Green, KY: Bowling Green University Press.

Rutherford, A. (1990) 'British penal policy and the idea of prison privatization', in D.C. McDonald (ed.) *Private Prisons and the Public Interest*. New Brunswick, NJ: Rutgers University Press.

Rutherford, A. (2000) 'An elephant on the doorstep: criminal policy without crime in New Labour's Britain', in P. Green and A. Rutherford (eds) *Criminal Policy in Transition*. Oxford: Hart Publishing.

Ryan, M. (1996) 'Private prisons: contexts, performance and issues', *European Journal on Criminal Policy and Research*, 4(3): 92–107.

Ryan, M. and Ward, T. (1989) *Privatization and the Penal System: The American Experience and the Debate in Britain*. Milton Keynes: Open University Press.

Sentencing Project (2002). *Prison Privatization and the Use of Incarceration: Briefing Sheet* 1.02, Washington DC: The Sentencing Project.

Taylor, R.B. (2001) *Breaking away from Broken Windows*. Boulder, CO: Westview Press.

Tomlinson, J. (1991) *Cultural Imperialism*. Baltimore, MD: Johns Hopkins University Press.

Tonry, M. (1999) 'Parochialism in US sentencing policy', *Crime and Delinquency*, 45(1): 48–65.

Tonry, M. (2001) 'Symbol, substance and severity in western penal policies', *Punishment and Society*, 3(4): 517–36.

Wacquant, L. (1999) 'How penal common sense comes to Europeans: notes on the transatlantic diffusion of the neoliberal doxa', *European Societies*, 1(3): 319–52.

Walker, R. (1999) 'The Americanization of British welfare: a case study of policy transfer', *International Journal of Health Services*, 29(4): 679–97.

Weiss, R. (1989) 'Private prisons and the state', in R. Matthews (ed.) *Privatizing Criminal Justice*. London: Sage.

Wilson, J.Q. and Kelling, G. (1982) 'Broken windows', *Atlantic Monthly*, March: 29–38.

Windelsham, Lord (1993) *Responses to Crime. Vol. 2*. Oxford: Oxford University Press.

Windelsham, Lord (1998) *Politics, Punishment and Populism*. New York, NY: Oxford University Press.

Wolman, H. (1992) 'Understanding cross-national policy transfers: the case of Britain and the United States', *Governance*, 5(1): 27–45.

Young, P. (1987) *The Prison Cell: The Start of a Better Approach to Prison Management*, London: Adam Smith Institute.

Chapter 8

Youth justice: globalisation and multi-modal governance

John Muncie

Conventional comparative criminology has long been beset with problems of partiality, Anglo-Americanism and a reliance on descriptive analyses of similarity and difference. Nevertheless interest in this area is beginning to burgeon, in part driven by the pragmatic and managerial appeal of discovering 'what works' in criminal justice. Yet all too often issues of national, regional and local culture are obscured. Questions of ideology and discourse are ignored. The twin concepts of globalisation and governance suggest some new points of departure. But while they have gradually permeated criminology, their presence has been stronger when applied to transnational organised crime and policing rather than in addressing processes of criminal justice reform. So how might they be employed in understanding contemporary transformations in systems of youth justice? Until the 1970s youth justice was dominated by an entrenched series of debates circulating around the often nebulous opposition of welfare and punishment. Since then sustained assaults on the social logics of the welfare state and public provision, particularly in Britain, the USA, Canada and Australasia, have brought profound shifts in economic, social and political relations associated with the 'free market'. In their wake has emerged a renewed emphasis on individual, family and community responsibility in matters of crime control. The concept of *globalisation* draws attention to the impact that these transformations have had on processes of policy convergence. The independence of the modern nation-state has been called into question. Are a global economy and universal criminal justice policies and practice undermining the autonomy of the state? Similarly, are we witnessing a shift from government to multiple sites and levels of *governance* of crime and disorder characterised by international and interorganisational *networks* of public, private, commercial, voluntary and community agencies?

Both concepts escape easy definition and are often used in a loose and eclectic fashion. While 'globalisation' usually directs our attention to macro-structural determinants of policy-making, 'governance' is concerned with how the macro is also micro managed, contested and resisted. Importantly governance means something more than a reference to 'government'. It draws attention to the multiple means through which populations are regulated, accept being governed and begin to govern themselves. It implies that power is not simply exercised through global or state dominance but through myriad institutions, procedures, reflections and calculations in which citizens are 'made up' and come to realise themselves. In its original formulation (Foucault 1991) governance refers to *any* act, means or tactic concerned with the regulation of conduct though it is usually employed in a more narrow fashion to raise questions of the individual/state interface. Globalisation, on the other hand, implies (in its 'strong' version) that there are uncontrollable economic forces which have come to shift power and authority away from communities and nations and towards 'external' transnational capital. Both concepts pose some thorny questions for the study of systems of youth justice. Policy-making in this area has traditionally been studied with regard to national sovereignty and the independence of the nation-state. Indeed criminal justice remains a powerful icon of sovereign statehood. The concept of globalisation can also be both illuminating and confusing. It is contested both empirically and conceptually. It seems to come with a wide diversity of definition and use (Clarke 2000; Yeates 2001). It sits alongside a number of competing terms, such as the following:

- Transnationalisation (the dissolving of national boundaries).
- Supranationalisation (the transcending of national limits).
- Internationalisation (exchanges of capital and labour).
- Universalisation (spread of information and cultural phenomena worldwide).
- Neoliberalisation (removal of regulatory barriers to international exchange/transfer).
- Westernisation (homogenisation, driven by advanced industrial economies).
- Anglo-Americanisation (homogenisation, driven by USA/UK alliance).
- Modernisation (the diffusion of managerial economics).

153

It is often unclear whether these are synonyms, whether globalisation is an umbrella term or whether it conjures up something quite distinctive. It is also unclear whether any of these concepts are indeed worldwide in applicability or whether they all simply direct our attention to transformations in neoliberal Anglophone – English speaking – countries. In other words the concept of globalisation may itself be peculiarly ethnocentric.

This chapter begins by assessing how far shifts in political economy, particularly that of capital mobility, across advanced industrialised countries can be assumed to have eroded the foundations of re-distributive welfare states and severely constrained the range of political strategies and policy options that individual states can pursue (Beck 2000). It examines the thesis that neoliberal conceptions of unregulated markets and international competitiveness have shifted power away from nation-states and narrowed their choice of strategic criminal justice and social policy options. The twin concepts of globalisation and governance suggest two inter-related transformations. First, that criminal justice policies are converging (at least across the 'global north'). A combination of macro-socioeconomic developments, in-itiatives in international law and accelerations in processes of policy transfer and diffusion can be viewed as symptomatic of a rapid con-vergence and homogenisation of criminal justice policies. The necessity of attracting international capital compels governments to adopt similar economic, social and criminal justice policies in part aided by geo-political mobility and subsequent policy transfer, diffusion and learning. Secondly, this homogenisation, it is contended, is underpinned by a fundamental shift in state/market relations. A loss or reconfiguration of the social is also evidenced in the processes whereby the market and international capital encourage the formulation of policies based less on principles of social inclusion and more on social inequality, de-regulation, privatisation, penal expansionism and welfare residualism. In effect, this thesis presages the decline of social democratic reformist politics and projects worldwide (Mishra 1999).

This chapter assesses the pertinence of such thematics to under-standing global, international, national and local shifts in contemporary youth justice policy and practice. It explores how youth justice, particularly in England and Wales, is embroiled in the collective impact of these multi-tiered modes of governance. It also reveals how the processes of convergence and transfer may not be as singular and one-dimensional as might be first assumed.

From welfare to neoliberal governance?

It has been widely claimed that since the 1960s penal welfarism has been undermined by the development of forms of neoliberal or 'advanced' governance (Bell 1993; Garland 1996; Rose 1996a, 1996b, 2000). This fundamental change in criminal and youth justice has been broadly characterised as placing less emphasis on the social contexts of crime and measures of state protection and more on prescriptions of individual/family/community responsibility. The shift has been captured in the notion of 'governing at a distance'. Welfarism has been increasingly critiqued for encouraging state dependence, overloading the responsibilities of the state and undermining the ability of individuals to take responsibility for their own actions. 'Old' notions of *social* engineering, *social* benefits, *social* work and *social* welfare, it is claimed, have been transformed to create responsible and autonomous (i.e. not welfare dependent) citizens (O'Malley 2000). A loss (or 'death') of the social thesis suggests a number of inter-related – sometimes contradictory – criminal justice processes:

- Changing governance to reflect market-like conditions and processes.
- Privatising the state sector and commodifying crime control.
- Widening material inequalities between and within states, thus creating new insecurities and fuelling demands for further centralised authoritarian law and order strategies.
- Devolving responsibility for government to individuals, families and communities: as captured in the notion of the 'the active citizen'.
- Exposing professional practice to fiscal accounting, audit, evaluation research and the ethos of 'what works'.
- Espousing scientific realism and pragmatic responses to crime and disorder in the hope that an image of an 'orderly environment' can be secured which in turn will help to attract 'nomadic capital'.

Numerous authors (for example, Wacquant 1999) then contend that these processes have had a growing impact on the homogenisation of criminal justice across western societies, driven in particular by the spread of neoliberal punitive penal policies from the USA (for the USA, see Krisberg and Austin 1993; for Canada, see Smandych 2001; for England and Wales, see Goldson 2000a; for Australia, see Cunneen and White 1995). In youth justice these shifts are generally recognised in a diminution of a welfare-based mode of governance in favour of various 'justice' based responsibilisation and managerial strategies (Muncie and

Hughes 2002). Six recurring and inter-related themes can be identified.

Diminution of welfare

By the late 1970s, liberal lawyers, civil libertarians and radical social workers were becoming increasingly critical of 'welfare based' procedures and sentencing. They argued that meeting the 'needs' of offenders acted as a spurious justification for placing excessive restrictions on individual liberty, particularly for young women, which were out of proportion either to the seriousness of the offence or to the realities of being in 'need of care and protection'. Social work interventions were considered not only to preserve explanations of individual pathology but also to undermine the right to natural justice. Young people were considered in double jeopardy, sentenced for their background as well as for their offence. In the wake of these criticisms a new justice-based model of corrections emerged. Its leading proponent, von Hirsch (1976), proposed that proportionality of punishment to fit the crime, determinacy of sentencing, equity and protection of rights through due process and an end to judicial, professional and administrative discretion be reinstated at the centre of youth and criminal justice practice. The idea of punishing the crime, not the person, had clear attractions for those seeking an end to the abuses of discretional power. Indeed, the impact of this 'back to justice' was reflected in youth justice reform in many western jurisdictions at the time. A focus on 'deeds' rather than 'needs' formally expunged many of the last vestiges of welfarism from the system.

Adulteration

This liberal critique of welfare coalesced with the concerns of traditional retributivists that rehabilitation was a 'soft option'. For them tougher sentencing would also enable criminals to get their 'just deserts'. Within the political climate of the 1980s notions of 'just deserts' and 'anti-welfarism' were politically mobilised by the right. The language of 'justice and rights' was appropriated as one of 'individual responsibility and obligation'. Accordingly Hudson (1987) has argued that the 'just deserts' or 'back to justice' movements that emerged in many western jurisdictions in the 1980s were evidence of a 'modern retributivism' rather than necessarily heralding the emergence of new liberal regimes and a positive rights agenda. As a result, by the 1990s particularly in the USA and England and Wales, 10–13-year-olds came to face almost the same sentencing powers as were previously restricted to those aged 14 or over. This 'adulteration' of youth justice has witnessed widespread dismantling of special court procedures which had been in place for much of the twentieth century to protect young people from the stigma and formality of adult justice (Fionda 1998). Since the 1980s (but beginning in Florida in 1978) most USA states have expanded the charges for which juvenile defendants can be tried as adults in criminal courts, lowered the age at which this can be done, changed the purpose of their juvenile codes to prioritise punishment and resorted to more punitive training and boot camps. In some states there is now no age limit at all to adult criminal prosecution and trial. Accordingly the numbers of under 18-year-olds committed to adult prisons in the USA has more than doubled since 1985, with nearly 60 per cent being of African-American origin (CNN News: 28 February 2000). The USA, along with Iran, remains the only state to retain the power to impose the death penalty on under-18s. In the UK the principle of *doli incapax* – which for many centuries had protected 10–14-year-olds from the full rigours of adult justice – was abolished in 1998 (Bandalli 2000). In Canada the Youth Criminal Justice Act 2001 prioritised punishment and accountability as youth justice's major rationales (Smandych 2001).

Risk factor prevention

In place of traditional attempts to isolate specific causes of crime has emerged a risk factor prevention paradigm which focuses attention on the *potential* for harm, disorder and misbehaviour (rather than crime itself). These risk factors include hyperactivity, large families, poor parental supervision, low achievement and family disharmony (Farrington 1996). It has been argued that these risks have a strong transatlantic replicability (Farrington 2000). Risk has been increasingly presented as a factual reality rather than as a complex construction mediated through interpretative judgements of what is considered to be the norms of acceptable behaviour. Boundaries between the deviant and non-deviant, between the public and the private have become blurred. Early intervention strategies designed to 'nip offending in the bud' have produced new criminal subjects and deviant 'others', precisely those marginalised and socially excluded who are the first victims of a global economy. The globalising appeal of zero-tolerance and community safety strategies ensure that crime and disorder increasingly come to dominate concerns about quality of life, urban renewal and social policy in general (Stenson 2000). Social problems are defined in terms of their criminogenic potential, and criminal justice systems are taking over some of the roles that were previously undertaken by welfare and child protection agencies (Crawford 2002).

Responsibilisation

Garland (1996) refers to a responsibilisation strategy involving 'central government seeking to act upon crime not in a direct fashion through state agencies (police, courts, prisons, social work, etc.) but instead by acting indirectly, seeking to activate action on the part of non-state agencies and organizations'. The message is that all of us – from property owners to manufacturers to school authorities, families and individuals – have a responsibility to reduce criminal opportunities and increase informal controls. Rose and Miller (1992) reasoned that this was not a simple case of state abrogation or of privatisation of public issues, but of a new mode of 'governing at a distance'. The state may issue directives, but responsibility for their enactment is passed down to local bodies and ultimately individuals themselves. In the field of youth justice this has developed into a notable devolution of youth justice policy (via localised youth offending teams) but also, in some contradiction of a 'governing at a distance' thesis, a significant strengthening of centralisation (via a national youth justice board). In tandem numerous aspects of social policy – whether regarding parenting, health, employment, housing – have become captured within a youth justice discourse. 'Joined up' partnership and multi-agency collaboration approaches draw all manner of 'early interventions' from preschool education to parenting classes into a crime discourse.

Actuarial justice

Youth justice has become progressively more disengaged from philosophies of welfare and/or justice in favour of improving internal system coherence through standardised risk assessment procedures, technologies of actuarial justice and the implementation of managerial performance targets. Rehabilitation or due process have been replaced by the rather less transformative rationales of processing complaints and applying punishments in an efficient and cost-effective manner. Indicators that measure 'outputs' rather than 'outcomes' have begun to take on a life of their own. They are not simply vehicles for policy implementation but have become an end in themselves (Feeley and Simon 1992; Garland 1996; Kempf-Leonard and Peterson 2000; McLaughlin *et al.* 2001).

Penal expansionism

An increasingly internationalised alliance of private industrial and penal interests has emerged that has a vested interest in penal expansion (Christie 2000). This is most notable in prison-building programmes and in the technological apparatus of crime control, such as CCTV and electronic monitoring. Juvenile codes have been reformulated to prioritise punishment. Certain groups are identified as a threatening and permanently excluded underclass about which little can be done but to neutralise and segregate them in 'Gulags of incapacitation'. In both England and Wales and the USA this has facilitated the expansion of secure units and punitive disciplinary penal regimes. Vengeance and cruelty are no longer an anathema to criminal justice (Simon 2001). Such developments are evidence of a 'reactionary thematisation of late modernity' through which politics and culture have become saturated with images of moral breakdown, incivility and the decline of the family (Garland 2001).

Collectively these processes suggest an acceleration of the governance of young people through crime and disorder (Simon 1997). The continual reworking and expansion of youth justice systems; a never-ending stream of legislation apparently dominating all other government concerns; the political use of youth crime as a means to secure electoral gain; the excessive media fascination – both as news and entertainment with all things 'criminal'; and the obsession with regulation whether through families, schools or training programmes all attest to the disorder attributed to young people as a central motif of governance. Neoliberal conceptions of family autonomy do not extend to children. They continue to be governed differently and are subject to compelling structures of dominance (Bell 1993). Such readings of contemporary youth justice give weight to the primacy of ascribing the multivariate modes of youth governance to neoliberal rationalities and technologies. These broad trends, recognisable in many western youth justice systems, lie at the heart of a neoliberal version of the globalisation thesis.

Policy transfers

Policy transfer can be considered as one of the most tangible effects of such processes. Numerous authors have remarked upon a growing similarity in criminal justice across western societies, driven in particular by neoliberalism and the spread of penal policies, particularly from the USA (Wacquant 1999; Christie 2000; Garland 2001; Jones and Newburn

2002). It has become more and more common for nation-states to look worldwide in efforts to discover 'what works' in preventing crime and to reduce reoffending. The talk then is of an emerging global youth justice. Much of this analysis relies on tracing the export of penal policies from the USA to other advanced industrial economies, such as England. Wacquant (1999), for example, identifies how numerous American state agencies, think-tanks, foundations, policy advisers, commercial enterprises and academics have worked in concert with their British counterparts (such as the Adam Smith Institute and the Institute of Economic Affairs) to forge a law and order policy consensus. From America, England has indeed imported aspects of zero-tolerance policing, curfews, electronic monitoring, naming and shaming, instant justice and punitive incarceration. Such USA/England convergence has come to dominate the literature on policy transfer. And on one level it certainly has pertinence. In the early days of opposition Labour persistently challenged and condemned the Conservatives' overt trans-atlantic policy transfers in both social and criminal justice matters. The left of centre preferred to look to Europe. However after Blair's visit to the USA in 1993, which presaged the new doctrine of 'being tough on crime and tough on the causes of crime', New Labour also shifted its focus from Europe to the New Democratic policies of the USA. Since the mid-1990s, not only compulsory and conditional welfare to work (workfare) but also *versions* of zero-tolerance policing, high-intensity disciplinary penal regimes, night curfews, electronic tagging, mandatory minimum sentences, the naming and shaming of young offenders and strict controls over parents are all assumed to have been transported wholesale to England. A tough stance on crime and welfare has become the taken-for-granted mantra to achieve electoral success. But as Sparks (2001) has put it, there may be inherent difficulties to this type of comparative analysis because of the 'distracting sway of the American case as a pole of attraction'.

Indeed it is also clear that youth justice in England and more widely across Europe has also been informed by contra penal trajectories such as those derived from the import of restorative justice conferencing pioneered in New Zealand and Australia. Scotland's 30-year-old experience of children's hearings has also been borrowed by England to inform its referral orders and youth offender panels (which went national in April 2002). The Northern Ireland criminal justice review (O'Mahony and Deazley 2000) advocates youth conferencing to be at the heart of its new approach to juvenile justice. In return, so the Youth Justice Board (2002) informs us, New Zealand has begun experimenting with the idea of English youth offending team partnerships. The transfer of policy is clearly not as one-dimensional or as one directional as authors, such as Wacquant (1999), might suggest.

Critics of US-inspired neoliberal globalisation would then point out countervailing tendencies at work in numerous youth justice systems across the world. Within restorative justice the talk is less of formal crime control and more of informal offender/victim participation and harm minimisation. These initiatives in part draw upon notions of informal customary practices in Maori, Aboriginal and Native American indigenous populations. They have come to find practical expression in various forms of conferencing in Australasia, in healing circles in Canada and in the processes that underpin the work of the Truth and Reconciliation Commission in South Africa. Both the United Nations and the Council of Europe have given restorative justice their firm backing. Indeed, various commentators detected an opening up of youth justice throughout most of Europe in the 1990s whereby custodial sanctions were on the decrease. Community safety, reparation, community work, courses in social training and so on together with compliance with United Nations rules and Council of Europe recommendations have all been advocated as means to achieve participative justice and to reduce the recourse to youth imprisonment. Most European countries also have a designated Children's Rights Commissioner with overall responsibility for young people and the formulation of specific 'protective' youth policies. Wales, Scotland and Northern Ireland have recently made similar appointments, but it has taken England until mid 2003 to even begin to give the issue serious consideration.

Restorative justice processes in New Zealand and in most Australian states are now established in statute as the fundamental rationale for youth justice. Their aim is to keep young people out of formal court processes by way of various types of family group conferences. Most academic research – driven in particular by policy entrepreneurs – speaks highly of such an approach in impacting on reoffending and on ensuring that both victim and offender are the *key* participants and decision-makers in determining any future action (Miers 2001; Morris and Maxwell 2001; Gelsthorpe and Morris 2002). In Australasia professional decision-making and formal court processing appear marginal to an extent not contemplated in most other western systems (with the notable exception of Scotland). Much of this, again, is probably due to an *alliance* between neoliberalism and a social democratic politics and thus a political willingness to hang on to vestiges of social welfarism (see O'Malley, Chapter 3). But we should be wary that this is some general panacea. Australian research, for example, has suggested that for indigenous populations it may lead to a double failure: failing to be law abiding and failing to act appropriately according to an indigenous justice script rewritten by whites (Blagg 1997). In general the danger remains that any form of compulsory restoration may degenerate into a ceremony of public shaming and degradation, particularly when it operates within a system of justice that is driven by punitive, exclusionary and coercive values and whose primary intent is the infliction of further harm (as currently seems to be the case in England and Wales). It also tends merely to reinforce notions of individual responsibility rather than those of social justice (White 2000). Nevertheless restorative justice retains the potential to offer a series of replacement discourses of 'social harm', 'conflict resolution', 'participatory justice' and 'redress' to challenge conservative neoliberal conceptions of punitive populism and an exclusionary retributive justice (De Haan 1990; Walgrave 1995; Crawford and Newburn 2002).

A basic comparison of American 'carceral hyperinflation' and a European emphasis on citizenship has frequently been made, with some nation-states, such as England, veering markedly to the former rather than the latter (see, for example, Pitts 2001). But the anti-welfare neo liberalism of the USA would seem to have little in common with other 'neoliberal' countries such as Canada, New Zealand, Australia and most of western Europe (see Chapter 3). Nevertheless it is probably no co-incidence that restorative justice and neoliberal ideologies have emerged simultaneously. Both proclaim an end to state monopoly and a revival of community responsibilisation. But certainly in England and Wales, among this growth industry of policy transfer and international exchange over the past decade, a lack of interest in Europe is notable (Muncie 2002). There are of course always exceptions to the rule. For example the English Intensive Supervision and Surveillance Programmes (introduced in 2001) were initially based on a scheme in the Netherlands, but again it is significant that there they were conceived as mechanisms for supervision and *support* rather than supervision and *surveillance.*

The notion of homogenised policy transfer has also been critiqued by those concerned not just with issues of structural convergence/ divergence but with the role of 'agency' in the formulation and implementation of specific policies (Nellis 2000; see Chapter 7). Detailed empirical examinations of policy-making in different countries reveal important differences in substance and significant differences in the processes through which policy is reformed and implemented. Jones and Newburn, for example, argue that the concept of zero tolerance associated with New York policing reforms in the early 1990s barely survived its import to the UK. The strategies adopted by the NYPD were only employed by some minor experiments in mainstream British policing. While in America zero-tolerance policing was heralded as a great success, particularly in reducing crime rates and particularly the number of firearms offences, the precise reasons for such a decline remain disputed. Many American cities (and western cities worldwide) witnessed falls in their recorded crime rates throughout the 1990s without the introduction of zero tolerance. It is now acknowledged that crime reduction in New York was also part of a longer trend in the decline of violent offences associated with the trade in crack cocaine. Nevertheless the idea of creating environments which discourage offending and incivility was enthusiastically imported into Britain in 1995 as part of Labour's new interventionist agenda. Its impact here, though, has been more on the level of political rhetoric, fuelled by a cross-party commitment to develop more punitively sounding policies that can be widely perceived as being 'tough on crime' (Innes 1999). Similarly Nellis' analysis of the transatlantic transfer of electronic monitoring from the USA to England in particular (but also to Singapore, some Australian states, Sweden and the Netherlands) makes clear that the terms ' inspiration' and 'emulation' rather than 'copying' best describe the processes involved. Nevertheless there may be problems in claiming policy transfer as a largely symbolic exercise. While policy may not travel wholesale it is always vital not to lose sight of the fact that the discursive also has material effects.

These lines of inquiry suggest that policy transfer is rarely direct and complete but is partial and mediated through national and local cultures which are themselves changing at the same time. Policy transfer can be viewed as simply a pragmatic response where nothing is ruled in and nothing ruled out. Authoritarian, restorative and actuarial justice might all be perceived as useful tactics to employ to get the crime rate down. Or they can be viewed as symptomatic of a system that has lost its way and no longer adheres to any fundamental values and principles, whether they are rooted in welfare, punishment, protection or rights. The logic of assuming we can learn 'what works' from others is certainly seductive. It implies rational planning and an uncontroversial reliance on a 'crime science' which is free of any political interference. But it also assumes that policies can be transported and are transportable without cognisance of localised cultures, conditions and the politics of space. Indeed some transfers in the English context seem only to have symbolic value in a world of gesture politics. No local child curfews have been put in place despite powers of some three years' standing and their subsequent extension from under-10s to 15-year-olds in 2001. Proposals for instant night courts and on-the-spot fines for unruly behaviour were declared unworkable and quietly dropped. Any legislation which clearly curbs judicial discretion, such as the three-strikes ruling for persistent burglars, has been largely ignored by the courts. In other areas such as the building of secure training centres the logic of 'what works' seems to be lost in a pandering to a highly politicised, in part media-driven, demand for expressive law and order. In other words in England and Wales youth justice has become a particularly complex melange of competing and contradictory policies which simultaneously exhibit a strong exclusionary punitive rationale alongside a momentum to implement forms of inclusionary and participative justice (Muncie 2002).

Policy transfer and international dialogue will probably become a more dominant aspect of youth justice if only because of the possibilities opened up by the growth in international telecommunications, the development of policy entrepreneurs (such as the Youth Justice Board in England and Wales) and the acceleration of intergovernmental policy networks. But at nation-state, regional and local levels things may look a bit different. Individual states continue jealously to guard their own sovereignty and control over crime control and punishment as do some regional state governments. Local implementation of key reforms may also reveal a continuing adherence to some traditional values and a resistance to change.

International conventions

The 1989 United Nations Convention on the Rights of the Child has established a near-global consensus that all children have a right to *protection*, to *participation* and to basic material *provision*. The only countries not to have ratified are Somalia and the USA. The convention builds upon the 1985 UN Standard Minimum Rules for the Administration of Youth Justice (the Beijing Rules) which recognised the 'special needs of children' and the importance of dealing with offenders flexibly. It promoted diversion from formal court procedures, non-custodial disposals and insisted that custody should be a last resort and for minimum periods. In addition the rules emphasised the need for anonymity in order to protect children from lifelong stigma and labelling. The convention cemented these themes in the fundamental right that in all legal actions concerning those under the age of 18, the 'best interests of the child shall be a primary consideration' (Article 3.1). Further it reasserts the need to treat children differently, to promote their dignity and worth with minimum use of custody and that children should participate in any proceedings relating to them (Article 12). In 1990 the UN Guidelines for the Prevention of Juvenile Delinquency (the Riyadh Guidelines) added that youth justice policy should avoid criminalising children for their minor misdemeanours. The European Convention on Human Rights (first formulated in 1953) provides for the due process of law, fairness in trial proceedings, a right to education, a right to privacy and declares that any deprivation of liberty (including curfews, electronic monitoring and community supervision) should not be arbitrary or consist of any degrading treatment. It was incorporated into British law following the Human Rights Act 1998 and implemented in 2000. Collectively these conventions and rules can be viewed as tantamount to a growing legal globalisation of youth justice. They have certainly been heralded as marking the importance of incorporating a rights consciousness in any contemporary youth justice reform (Bala *et al*. 2002).

Yet, as Freeman (2002) notes, the implementation of these directives has often been half-hearted and piecemeal. Several countries have filed reservations to particular elements of the UN convention and claimed that they are not bound to all its provisions. The English case is typical. For example, in the gamut of New Labour youth justice reforms from 1998 onwards no directive has ever been given to the courts or youth offending teams that child welfare should be of 'primary consideration'. The UN has consistently, and most recently in 2002, advised the UK to raise its age of criminal responsibility but New Labour has stubbornly refused to do so. Indeed somewhat perversely it has instead moved in the opposite direction by abolishing the principle of *doli incapax*. The UN convention stipulates that children should be protected from custody whenever possible and when deprived of liberty should be treated with humanity. In England three new privately managed secure training centres for 12–14-year-olds have been built since 1998. It is only financial constraints that hinder their expansion. Young offender institutions have long been condemned as 'corrosive', leading to high rates of self-harm and suicide and subjecting young people to 'inhuman and degrading treatment' (*Guardian*: 30 November 2002). The UN's 2002 observations on the UK's implementation of the convention also expressed concern at the increasing numbers of children in custody, at earlier ages for lesser offences and for longer periods, together with custodial conditions that do not adequately protect children from violence, bullying and self-harm (www.amnestyusa.org/news/2002/uk). Article 6 of the Human Rights Act provides for the right to a fair trial with legal representation and a right to appeal. The introduction nationwide of referral orders with lay youth offender panels deliberating on 'programmes of behaviour' with no legal representation might appear to be in denial of such rights. Article 8 confers the right to respect for private and family life and protects families from arbitrary interference. Parenting orders, child curfews and anti-social behaviour orders, in particular, would again appear to be in contempt (Freeman 2002). More seriously, many of the principles of restorative justice which rely on informality, flexibility and discretion sit uneasily against legal requirements for due process and a fair and just trial. Rights may be given to the victim or the community to receive reparation, but juridical rights guaranteeing constraint against the child offender may be removed. This is compounded by preventive early interventions directed at those thought to be 'at risk'. Prevention has no boundaries and makes the system insatiable. But in response to the UN Committee on the Rights of the Child in 1999, Labour has claimed that early intervention is an 'entitlement' and that such pre-emptive policies contribute to 'the *right* of children to develop responsibility for themselves'. In these ways a discourse of rights is appropriated to justify degrees of authoritarianism that are clearly far removed from UN intentions. There are other grounds for considering that the rights of children and parents are being bypassed in recent English legislation. New Labour claims to be supportive of parents and protective of children but its preventive rhetoric is backed by coercive powers. Civil orders are backed up by stringent criminal sanctions. By equating 'disorder' with crime, the reach of youth justice is broadened to take in those below the age of criminal responsibility and the non-criminal as well as the known offender.

Clearly it is possible to claim an adherence to the principle of rights while simultaneously pursuing policies which exacerbate structural inequalities and punitive institutional regimes. Relying on international statements of due process and procedural safeguards can do little to deliver justice on the ground. The development of a positive rights agenda remains limited (Scraton and Haydon 2002). Moreover little attention has been given to the extent to which legal globalisation itself is a concept driven by western notions of 'civilised' human rights. Far from opening up challenges to neoliberalism, rights agendas may simply act to bolster western notions of individuality and freedom while implicitly perpetuating postcolonial notions of a barbaric and authoritarian 'global east' or 'global south'. The issue remains of how far international law can, or is even designed to, challenge the punitive excesses associated in particular with conservative neoliberal states.

National cultures and legislative sovereignty

There are relatively few rigorous comparative analyses of youth justice. In many respects this is not surprising. Doing comparative research is fraught with difficulties (Nelken 1994, 2002). The classification and recording of crime differ and different countries have developed different judicial systems for defining and dealing with young offenders. What is classified as penal custody in one country may not be in others though regimes may be similar. Not all countries collect the same data on the same age groups and populations. None seem to do so within the same time periods. Linguistic differences in how the terms 'minor', 'juvenile', child' and 'young person' are defined and operationalised further hinder any attempt to ensure a sound comparative base. However even a cursory look at some of the most basic statistical data highlights national diversity rather than global similarity and in doing so attaches another layer of caveats to a totalising neoliberal globalisation thesis.

At what age can a young person be held criminally responsible? The UK countries stand out as having some of the lowest ages of criminal responsibility in the EU. These range from 8 in Scotland and 10 in England and Wales to 15 in Denmark, Norway, Finland and Sweden and 18 in Belgium and Luxembourg (see Figure 8.1). Notable in England and Wales of course has been the abolition of *doli incapax* despite recurring complaints from the UN. In contrast Ireland raised its age of criminal responsibility from 7 to 12 in its Children Act 2001. Spain has also recently moved in the opposite direction by increasing the age of responsibility from 12 to 14 in its Juvenile Responsibility Act 2001 (Rechea 2002). Interestingly, too, most central and eastern European countries have relatively high ages of responsibility (most in accord with Russia's 16) but at least six (Estonia, Latvia, Ukraine, Moldova, Poland, Macedonia) are currently considering whether to lower this to 14 or below (Asquith 1996).

Of the statistical data that are available most are directed at recording head counts and rates of youth custody. The Council of Europe (1998), for example, has recorded that, in 1996, with the exception of Ireland and Turkey, England and Scotland have the highest percentage of their prison population under the age of 21, with Scotland at 19 per cent; England 18 per cent; France 10 per cent; Italy 4.5 per cent; and Finland 4 per cent (see Figure 8.2). There seems to be something of a correlation here: those countries with the lowest ages of responsibility also have more of their prisons filled with young people.

Data derived from the International Centre for Prison Studies (2002)

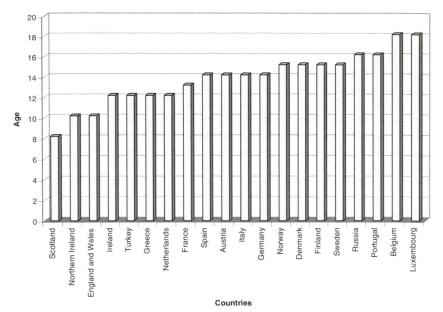

Figure 8.1   Ages of criminal responsibility in Europe

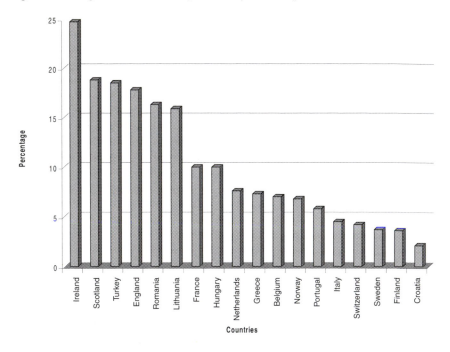

Figure 8.2   Percentage of the prison population under 21 years of age in Europe (1996 figures)

are again partial and range across some four years but also reveal the remarkable extent to which England and Wales locks up more young people than any of its European neighbours. Figures are not available for the same dates, but it is notable that in March 2002 there were over 2,500 young people in prison in England and Wales compared to some 600 in France in May. At the other extreme, in Norway, Finland and Sweden in 2000 the numbers were all below 15 (see Figure 8.3). Further breakdowns of penal populations from the UN Survey on the Operation of Criminal Justice Systems (2002) provide rates of imprisonment per 100,000 of youth population. These statistics show a rate of 38.40 per 100,000 in the USA and 18.26 per 100,000 in England and Wales compared to 0.11 in Denmark, 0.07 in Norway and 0.02 in Belgium (see Figure 8.4).

Any such basic comparative analysis cannot help but point up the atypicality and exceptional nature of the USA and England and Wales. It also underlines the UN's concern that England and Wales is increasingly locking up children for lesser offences and for longer periods of time. Not only has youth justice in England and Wales become more complex but there is no doubt that it has also become more punitive. The numbers sentenced to youth custody has almost doubled in a decade from some 5,000 in 1993 to nearing 9,000 in 2002. This has occurred despite the fact that the recorded youth crime rate has been declining, not rising over the period. Indeed international research has consistently found that there is no correlation between crime rates and custody rates (Council of Europe 2000). Locking up young people is driven by something other than crime. The use of custody appears politically, rather than pragmatically inspired: prison 'works' at a political and symbolic level even when it is a demonstrable failure.

This begs the question of why some nation-states, such as England and Wales, are so markedly different? How has the majority of Europe apparently been able to develop more imaginative and less harmful responses to youth offending? The clues to address these questions are part ideological, part cultural and part political. While it may be impossible to present a typology of European youth justice systems, five contrasting features might be developed. These are the relative import of the welfare principle, tolerance, republicanism, restoration and repenalisation. All suggest widely divergent future directions for youth justice in Europe (and elsewhere?).

The welfare principle

Belgium and Scotland stand out as examples where the primacy of the welfare principle remains the fundamental rationale for youth justice. In

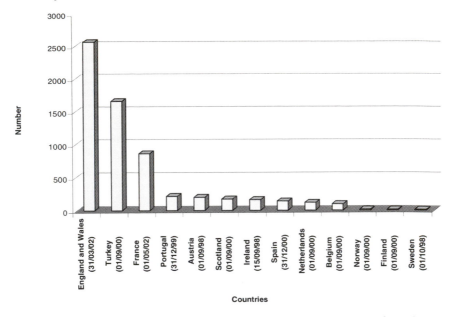

Figure 8.3   Number of young people aged under 18 in prison at selected dates (1998–2002) in Europe

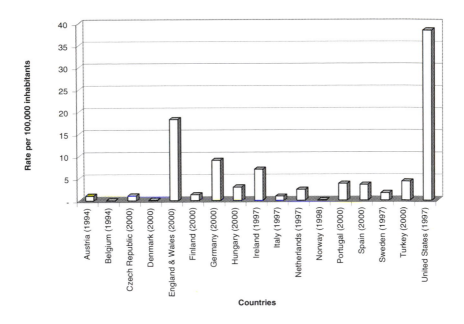

Figure 8.4   Juveniles admitted to prison: selected European countries and USA (1994/1997/1998/2000)

Belgium special youth brigades exist in most police forces, often staffed by officers holding social work diplomas. All judicial interventions are legitimated through an educative, rather than punitive, responsibilising discourse. While in practice some welfare measures are backed by punitive and coercive powers, it remains impossible to impose legal penalties on those aged under 16 (Walgrave and Mehlbye 1998). Equally, it is not always fully acknowledged that Scotland abolished the juvenile court in 1968 and has been operating with a welfare tribunal for the majority of under 16-year-old offenders for the past 30 years. It has not been without its critics, not least because of the lack of legal safeguards and the apparent tendency for the adult courts to deal with those aged 16 and over with undue severity. Scotland continues to have a high percentage of its prison population dedicated to under 21-year-olds. Nevertheless the hearing system has ensured that child welfare considerations hold a pivotal position for younger offenders and provides a credible alternative to the punitive nature of youth justice pursued in many other jurisdictions (McAra and Young 1997; Smith 2000; Whyte 2000).

Tolerance

In Holland, youth prison populations were reduced in the 1970s by limiting penal capacity, emphasising rehabilitation and supporting a culture of tolerance (Downes 1988; Komen 2002). HALT projects begun in Rotterdam in 1981 and various other social crime prevention initiatives appear to have had an impact on vandalism, truancy and shoplifting by replacing judicial intervention with reparation schemes and advice agencies to improve youth's 'survival skills'. In Finland the young offender prison population has been reduced by 90 per cent since 1960 without any associated rise in known offending. This was achieved by suspending imprisonment on the condition that a period of probation was successfully completed. Immediate 'unconditional' sentencing to custody is now a rarity (National Research Institute 1998; Kuure 2002). The Norwegian criminologist, Nils Christie, has argued that this dramatic shift has been made possible by a conscious effort on the part of successive Finnish governments to formulate a national identity closer to that of other Scandinavian states (Christie, cited in Karstedt 2001). In Trondheim, Norway, in 1994 a 5-year-old girl was murdered by two 6-year-old boys. The exceptionality of this case mirrored that of the murder of James Bulger by two 10-year-old boys a year earlier in England. In the seven subsequent years public, media and political outcry remained unabated in the UK, continually dwelling on the 'leniency' of their sentence, their 'privileged' access to specialised rehabilitation and their eventual 'premature' release under a cloak of fearful anonymity. In Norway the murder was always dealt with as a tragedy in which the local community shared a collective shame and responsibility. The boys were never named. They returned to school within two weeks of the event (Muncie 2002).

Republicanism

In France in the 1980s the Mitterand government responded to a series of violent disturbances in Lyon and Marseilles, not by implementing more authoritarian measures but by developing means of education and vocational opportunity and avenues for local political participation and incorporation. The Bonnemaison initiative involved the recruitment of older youth (*animateurs*) to act as paid youth workers with youngsters in the ghetto suburbs. These were connected with residents and local government officials to form crime prevention committees designed to address issues of citizenship and urban redevelopment as well as those of security. It is widely assumed that such strategies, based on local democratic representation rather than repression, were at least initially successful in achieving a greater integration particularly for children of North African origin (King and Petit 1985; King 1988, 1991; Pitts 1995, 1997). Since the 1980s, however, there is compelling evidence of a greater convergence of French and English crime prevention strategies made up of a patchwork of zero-tolerance policing and of situational and social methods (Crawford 2001; Roche 2002). In particular the right-wing government of Alain Juppe from 1993 to 1997 provided no new dynamic for a social crime prevention policy, instead prioritising a zero-tolerance police-led approach. It is a policy that was continued by the left-wing Jospin government. The socioeconomic conditions that produce youth marginalisation and estrangement are no longer given central political or academic attention (Bailleau 1998). Nevertheless writers such as Pitts (2001) continue to maintain that a culture of French *republicanism*, driven by notions of social *solidarity* and *integration*, ensures more of a lasting rejection of American punitiveness than seems to be possible or politically acceptable in countries such as England. In Italy, judges have an additional power to grant a 'judicial pardon' which together with policies of 'liberta controllata' (a form of police supervision) and a greater willingness to defer control to families means that young people are incarcerated only for a very few serious violent offences (Dunkel 1991; Ruxton 1996; Nelken 2002). For Melossi (2000) this is driven by an Italian cultural tradition of soft paternal authoritarianism linked to low levels of penal repression. Comparing penal policy in Italy and the USA, he is drawn in part to the relative impact of Catholic paternalism and radical Protestantism in informing each country's cultural repertoire. This 'cultural embeddedness' (see Melossi, Chapter 5) may not determine penal policy but provides the parameters in which the purpose and meaning of punishment are understood.

Restoration, reconciliation and conflict resolution

There has been a substantial growth in interest in restorative justice across Europe in the past 20 years. The Council of Europe has recommended to all jurisdictions that mediation should be generally available, that it should cover all stages of the criminal justice process and that it should be autonomous to formal means of processing. Weitekamp (2001) argues that its influence has been particularly strong in those jurisdictions with no prior provision for victim support. Austria is often cited as being at the forefront of such developments. Following the Juvenile Justice Act 1989, 50 per cent of cases suitable for prosecution were resolved by out-of-court mediation and by informal negotiations between offender, victim and mediator to achieve reconciliation (Justice 2000).

Repenalisation

Notwithstanding these developments reform in most countries of the 'global north' also seems to be progressively underpinned by versions of neoliberal politics and strategies of responsibilisation. In the past decade many European countries have reported a distinct hardening of attitudes and criminal justice responses to young offending driven in part by the growth of right-wing politics throughout Europe. For example, there has been a dramatic reversal in Dutch penal policy from the mid-1980s onwards. Once heralded as a beacon of tolerance and humanity, Holland embarked on a substantial prison-building programme linked to a tendency to expand pre-trial detention and to deliver longer sentences on conviction (Pakes 2000). The conditions governing the possibility of transferring juvenile cases to an adult court have also been relaxed. For Junger-Tas (2002) these shifts are driven by neoliberal market reform, mass immigration, changes in the labour market and a related lowering of the tolerance level for crime and violence. Fear and insecurity fuel demand for a 'norm-enforcing system' that is both retributive and interventionist. In the Netherlands restorative justice has little presence. Tham (2001) reports similar shifts in the 1990s across many European social democracies, including Italy,

Germany and the Scandinavian countries. In Denmark penalties have been explicitly increased for crimes committed by young people, while in Sweden policies of rehabilitation have been replaced by 'just deserts' and an expansion of penal legislation. While this has yet to produce any notable expansion in prison populations, Tham (2001) detects a break up of social democratic welfare humanitarianism and the emergence of a new moralism of 'zero tolerance' associated with the disciplinary techniques of the free market. Essentially a 'Weberian means-end rationality is drifting towards a policy inspired by populism and a Durkheimian problem of order' (Tham 2001: 422). Social Democratic governments are increasingly turning to law and order as a means of providing symbols of security and to enhance their own chances of electoral support. Such analysis clearly resonates with the expansion of interventionist and authoritarian policies ushered in by New Labour in England. But here they have been employed with a much greater punitive effect (Muncie 2001; Goldson 2000a; 2002). While many European countries may have added punitive elements to their legislation in the 1990s, none have moved to such a dramatic re-penalisation of young offending as that witnessed in the USA and in England and Wales. The philosophy of child protection continues to hold sway in most European countries.

These brief case studies illustrate some important national divergences and similarities but we should be mindful of the dangers that such static snapshots might provide. They do though offer various clues about why there are marked variations in youth justice policy and youth custody, even when limited to Europe. The answer seems to lie primarily with securing the political will to experiment with alternative forms of conflict resolution, coupled with a cultural sensibility that imprisoning young people is not only harmful but also self-defeating. To understand more fully the atypical American and English cases we need to look more closely at what drives their recurring punitive mentality: at the levels of public fascination with all things criminal, with media that consistently mobilise around law and order and with political parties of all persuasions that seem incapable, even in an era of 'what works', to rise above popular punitiveness.

Local sensibilities and resistances

The 'catastrophic' images raised by some neoliberal readings of governance may help us to identify significant macro-social changes, but are less attuned to resistance to change, to contradictions within neoliberalism and its often hybrid nature, to the inherent instability of neoliberal strategies and to the simultaneous emergence of other competing transformational tendencies (Muncie and Hughes 2002). Neoliberalism not only has a global impact but also, under the rubric of 'governing at a distance', has encouraged the proliferation of 'local solutions' to local problems. Fully to understand the workings and influences on youth justice we need to be attuned to the twin and contradictory processes of *delocalisation* and *relocalisation* (Crawford 2002). The risks and hazards of globalisation have simultaneously produced a 'retreat to the local' and nostalgia for tradition and community. The local governance of crime and insecurity is evidenced in the prolific discourses of 'community safety' in the UK and of 'urban security' across Europe (Hughes 2002). Both are informed by notions of community participation, proactive prevention, informalism, partnership and multi-agency collaboration. Given that they are directed not only at crime but also incivilities and the anti-social, it is not surprising that their usual target is the (mis)behaviour of young people, particularly in 'high risk' neighbourhoods. Yet what emerges from studies of the actual conduct of governance in particular localities is not uniformity, but diversity. Again, the possibility of identifying coherent and consistent patterns in (youth) governance is called into question (Hughes and Edwards 2002).

Broad governmental mentalities – whether global or national – will always be subject to revision when they are activated on the ground. Policy transfer will be piecemeal and reconfigured in local contexts. Whatever the rhetoric of government intention, the history of youth justice (e.g. in England and Wales) is also a history of active and passive resistance from pressure groups and from the magistracy, the police and from youth justice workers through which such reform is to be effected. At one level this is reflected in the wide disparities between courts in the custodial sentencing of young people. These range in England and Wales from one custodial sentence for every ten community sentences in the south west to one in five in the West Midlands and the north west. On another level it is reflected in the haphazard implementation of national legislation and youth justice standards in different localities (Holdaway *et al*. 2001). There is always a space to be exploited between written and implemented policy. The translation of policy into practice depends on how it is visioned and reworked (or made to work) by those empowered to put it into practice. As a result youth justice practice is likely to continue to be dominated by a complex of both rehabilitative 'needs' and responsibilised 'deeds' programmes. Joined-up strategic co-operation will often coexist with sceptical and acrimonious relations at a practitioner level (Liddle and Gelsthorpe 1994). The involvement of lay volunteers may facilitate the development of localised practices which are relatively immune to national managerial directives (Crawford and Newburn 2002). A social work ethic of 'supporting young people' may well subvert any partnership or national attempt simply to respon-sibilise the young offender. This is also because many of the 'new' global, neoliberal targets for intervention – inadequate parenting, low self-esteem, poor social skills, poor cognitive skills – are remarkably similar to those targets identified by a welfare mode of governance. The incongruity between such latent welfarism and the retributive nature of penal expansionism may well create some space in which the complex welfare needs of children in trouble can be re-expressed (Goldson 2000b). Equally an ill-defined rhetoric of crime prevention can enable social programmes to be re-elevated as those most likely to secure 'community safety'. Thus even in the USA – reputedly the bastion of conservative neoliberalism – we can still find numerous programmes funded by justice departments and run by welfare/police partnerships which appear more concerned with social support (e.g. providing housing, health care, employment opportunities) rather than overt crime control. Moreover such reinventions of the social can also be based on long-term and large-scale programmes which address such issues as poverty, powerlessness, discrimination and so on, which fly in the face of neoliberal, short-term, 'what works' evaluative, or neoconservative punitive, agendas. Long-range projects of 'the social' can survive or be reborn (O'Malley 2000).

Rather than an inexorable global conquest of American-inspired neoliberal rationalities and technologies, this analysis of youth justice gives weight to a succession of local encounters of complicity and resistance. It ensures that the role of 'agency' is centred in understanding processes of policy implementation.

Conclusion

Youth justice may be becoming more globalised through the impact of neoliberalism, policy transfer and international conventions, but at the same time it is becoming more spatialised through national, regional and local enclaves of difference, coalition and resistance. Individual nation-states are undoubtedly being challenged by these developments. But clearly there are discrete and distinctive ways in which neoliberalism finds expression in conservative and social democratic rationalities and in authoritarian, actuarial or restorative technologies. Globalising forces may straddle (part of) the world but also have to manifest themselves at the national and local levels, at all of which they may be subject to multiple translations or oppositions. Globalisation is always only one among many influences on policy. Above all the global/national/local are not exclusive entities: the key issue is how they are experienced in plurality in different contexts. Global neoliberal pressures are mediated through national, regional and local identities and sensibilities. A mutually transforming relationship among global and local processes prefigures plurality as a driving context for policy implementation (Yeates 2002). Governance is not only multi-tiered and multi-levelled (on a globalised vertical plane) but is also multi-sphered and multi-modal (on a governmental horizontal plane). It cannot be simply reduced to global economic transformations. Global processes are mediated by distinctive national cultures and sociocultural norms. It is impossible to identify any pure models of youth justice. In every country and in every locality youth justice is 'made up' through unstable and constantly shifting political–cultural alliances between neoliberal, conservative and social democratic mentalities. The end result is ongoing processes of multiplicity (as well as uniformity), divergence (as well as convergence) and contingency (as well as determinism). This hybridity activates multiple lines of invention, contestation and contradiction in policy-making and implementation.

Globalisation does not simply produce uniform or homogenising outcomes. It also produces social differentiation, segmentation and dislocation. While the nation-state may well be in a process of being reconstituted by international (e.g. UN conventions, European integration), national (e.g. privatisation) and local (e.g. community partnerships/networks) pressures, it nevertheless holds on to criminal justice as a powerful symbolic display of its own sovereignty. Nowhere is this more clearly seen than in the USA and its outright opposition to the authority of international courts. Questions of who is criminalised and how are they to be dealt with are political and cultural decisions. The forces of globalisation, such as neoliberal economics and inter-national human rights conventions, cannot be ignored, but neither should the processes through which these forces come to have practical effect in different localities and communities.

Essentialist conceptions of globalisation imply homogeneity and hegemonic dominance, but globalisation is but one element in a series of complex processes and political strategies that make up the multi-modal landscape of youth justice.

Acknowledgements

Thanks to my colleagues at the Open University – John Clarke, Gordon Hughes and Eugene McLaughlin – for their helpful comments on this chapter while it was in draft.

References

Asquith, S. (1996) *Juvenile Justice and Juvenile Delinquency in Central and Eastern Europe*. University of Glasgow, Centre for the Child and Society (http://eurochild.gla.ac.uk).

Bailleau, F. (1998) 'A crisis of youth or of juridical response?', in V. Ruggiero *et al.* (eds) *The New European Criminology*. London: Routledge.

Bala, N., Hornick, J., Snyder, H. and Paetsch, J. (eds) (2002) *Juvenile Justice Systems: An International Comparison of Problems and Solutions*. Toronto: Thompson.

Bandalli, S. (2000) 'Children, responsibility and the new youth justice', in B. Goldson (ed.) *The New Youth Justice*. Lyme Regis: Russell House.

Beck, U. (2000) *What is Globalisation?*. Cambridge: Polity Press.

Bell, V. (1993) 'Governing childhood: neo-liberalism and the law', *Economy and Society*, 22(3): 390–403.

Blagg, H. (1997) 'A just measure of shame? Aboriginal youth and conferencing in Australia', *British Journal of Criminology*, 37(4): 481–501.

Christie, N. (2000) *Crime Control as Industry*. London: Routledge.

Clarke, J. (2000) 'A world of difference? Globalisation and the study of social policy', in G. Lewis *et al.* (eds) *Rethinking Social Policy*. London: Sage.

Council of Europe (1998) *Penological Information Bulletin, 21.*

Council of Europe (2000) *European Sourcebook of Crime and Criminal Justice Statistics*. Council of Europe.

Crawford, A. (1997) *The Local Governance of Crime: Appeals to Community and Partnership*. Oxford: Clarendon Press.

Crawford, A. (2001) 'The growth of crime prevention in France as contrasted with the English experience', in G. Hughes *et al.* (eds) *Crime Prevention and Community Safety: New Directions*. London: Sage.

Crawford, A. (2002) 'The governance of crime and insecurity in an anxious age: the trans-European and the local', in A. Crawford (ed.) *Crime and Insecurity: The Governance of Safety in Europe*. Cullompton: Willan.

Crawford, A. and Newburn, T. (2002) 'Recent developments in restorative justice for young people in England and Wales: community participation and representation', *British Journal of Criminology*, 42(3): 476–95.

Cunneen, C. and White, R. (1995) *Juvenile Justice: An Australian Perspective*. Melbourne: Oxford University Press.

De Haan, W. (1990) *The Politics of Redress*. London: Unwin Hyman.

Dolowitz, D. (ed.) (2000) *Policy Transfer and British Social Policy: Learning from the USA?*. Buckingham: Open University Press.

Dolowitz, D. and Marsh, D. (2000) 'Learning from abroad: the role of policy transfer in contemporary policy making', *Governance*, 13(1): 5–24.

Downes, D. (1988) *Contrasts in Tolerance*. Oxford: Oxford University Press.

Dunkel, F. (1991) 'Legal differences in juvenile criminology in Europe' in T. Booth (ed.) *Juvenile Justice in the New Europe*. Social Services Monograph. Sheffield: University of Sheffield.

Farrington, D. (1996) *Understanding and Preventing Youth Crime. Social Policy Research Findings* 93. York: Joseph Rowntree Foundation.

Farrington, D. (2000) 'Explaining and preventing crime: the globalisation of knowledge', *Criminology*, 38(1): 1–24.

Feeley, M. and Simon, J. (1992) 'The new penology: notes on the emerging strategy of corrections and its implications', *Criminology*, 30: 449–74.

Fionda, J. (1998) 'The age of innocence? The concept of childhood in the punishment of young offenders', *Child and Family Law Quarterly*, 10(1): 77–87.

Foucault, M. (1991) 'Governmentality', in G. Burchell *et al.* (eds) *The Foucault Effect: Studies in Governmentality*. Hemel Hempstead: Harvester.

Freeman, M. (2002) 'Children's rights ten years after ratification', in B. Franklin (ed.) *The New Handbook of Children's Rights*. London: Routledge.

Garland, D. (1996) 'The limits of the sovereign state', *British Journal of Criminology*, 36(4): 445–71.

Garland, D. (2001) *The Culture of Control*. Oxford: Oxford University Press.

Gelsthorpe, L. and Morris, A. (2002) 'Restorative youth justice: the last vestiges of welfare?, in J. Muncie *et al.* (eds) *Youth Justice: Critical Readings*. London: Sage.

Goldson, B. (ed.) (2000a) *The New Youth Justice*. Lyme Regis: Russell House.

Goldson, B. (2000b) 'Children in need or young offenders?', *Child and Family Social Work*, 5: 255–65.

Goldson, B. (2002) 'New punitiveness: the politics of child incarceration', in J. Muncie *et al.* (eds) *Youth Justice: Critical Readings*. London: Sage.

Grisso, T. and Schwartz, R.G. (eds) (2000) *Youth on Trial*. Chicago, IL: University of Chicago Press.

Holdaway, S., Davidson, N., Dignan, J., Hammersley, R., Hine, J. and Marsh, P. (2001) *New Strategies to Address Youth Offending: The National Evaluation of the Pilot Youth Offending Teams. Research Directorate Occasional Paper* 69. London: Home Office.

Hudson, B. (1987) *Justice through Punishment*. Basingstoke: Macmillan.

Hughes, G. (2002) 'Plotting the rise of community safety', in G. Hughes and A. Edwards (eds) *Crime Control and Community*. Cullompton: Willan.

Hughes, G. and Edwards, A. (eds) (2002) *Crime Control and Community: The New Politics of Public Safety*. Cullompton: Willan.

Innes, M. (1999) 'An iron fist in an iron glove? The zero tolerance policing debate', *Howard Journal*, 38(4): 397–410.

International Centre for Prison Studies (2002) *World Prison Brief* (www.kcl.ac.uk/depsta/rel/icps/worldbrief).

Jones, T. and Newburn, T. (2002) 'Policy convergence and crime control in the USA and the UK', *Criminal Justice*, 2(2): 173–203.

Junger-Tas, J. (2002) 'The juvenile justice system: past and present trends in western society', in I. Weijers and A. Duff (eds) *Punishing Juveniles*. Oxford: Hart Publishing.

Justice (2000) *Restoring Youth Justice: New Directions in Domestic and International Law and Practice*. London: Justice.

Karstedt, S. (2001) 'Comparing cultures, comparing crime: challenges, prospects and problems for a global criminology', *Crime, Law and Social Change*, 36(3): 285–308.

Karstedt, S. and Bussman, K.-D. (eds) (2000) *Social Dynamics of Crime and Control*. Oxford: Hart Publishing.

Kempf-Leonard, K. and Peterson, E. (2000) 'Expanding realms of the new penology: the advent of actuarial justice for juveniles', *Punishment and Society*, 2(1): 66–97.

King, M. (1988) *How to Make Social Crime Prevention Work: The French Experience*. London: NACRO.

King, M. (1991) 'The political construction of crime prevention: a contrast between the French and British experiences', in K. Stenson and D. Cowell (eds) *The Politics of Crime Control*. London: Sage.

King, M. and Petit, M.-A. (1985) 'Thin stick and fat carrot – the French juvenile system', *Youth and Policy*, 15: 26–31.

Komen, M. (2002) 'Dangerous children: juvenile delinquency and judicial intervention in the Netherlands, 1960–1995', *Crime, Law and Social Change*, 37: 379–401.

Krisberg, B. and Austin, J. (1993) *Reinventing Juvenile Justice*. London: Sage.

Kuure, T. (2002) 'Low custody in Finland.' Paper delivered to the Children Law UK/NACRO Conference, 'Reducing custodial sentencing for young offenders: the European experience', London, 23 October.

Lacey, N. and Zedner L. (2000) 'Community and governance: a cultural comparison', in S. Karstedt and K.-D. Bussman (eds) *Social Dynamics of Crime and Control*. Oxford: Hart Publishing.

Liddle, M. and Gelsthorpe, L. (1994) *Crime Prevention and Inter-agency Co-operation. Crime Prevention Unit Paper* 53. London: Home Office.

McAra, L. and Young, P. (1997) 'Juvenile justice in Scotland', *Criminal Justice*, 15(3): 8–10.

McLaughlin, E., Muncie, J. and Hughes, G. (2001) 'The permanent revolution: New Labour, new public management and the modernisation of criminal justice', *Criminal Justice*, 1(3): 301–18.

Melossi, D. (2000) 'Translating social control: reflections on the comparison of Italian and North American cultures', in S. Karstedt and K.-D. Bussman (eds) *Social Dynamics of Crime and Control*. Oxford: Hart Publishing.

Mérigeau, M. (1996) 'Legal frameworks and interventions', in W. McCarney (ed.) *Juvenile Delinquents and Young People in Danger in an Open Environment*. Winchester: Waterside Press.

Miers, D. (2001) *An International Review of Restorative Justice. Crime Reduction Research Series Paper* 10. London: Home Office.

Mishra, R. (1999) *Globalisation and the Welfare State*. Cheltenham: Edward Elgar.

Morris, A. and Maxwell, G. (eds) (2001) *Restorative Justice for Juveniles*. Oxford: Hart Publishing.

Muncie, J. (1999) *Youth and Crime: A Critical Introduction*. London: Sage.

Muncie, J. (2001) 'A new deal for youth? Early intervention and correctionalism', in G. Hughes *et al.* (eds) *Crime Prevention and Community Safety: New Directions*. London: Sage.

Muncie, J. (2002) 'Policy transfers and what works: some reflections on comparative youth justice', *Youth Justice,* 1(3): 27–35.

Muncie, J. and Hughes, G. (2002) 'Modes of youth governance: political rationalities, criminalisation and resistance', in J. Muncie *et al.* (eds) *Youth Justice: Critical Readings*. London: Sage.

National Research Institute of Legal Policy (1998) *Regulating the Prison Population. Research Communications* 38. Helsinki: NRILP.

Nelken, D. (1994) 'Whom can you trust? The future of comparative criminology', in D. Nelken (ed.) *The Futures of Criminology*. London: Sage.

Nelken, D. (2002) 'Comparing criminal justice', in M. Maguire *et al.* (eds) *The Oxford Handbook of Criminology* (3rd edn). Oxford: Oxford University Press.

Nellis, M. (2000) 'Law and order: the electronic monitoring of offenders', in D. Dolowitz (ed.) *Policy Transfer and British Social Policy*. Buckingham: Open University Press.

O'Mahony, D. and Deazley, R. (2000) *Juvenile Crime and Justice: Review of the Criminal Justice System in Northern Ireland. Research Report* 17. Belfast: Northern Ireland Office.

O'Malley, P. (2000) 'Criminologies of catastrophe? Understanding criminal justice on the edge of the new millennium', *Australian and New Zealand Journal of Criminology,* 33(2): 153–67.

O'Malley, P. (2002) 'Globalising risk? Distinguishing styles of neo-liberal criminal justice in Australia and the USA', *Criminal Justice,* 2(2): 205–22.

Pakes, F. (2000) 'League champions in mid table: on the major changes in Dutch prison policy', *Howard Journal,* 39(1): 30–9.

Pitts, J. (1995) 'Public issues and private troubles: a tale of two cities', *Social Work in Europe,* 2(1): 3–11.

Pitts, J. (1997) 'Youth crime, social change and crime control in Britain and France in the 1980s and 1990s', in H. Jones (ed) *Towards a Classless Society*. London: Routledge.

Pitts, J. (2001) *The New Politics of Youth Crime: Discipline or solidarity?*. Basingstoke: Palgrave.

Rechea, C. (2002) 'Juvenile justice in Spain.' Paper delivered to the Children Law UK/NACRO conference, 'Reducing custodial sentencing for young offenders: the European experience', London, 23 October.

Roche, S. (2002) 'Toward a new governance of crime and insecurity in France', in A. Crawford (ed.) *Crime and Insecurity: The Governance of Safety in Europe.* Cullompton: Willan.

Rose, N. (1996a) 'The death of the social? Refiguring the territory of government', *Economy and Society,* 25(3): 327–46.

Rose, N. (1996b) 'Governing "advanced" liberal democracies', in A. Barry *et al.* (eds) *Foucault and Political Reason.* London: UCL Press.

Rose, N. (2000) 'Government and control', *British Journal of Criminology,* 40: 321–39.

Rose, N. and Miller, P. (1992) 'Political power beyond the state: problematics of government', *British Journal of Sociology,* 43(2): 173–205.

Ruxton, S. (1996) *Children in Europe.* London: NCH Action for Children.

Scraton, P. and Haydon, D. (2002) 'Challenging the criminalisation of children and young people: securing a rights based agenda', in J. Muncie *et al.* (eds) *Youth Justice: Critical Readings.* London: Sage.

Simon, J. (1997) 'Governing through crime', in L. Friedman and G. Fisher (eds) *The Crime Conundrum.* Boulder, CO: Westview Press.

Simon, J. (2001) 'Entitlement to cruelty: neo-liberalism and the punitive mentality in the United States', in K. Stenson and R.R. Sullivan (eds) *Crime, Risk and Justice.* Cullompton: Willan.

Smandych, R. (ed.) (1999) *Governable Places: Readings on Governmentality and crime control.* Aldershot: Ashgate.

Smandych, R. (ed.) (2001) *Youth Justice: History, Legislation and Reform.* Toronto: Harcourt.

Smith, D. (2000) 'Learning from the Scottish juvenile justice system', *Probation Journal,* 47(1): 12–17.

Sparks, R. (2001) 'Degrees of estrangement: the cultural theory of risk and comparative penology', *Theoretical Criminology,* 5(2): 159–76.

Stenson, K. (2000) 'Crime control, social policy and liberalism', in G. Lewis *et al.* (eds) *Rethinking Social Policy.* London: Sage.

Stenson, K. and Sullivan, R. (eds) (2001) *Crime, Risk and Justice.* Cullompton: Willan.

Tham, H. (2001) 'Law and order as a leftist project? The case of Sweden', *Punishment and Society,* 3(3): 409–26.

United Nations Office for Drug Control and Crime Prevention (2002) *The Seventh Survey on Crime Trends and the Operations of Criminal Justice Systems* (www.odccp.org/odccp/crime-cicp-survey-seventh.html).

Vaughan, B. (2000) 'The government of youth: disorder and dependence', *Social and Legal Studies,* 9(3): 347–66.

Von Hirsch, A. (1976) *Doing Justice.* New York: Hill & Wang.

Wacquant, L. (1999) 'How penal common sense comes to Europeans: notes on the transatlantic diffusion of the neoliberal doxa,' *European Societies,* 1(3): 319–52.

Walgrave, L. (1995) 'Restorative justice for juveniles: just a technique or a fully fledged alternative?' *Howard Journal,* 34(3): 228–49.

Walgrave, L. and Mehlbye, J. (eds) (1998) *Confronting Youth in Europe – Juvenile Crime and Juvenile Justice*. Copenhagen: Institute of Local Government Studies.

Weitekamp, E. (2001) 'Mediation in Europe: paradoxes, problems and promises' in A. Morris and G. Maxwell (eds) *Restorative Justice for Juveniles*. Oxford: Hart Publishing.

White, R. (2000) 'Social justice, community building and restorative strategies', *Contemporary Justice Review*, 3(1): 55–72.

Whyte, B. (2000) 'Youth justice in Scotland', in J. Pickford (ed.) *Youth Justice: Theory and Practice*. London: Cavendish.

Yeates, N. (2001) *Globalisation and Social Policy*. London: Sage.

Yeates, N. (2002) 'Globalisation and social policy: from global neo-liberal hegemony to global political pluralism', *Global Social Policy*, 2(1): 69–91.

Youth Justice Board (2002) *Youth Justice Board News*. September.

Chapter 9

Importing criminological ideas in a new democracy: recent South African experiences

Dirk van Zyl Smit and Elrena van der Spuy

Introduction

Criminological ideas have long been imported into South Africa. Both Afrikaner Nationalists in the 1930s and aspiring radical supporters of majority rule in the 1970s and 1980s turned to the grand criminological theories of their time. Thus the overtly racist criminological ideas that were widely available internationally in the 1930s were used to underpin the Afrikaner Nationalist school of criminology. In turn, this school both shaped the core ideology of Afrikaner Nationalism itself, and emerged thereafter as a 'practical' criminology in the heyday of apartheid in the 1950s and 1960s (Van Zyl Smit 1990, 1999).

Similarly, an affinity with the ideas of what one may loosely call critical or radical criminology flourished among a small group of intellectuals in the 1970s and 1980s. In the climate of political change in the early 1990s this criminology, supplemented by communitarian idealism and feminism, was given considerable publicity and appeared to be growing in influence. When the new democratic government came into power in 1994 it was notable that its early policy pronouncements were cast in terms of community and restorative justice. Various pilot projects to encourage community justice initiatives were quickly developed. Perhaps most dramatically of all, the Truth and Reconciliation Commission, which was set up in 1995, could be seen, in spite of all its shortcomings, as a giant initiative in restorative justice (Villa-Vincencio 1999; Parmentier 2001).

In practice, both these very different groups of criminological idealists were confronted, when they gained the ear of those in power, with the reality of the extant South African criminal justice system. Our concern here is not with the experience of the now entirely impotent, if not defunct, school of Afrikaner Nationalist criminology. But it is worth noting that, in spite of the explicit and successful strategy of the Afrikaner secret society, the *Broederbond,* in installing white Afrikaner sympathisers in key positions in the police, the judiciary and the prisons service, the criminal justice system still remained open to a wide range of other influences. These ranged from 'neutral' ideas about professionalism and techniques of crime control to much more complex ideals of equal justice in 'ordinary criminal law' that, notwithstanding massive substantive inequalities, continued to be espoused by the senior judiciary.

A single example will suffice. General Victor Verster, the man who gave the prison service its militaristic shape that was to survive into the 1990s, and who lent his name to the prison from which Nelson Mandela was released, represented South Africa at the United Nations meetings which produced the 1955 Standard Minimum Rules for the Treatment of Prisoners (Van Zyl Smit 1992). The Prisons Act 1959 was clearly drafted by someone who had the rules and the English Prison Act 1953 at his elbow. Almost as an afterthought some explicitly racist provisions were added providing not only for segregation of prisoners on racial lines but also for differences in their diet and uniform as well as in the rank structure of prison officers. The effects of these provisions were truly dire, as a generation of prison autobiographies revealed, but the importance of the underlying structure should not be underestimated. In the late 1980s, even before the course for majority rule had been set by President de Klerk's speech of 2 February 1990, the racial references in the legislation were being removed and indeed segregation among prisoners on racial grounds was abolished (with relatively few problems) before the first elections based on universal suffrage. It is worth emphasising that no major restatement of legislative purpose or fundamental revision was required to make the primary legislation look like a conventional, conservative legal framework for an 'ordinary' prison system.

In some ways the opportunities for change in the South African criminal justice system that presented themselves in the 1990s were a reprise of the 1950s. There was again an explicit policy (albeit on much more acceptable grounds) that new people should be brought into positions of power not only in political positions but also in key administrative posts in the system. Once again, a group of criminologists steeped in a particular 'outside' tradition had considerable access to the corridors of power. But once again the new people and the new ideas were up against an existing system that could not be wished away. Nor could its personnel be summarily replaced, let alone its plan that included prisons deliberately built, for ideological reasons, to house blacks in large communal cells.

Of course there were differences. The first of these was that the criminology that had the ear of the authorities was in some ways the antithesis of the Afrikaner Nationalist criminology of the 1950s. The second was that foreign funding (Van der Spuy 2000) now flowed directly to South Africans intimately involved in making criminal justice policy. The donors were overwhelmingly the major representatives of the west. With its long-standing links to South Africa, various arms of the British aid programme were among the early major donors, in the field of police training for example. Donors displayed different emphases and specialisations: USAID, for example, awarded a major multi-million grant to the reform of the justice sector soon after 1994. The UK, the EU, the Scandinavian countries, France and Belgium gave proportionately more in technical and financial assistance to the police. Along with foreign donors came international policing academics and consultants, some of whom indeed had perceived that police reform was set to become a major item on any new democratic government's agenda and had arrived on the scene in the early 1990s. The result was a melange of donor-assisted projects in both the policing and justice ministries, with little co-ordination or strategic framework (Van der Spuy et al. 1998). The outcome was the injection of a wide range of criminal justice ideas and methodologies among which it is hard to discern an underlying agenda.

While some of the foreign funding went to professional crimi-nologists both in universities and in private research agencies,[1] most of it was aimed directly at participants in the criminal justice system. In both instances the effect of the funding was to increase the capacity of South African institutions to produce criminological research findings. The new private research agencies in particular have contributed relatively sophisticated victim research and analysis of criminal statistics and added a professional dimension to criminal justice policy formulation. With much of the foreign funding came also assumptions about how a criminal justice system should operate. These were often underpinned, we would suggest, by a very different criminology from that which the new majority government adopted in its approach to criminal justice.

The criminology espoused by donor governments was rarely made explicit. Indeed, given its genesis in the day-to-day interaction of international agencies and 'experts' with the local officials of the criminal justice system, it was not a coherent set of criminological ideas.

It brought to bear, rather, the pragmatic intentions and administrative pessimism of the donor partners. These ideas found a sympathetic audience among local official constituencies, who quickly learnt the bitter lesson that the ideals that they held prior to the assumption of power were not immune to the pressures of office.

This emergent bureaucratic criminology developed a primary concern with ensuring that the remodelled state apparatus focused on catching and punishing criminals efficiently – with ensuring that individuals did not commit with impunity the types of crime that were of particular concern to the donors. Ultimately it has been this emergent criminology of practitioners that has had more impact than the ideal of a more egalitarian and communitarian, and therefore less crime-ridden, society that underpinned the radical criminology of the early 1990s. The extent of the dominance of this bureaucratic criminology, however, remains an open question.

One caveat before we enter into an account that may support our claim. Resources both ideological and material in South Africa, as elsewhere, were, and are, distributed unevenly across the criminal justice system. The impact of new ideas may therefore have been expected to vary considerably in the different agencies. Some initiatives, such as those to introduce asset forfeiture and reform juvenile justice, cut across the areas of responsibility of various agencies. In what follows we have to be selective: a full history of the impact of ideas in South Africa would require a much more comprehensive account of the underlying state of crime and criminal justice than is possible here. Instead we present a number of illustrative examples.

Police and policing

Reform of the apartheid police had been high on the agenda even before the transfer of power in 1994. The ideas that were to shape the first few years of policy reform had incubated on the one hand among academics, some of them activists who had had first-hand experience of the varieties of pre-1990 police repression. But even the generals of the pre-1994 South African police realised the need for new policies. The latter, in what was to prove to be an act of anticipatory socialisation, had adopted the idea of community policing by the late 1980s and given it a trial run in pre-independence Namibia.[2]

From the early 1990s to 1997 the project of police reform was informed by notions of community policing, police accountability and the infusion of human rights ideas strongly advocated by a number of international policing advisers (Brogden and Shearing 1993; Weitzer 1993). The first tentative steps taken by the pre-1994 police high command were intensified by measures agreed upon during the 1993 negotiations for an interim Constitution,[3] and in a series of policy documents thereafter.[4] Considerable effort was made to translate the core principles associated with community policing (consultation, partnership and community oversight) into institutional practice. In this period, community police forums, consisting of station commanders and members of the local community, became the key institutional mechanisms through which local accountability was to be enacted. The establishment of community police forums became a statutory requirement, entrenched in both the interim Constitution and the South African Police Service Act 1995.[5]

In the initial phase the paradigm of community policing was intended to serve the strategic purpose of legitimating the former, colonial-style public police through reform of its core institutions. In the same period, a 'holistic' policy framework for crime prevention was being constructed along more radical lines. The spirit of such thinking was encapsulated in the National Crime Prevention Strategy (NCPS) (Department of Safety and Security 1996). The NCPS was designed by an interdepartmental team, assisted by consultants and foreign advisers. The gist of the strategy was that crime policy had to be embedded in a macro-developmental framework that would address structural inequities, if it were to have any chance at success. It was in this sense the epitome of the progressive criminology prevailing at the key English-speaking academic and non-governmental institutions concerned with police reform.

Even as the NCPS was being adopted to general acclaim, its very premises were being undermined by the leading actors concerned with police reform – both politicians and the police executive. One criminologist-turned-practitioner who had been directly involved in the drafting of the NCPS has given the following verdict:

> The implementation of the NCPS in fact never matched up to its original motive – to initiate *prevention* efforts as a way of reducing the burdensome caseload which was constantly mitigating efforts at institutional reform of the criminal justice system. Rather than *prevention* becoming a watchword, the theme of this wave of reform became *co-ordination*, as part of the desperate attempt to 'fix' the criminal justice system so that it could deal with the massive numbers of victims and suspects, and thereby deter other potential offenders (Rauch 2002: 9).

By 1998 politicians were speaking of crisis management in the police. They confirmed public perceptions of a police force that was under threat in just about every way (*Hansard* 1998: col. 3244–8). High crime rates, rising public unease about crime and harsh budgetary constraints combined to rule out truly sweeping reform. The scene was set for a new phase in policing policy: a dwindling emphasis on community policing, and a much narrower and state-centered approach to police reform. The most substantive exposition of the latest policing methodology that has evolved since 1997 is that of the National Crime Combating Strategy of 2000. A comparison of the form and content of the National Crime Prevention Strategy of 1996 with the National Crime Combating Strategy of 2000 neatly illustrates the shift in policing paradigms that has taken place. Underlying these shifts were a variety of factors and forces.

From 1997 onwards the objective of police reform was redefined, from broadly based political legitimacy to police effectiveness; from the technocratic idealism of the NCPS to 'back to basics' in the 'battle against crime' (*Hansard* 1998: col. 3248). One indication of the rapid obsolescence of the NCPS is to be found in the 1998 White Paper on Safety and Security (Department of Safety and Security 1998). With an emphasis on 'pragmatic policy' which would empower the 'front-liners' to 'deliver', the White Paper reasserted the law enforcement role of the public police and hived off the responsibilities for social crime prevention to local authorities. The emphasis in the White Paper was now on an increase in the effectiveness of criminal investigation, rather than on a reconfigured police force acting organically with 'the community'.

The drift towards a technocratic disposition gained momentum within the South African Police Service (SAPS) with the appointment in August 1997 of Meyer Kahn, a corporate businessman, as chief executive officer. Kahn promised to apply basic managerial procedures in order to combat civil service inertia. South African big business was an early player in the field of police reform, contributing large sums to the 'Business against Crime' initiative that channelled funds and expertise to the policing sector (*Hansard* 1999: col. 2582). The result was the importation of many familiar managerial credos. The SAPS was introduced to 'policing by objectives' and 'performance-based indicators' intended to increase the efficiency of this intractable bureaucracy. Thus not only the programmes of the international donor community but also the latest managerial techniques that South African big business had adopted from its western counterparts were deployed – with limited success – towards the goal of improving policing capacity.

The trend was intensified after the second democratic elections in 1999, when a new tough-talking minister, complemented by an equally aggressive new Commissioner of Police, promised a return to the "core business" of policing – namely, to enhance law enforcement (*Hansard* 1999: col. 2586). The policing elite began to place far less emphasis on broad policy frameworks, to refocus policing responsibilities on law enforcement and to invest its limited resources on some indispensable policing capacity, such as investigative skills and intelligence gathering. The conduit for the latest attempt at modernising public service systems was the Integrated Justice System (IJS) initiative, which concentrated on law enforcement and the administration of justice, largely ignoring the social dimensions of crime.

Donor assistance reinforced this shift from a concern with community policing (most notably by a major project that recast the basic training of new recruits in 1995) to a new emphasis on managerial skills, and the importation of a variety of policing technologies to fight transnational crime. As a technicist approach, which emulated public service developments in the First World War, the IJS initiative fitted well with this revision of donor priorities. Thus 'fixing the system' became a prominent focus of donor aid programmes after 1997. For the managerialists, as Rauch (2002: 13) observes, 'community consultation, participation and accountability were seen … as onerous and obstructing the development of a more streamlined and effective criminal justice "machine" …'. It would, however, be wrong to exaggerate the role of the donor community in reversing previous policy directions. In the main donors reacted to, rather than moulded, the changing perceptions of what needed to be done that were emerging among the top echelons of the police hierarchy, while also taking advantage of the growing internal concern with transnational organised crime.

There were also underlying social conditions that propelled police reform in narrower, more statist directions. Three factors appear to have been central. First, there was a steady growth in public concern about crime and perceptions of 'criminal anarchy' and police incapacity. Many leaders in the public sector shared this concern. Violent crime was no respecter of persons, and the new elite was as much a victim of luxury car hijackings and violent burglary as private citizens. Likewise, high-profile cases of criminal attacks on foreign businessmen and diplomats underlined the threat that social disorder represented to the newly cosmopolitan democracy. The debilitating effects of violent crime in particular on local and international investment necessitated a tougher state response to counteract perceptions that it was unable to act decisively. Already in 1995 the then President Nelson Mandela in a major address had stressed the government's intention to 'take the war to the criminals' (*Hansard* 1995: col. 12). This 'war on crime' rhetoric was to become all the more strident as serious crime rates failed to drop in the late 1990s.

Secondly, the emergence of new crime threats and their impact on the stability of the newly found democracy shaped the agenda for police reform. A relatively closed, out-of-the-way country under apartheid, South Africa after 1994 experienced massive increases in visitors, immigrants and international linkages. Not all these were benign. The traffic in hard drugs, hitherto a scarce commodity in the country, boomed after 1994. Cross-border smuggling of high-value items such as stolen vehicles rose rapidly. The spectre of 'organised' crime, hitherto largely a domestic affair, suddenly took on worldwide proportions. Encouraged by western countries such as the USA and the UK, political concern with organised crime opened up new priorities for anti-crime strategies. Boosting the capacity of the state to make 'war on organised crime' became a central preoccupation in the last years of the 1990s. After 1998 diplomatic pressure and technical assistance from various international quarters (the UK, UN, USA) combined to shape crime policies, legal-administrative regimes and operational strategies of the law enforcement agencies in South Africa as well as within the larger southern African region (Van der Spuy 1997, 2000). The unfamiliar experience of dealing with sophisticated cross-border criminal organisations appears to have been the main factor intensifying tendencies towards policy convergence (Bennett 1991) and thus moving local policing policy and practice nearer to the international norm. New institutional networks such as the Southern African Regional Police Chiefs Co-ordinating Organisation (SARPCCO) were instrumental in this regard. Increasingly, international agreements such as the Palermo Convention on Transnational Crime dictated adaptations of local policing priorities. This trend was reinforced by the influx of inter-national agencies such as the UNDP.

It would however be premature to conclude that this was a case of the imposition of metropolitan ideas, and hence self-interest, on a hapless Third World country. For South African elites, convergence appears to have been perceived as much a matter of self-interest as a pandering to powerful western forces. With international aid to South Africa running at a mere 2 per cent of the national budget (Van der Spuy 2000), donors were in no position to use their financial clout to dictate particular reforms. Nor were the transfer of technology and the latest managerial methods without their own inherent problems. Here, as elsewhere, the very latest public sector techniques derived from the west often failed to meet the difficulties of policing an intractably uncivil society. As other commentators have noted, the influence of these western models (underpinned often with international aid packages) may have transformed the rhetoric rather than the reality of operational policing (Dixon 2000).

Thirdly, the escalation of urban violence and low-intensity wars between gangs and vigilante groupings on the Cape Flats, and the resultant changes in security definitions of the 'threat' also pushed police reform in a very specific direction. The conviction grew in official circles that the state required new strategies, RICO-type laws and specialist units, to meet the challenge of 'urban terrorism' as it presented itself on the streets of greater Cape Town after 1996 (Schönteich 2000).

The philosophy and practices of the new phase have culminated in the National Crime Combating Strategy. The shift from a National Crime Prevention Strategy of four years earlier to a Crime Combating Strategy is of more than semantic importance. Prominent concerns of the latest consolidated three-year plan to combat crime include those of organised crime and public disorder. The plan contains a two-part strategy (Department of Safety and Security 2000). First, a geographic targeting of high-crime areas involves saturation policing of 140 'hotspots' in 68 Crime Combating Zones with the view to 'stabilising flashpoints'. Secondly, the organised crime strategy entails more specific targeting of organised crime groupings through the regrouping of specialist units. The recourse to specialisation is epitomised by the formation of an elite integrated policing and prosecutorial unit, the Directorate of Special Operations (the 'Scorpions'). In the view of some, the establishment of the Scorpions amounts to the search for solutions outside the main-stream police bureaucracy through the creation of a second police agency modelled loosely on the FBI (Justice and Constitutional Affairs Portfolio Committee 2000).

But will tough talk and muscular action in the 'war on crime' yield the desired effects? Judging by the content of the Minister of Safety and Security's speech to Parliament in mid-2001, there is new realism about policing. 'Quick-fix solutions', warned the minister, did not exist (Hansard 2001: col. 4285-92). Socioeconomic development, he explained, was the crucial factor in preventing crime. Minister Tshwete lamented that everyone had underestimated just how difficult it would be to transform the SAPS. Ironically, the spectre of the NCPS walked again, as the minister stressed that the National Crime Combating Strategy was also situated within a developmental framework. Anti-crime offensives would depend for their success on poverty alleviation. The newly unveiled Urban Renewal Strategy and the Integrated Rural Development Programme by their nature, reminded the minister, could not deliver in the short term.

Thus reform in the police seems to have turned full circle, from idealism to managerialism. Not all hopes of reform have been abandoned. Optimistic claims continue to be made that community-based peace committees can play an important role in ordering urban townships quite independently of the criminal justice system (Kempa and Shearing 2002; Roche 2002). The South African Law Commission has continued to work on a framework that may allow 'alternative policing' of this kind to flourish. The future of policing in South Africa is far from settled.

Prisons

The prisons service began the 1990s with a somewhat cosmetic change. In 1991 it became a separate government department, restyled the Department of Correctional Services with its own cabinet minister. This was linked to the announcement that the new department would be run according to 'business principles'. In fact there were no major new ideas in this change. The newly named Department of Correctional Services remained a tightly centralised, quasi-military bureaucracy, which continued to outlaw the nascent trade union of black prison officers (Van Zyl Smit 1992).

The most important source of fresh ideas in the prison sphere was initially the courts. The scope and nature of prisoners' rights had long been areas of struggle in South Africa (Van Zyl Smit 1987). Political prisoners, who were the only prisoners with the resources to go to law, had used rights-based arguments to improve their conditions of detention. They lost more often than they won. In the process prisoners' rights were generally defined more narrowly than in the past. But there were exceptions. Most notably, as early as 1979, a dissenting judgment by Judge Corbett in the leading case of *Goldberg* v. *Minister of Prisons* (1979) recognised that even sentenced political prisoners retain the rights of ordinary citizens except those that are taken away from them by law and as a necessary consequence of imprisonment. By the 1990s Corbett had become Chief Justice and in 1993 the Appellate Division (then the court of final instance) reversed its earlier line of reasoning. Relying heavily on Corbett's judgment and with specific reference to the recognition of prisoners' rights in foreign jurisdictions, the Appellate Division reasserted prisoners' rights in terms that would be acceptable in most liberal democracies (*Minister of Justice* v. *Hofmeyr* 1993).

This liberal position was consolidated shortly thereafter in the Bill of Rights that formed part of the interim Constitution, under which the first, democratically elected government functioned after May 1994. These constitutional rights which were to be re-enacted substantially unchanged in the final Constitution of 1996 went further than is usual in bills of rights. The Constitution specified, for example, not only that all prisoners had to be detained in conditions of human dignity but also spelt out that these included 'provision, at state expense, of adequate accommodation, nutrition, reading material and medical treatment'.[6]

The immediate response of the Department of Correctional Services to the change of regime was to produce new policy proposals. The 1994 *White Paper on the Policy of the Department of Correctional Services in the New South Africa* was a bland document, with little indication yet of a clear official line. It did, however, respond to the shift in the legal status of prisoners and suggest that a new legislative framework was required (Department of Correctional Services 1994). The newly appointed parliamentary committee on correctional services was somewhat suspicious of the bureaucrats of the old regime, who had drafted the white paper. It therefore gave unusually much credence to one of the responses to it, the so-called *Alternative White Paper*, which emphasised the importance of having a reduced prison population accommodated by a less secretive, demilitarised prison system that would be accountable to the public (Penal Reform Lobby Group 1995). The *Alternative White Paper* was a combined submission by various human rights and prisoners' rights organisations, joined somewhat surprisingly by the technically still banned union of correctional officials, the Police and Prison Officer's Civil Rights Union (POPCRU).

POPCRU needs some explanation. It emerged in the late 1980s as a trade union for police and prison officers who wanted to associate themselves with the emergent liberation movement. Initially, and particularly in the period between 1990 and 1994, it aspired to be more than a mere interest group: the words 'civil rights' in its title were significant. Support from an alliance of prisons officers' unions and anti-apartheid activists from the Netherlands encouraged it to oppose the militarisation of the prison service and to adopt an approach towards prisoners that would stress social upliftment rather than mere control (Van Zyl Smit 2001a).

Two important initiatives flowed from the white paper process: the one was a total overhaul of the legislative basis for the correctional system, the other was the creation of a Transformation Forum in which various stakeholders were to combine to reshape the Department of Correctional Services itself. In practice, the two processes went largely separate ways. At an early stage a decision was taken to exclude labour matters from the legislation, for it was understood that, once the service had been demilitarised, these matters would be regulated by ordinary public service legislation.

Initially the Transformation Forum seemed open to new ideas about how prisons should be run. Generously funded by the Danish government, this group was chaired by the African National Congress (ANC) politician Carl Niehaus, who was also chair of the parliamentary committee on correctional services and an ex-political prisoner himself. It consisted of a strange mixture of old-regime prison staff generals, former 'common law prisoners', trade union activists and idealistic penal reformers. The forum toured the world in order to study progressive prison practices. In South Africa, though, they were upstaged. Demilitarisation was introduced by ministerial fiat[7] rather than as part of the wider transformation process that the forum had envisaged (Giffard 1999).

The meetings of the Transformation Forum became increasingly fractious. Instead of dealing with ideas it became a forum for trade union pressures for immediate transformation of the personnel of the prisons service (more bluntly, getting black personnel into positions of power as soon as possible). The white Commissioner of Correctional Services, a career prison officer who had been appointed to manage the transition process for five years, resigned before the end of his term and was replaced by a new black commissioner, who had limited experience of prison administration. Tensions continued at the political level. Eventually Niehaus was appointed ambassador to the Netherlands and the Transformation Forum collapsed.

The disbanding of the Transformation Forum signalled the end of a particular phase of idealistic communitarianism in which prison reformers, who adopted an empathetic approach to prisoners as perceived fellow victims of social disadvantage, were highly influential. The shift manifested itself in various ways: at one level one could say simply that individualist American correctional ideas became more influential than more communitarian continental European notions. The American ideas had long been current: Minister Mzimela had personal links with the USA as he had been a prison chaplain in Atlanta while in exile, and had American-influenced advisers from the start. These influences manifested themselves in two important ways: viz. in a new managerialism, including an interest in privatisation, which was also supported strongly by the British government (Berg 2001; Goyer 2001), and in explicit support for more repressive regimes. Leading figures, both the Minister of Correctional Services and the Commissioner, began speaking about prisoners in derogatory terms as being worse than animals fit only to be housed down mine shafts and in super-maximum security prisons (*Cape Times* 1996; Van Zyl Smit 2001b). The most expensive prison development during this time was an ultra-high security prison built at vast cost. However, not all the American ideas were invariably repressive. Some of the American-style ideas, such as unit management in prison, had a genuine attraction for those prison officers who wanted a more pastoral role (Luyt 1999). These were the exception. At the same time prison officer unionism lost its idealistic dimension and degenerated largely into an extraordinarily vicious power struggle, with officers in some instances murdering each other to gain control of sections of the service (Sekhonyane 2002).

Meanwhile, legal developments continued. A new comprehensive Correctional Services Act (Act 111 of 1998) was eventually adopted by Parliament. Broadly modelled on Canadian and German legislation, it retained an explicit commitment to enabling sentenced prisoners to lead a crime-free life in the future. It also introduced detailed community corrections provisions and an elaborate community-participatory parole system (Van Zyl Smit 2001a). The courts too continued to extend the ambit of prisoners rights: Provincial Divisions of the High Court held that prisoners had the right to expensive medical treatment for HIV/AIDs from the authorities, even where it was not available to the public at state expense on the outside (*Van Biljon* v. *Minister of Correctional Services* 1997). Sentenced prisoners were granted a right to have electricity provided for their private electrical appliances to which they were entitled in terms of a privilege scheme (*Strydom* v. *Minister of Correctional Services* 1999). The Constitutional Court ruled that prisoners' right to vote could not be removed by regulation (*August and Another v. Electoral Commission* 1999). In 2002 the Supreme Court of Appeal weighed in with a judgment which declared unlawful a newly intro-duced regime that would have placed prisoners awaiting trial in a worse position than some sentenced prisoners (*Minister of Correctional Services* v. *Kwakwa* 2002).

All these legal developments have had only a limited impact. There is some evidence, for example, that the judgment on the treatment of prisoners suffering from HIV/AIDS has not been implemented fully (Geer and Ngubeni 2002). By the end of 2002 the only aspects of the legislative framework that had been put into operation were the provisions for private prisons and the system of judicial inspection. This extraordinary delay suggests that neither prisoners' rights nor public participation are high priorities.

As in the case of the police, the preliminary conclusion on develop-ments in prisons is mixed. Recently there has been some attempt to back away from the punitive excesses of the late 1990s. Prisons Commissioner

Sithole was forced to resign at the end of 1999 amid widespread allegations of corruption. Minister Mzimela had been replaced earlier by a more moderate successor. After Sithole's resignation there was a series of new commissioners: appointed, in some instances it is said, by the President, directly in order to combat corruption. In late 2001 President Mbeki also appointed a judicial Commission of Inquiry into Alleged Incidents of Corruption, Maladminstration, Violence or Intimidation in the Department of Correctional Services.[8] Although the final report of the commission is unlikely to appear before late 2004, it has unearthed some startling evidence of corruption and other crimes (Sekhonyane 2002). Understandably, perhaps, the several new commissioners have focused on clean administration and emphasised the priority of reducing escapes. At the same time two large private prisons have been added to the prison system (Department of Correctional Services 2002).

Although the focus of the Department of Correctional Services has shifted to efficient implementation of punishment, some of the idealism remains. It is still likely that the full Correctional Services Act 1998 will be brought into operation in the near future. Moreover, communitarian ideas, if not practice, have enjoyed something of a revival with the recent emphasis in official circles on the notion of the 'restorative prison' (Giffard 2002).

The judiciary

The interaction of the judiciary with new ideas on criminal justice has been somewhat different from that of the police and prison authorities. In the early 1990s it was a much more confident institution.[9] Judges and magistrates were secure in the tenure of their offices and the senior judiciary at least believed that they themselves had always been independent from government. The creation of the Constitutional Court as a court of final instance in constitutional matters was not perceived by other judges as a threat to the judicial system. It was staffed from the beginning by judges (several of them had been judges under the old regime) who generally enjoyed the respect of most of their senior colleagues in other courts. As a result the judiciary could look freely, as the new Constitution explicitly encouraged them to do, at international and comparative jurisprudence. The Constitutional Court in particular has done so and its judgments abolishing capital and corporal punishment set the tone for legal debates about criminal justice in the early years of the new government (S v. *Makwanyane* 1995; S v. *Williams* 1995). Pressures on the judiciary to adhere more closely to communitarian values have been relatively indirect. Juries for example have not been introduced and the increased use of lay assessors has not directly threatened the authority of high court judges or career magistrates who hear most criminal cases (Seekings and Murray 1998).

In spite of these advantages, since the late 1990s in particular, the judiciary as an institution has come under similar pressures to the police and the prisons. There has been widespread criticism of the courts both for taking too long to process cases and for being soft on crime by granting bail too easily and imposing sentences that are too light. The efficiency criticisms are undoubtedly justified. The number of prisoners awaiting trial has almost tripled in the last eight years while the number of cases reaching the courts has remained constant (Van Zyl Smit forthcoming). The courts are not the only source of this delay. But in much public debate the lack of efficiency has been blamed on the constitutional principles applied by the courts rather than on mal-administration. The attacks on the granting of bail have also been cast in terms that seek to argue that the courts are not sufficiently sensitive to public opinion when they grant bail.

On the question of criminal procedural rights the courts have sometimes been weak. They have accepted as constitutional new bail legislation, which allows public opinion to be considered in a bail decision, and have not paid sufficient attention to the right to a speedy trial. In the case of bail in particular they have upheld draconian restrictions, even where they have recognised that such restrictions would not pass constitutional muster in comparable constitutional democracies (Sarkin et al. 2000).

On sentencing their response has been more subtle. They have asserted the constitutional principle that sentences should not be grossly disproportionate to the crime committed and have used this argument to hold that courts should be able to depart relatively freely from mandatory minimum sentences that the legislature has sought to impose (S v. Dodo 2001; S v. Malgas 2001).

One may also criticise the courts in other areas. Neil Boister (2003), for example, has argued that the South African courts have accepted laws that allow assets that were allegedly the proceeds of crime to be declared forfeit to the state too readily. In part this has happened, he suggests, because South African courts in their desire to support crime control and to be 'good international citizens' have accepted too easily that international conventions incorporate the due process standards to which the South African Constitution adheres.

In spite of these criticisms one can still conclude cautiously that South African constitutional jurisprudence continues to be a source of ideas for those who wish to defend individual liberties against excessive crime control. One example is the history of the amendment of s. 49 of the Criminal Procedure Act, which notoriously provided very wide justifications for the police (and indeed private citizens) to rely on the statutory defence of 'justifiable homicide' when killing someone in the course of arrest or crime prevention. Parliament amended this provision in 1996, introducing in its stead very strict Canadian-style limits on all such killings. *After* the legislation was passed, the police, certainly with the tacit support of their minister, fought a rear-guard action against its implementation (on the official website of the police legal advisers!). Eventually in 2002 the Constitutional Court intervened (*S* v. *Walters* 2002) and, in the face of opposition from the police,[10] declared the justifiable homicide aspects of the provision unconstitutional.

Of equal importance is that the generous view taken of the importance of sociopolitical rights by the Constitutional Court provides a fertile intellectual ground for those who want to assert a more humane criminal justice system in the face of pressure for efficient crime control. Both the decision that the government can be compelled to provide drugs that will reduce the risk of pregnant mothers transmitting HIV infection to their unborn children (*Minister of Health* v. *Treatment Action Campaign (no 2)* 2002) and the duty placed on the state to develop an adequate housing programme for the indigent (*Government of South Africa* v. *Grootboom* 2001) are indications that the Court is prepared to impose duties on the state to take positive action. Such duties may be extended to the criminal justice area too. In fact the Court has done so, where it has held that the state could be held liable for the criminal behaviour of a third party where it had not taken reasonable steps to prevent it (*Carmichele* v. *Minister of Safety and Security* 2001).

In our view the overall balance is positive. In spite of the many references by the Court to decisions in other jurisdictions it is reasonable to claim that the decisions of the South African Constitutional Court are less a product of imported ideas than a uniquely South African contribution to international jurisprudence on social justice. The intellectual confidence of the small elite that has shaped this jurisprudence is probably the most important reason for its independent development.

Child justice

Our final example of the interplay of the communitarian, liberal and repressive ideas that have been exported to South Africa is to be found in the sphere of juvenile or child justice. In the struggle for liberation juvenile justice had a vanguard function in South Africa in that the ill-treatment and imprisonment of children by the old regime was seen as one of the basic inequities that should be set right (Van Zyl Smit 1999). It was a campaign with which President Mandela was personally associated. The failure of the attempt to remove young children from prison after 1994, or even to reduce the numbers of those held there, in spite of numerous amendments to the law, may be seen as defeat for all reform in this area. The sheer persistence of such long-standing problems is captured in a recent compendium of statistics pertaining to children in conflict with the law (Muntingh 2003).[11] It provides tangible proof of an increasingly punitive dispensation for young offenders in recent years.

Yet reform has continued. Anne Skelton (2002) has described how a group of reformers (of whom she has been a prominent member) managed to protect the juveniles against the excesses of mandatory sentences and to hold on to restorative ideals in their proposals for juvenile justice reforms. The communitarian ideals and associated principles are well represented in the Child Justice Bill currently before Parliament.[12] Particularly influential have been the increased inter-national recognition of the rights of the child (Sloth-Nielsen 2001) and the application of the ideals of restorative justice to children. Charismatic proponents of restorative justice saw South African juvenile justice reform as an area in which their ideas could be applied (Zehr 1997). The history of juvenile justice in South Africa and the emotive nature of the issues involved provided South African reformers with a unique opportunity to build on these international initiatives. Juvenile justice has attracted particularly dedicated South African moral entrepreneurs who have exploited their opportunities to the full.

What can be deduced from the deliberations currently underway before the parliamentary committee responsible for the details of the bill? Two general impressions seem warranted. The first is that there is broad-based acceptance of the need for legislative reform in pursuit of a special dispensation for child justice. Secondly, a measure of consensus also seems to exist with regards to the importance of general restorative justice principles and the desirability of diversion from the criminal justice system. Controversy, however, has stalked the debate concerning the kinds of cases appropriate for diversion. On this score the proponents of crime control have argued that diversion may not be constitutionally appropriate for serious crimes (Justice and Con-stitutional Development Portfolio Committee 2003). This argument seems to be dominant. The committee has recommended that specific serious offences be excluded from the ambit of diversion. The sentencing provisions of the bill are still to be discussed. At this point child justice lobbyists are uncertain whether the blanket prohibition on imprison-ment for children under 14 and the total ban on life imprisonment for children advocated in the bill will remain intact. A further concession to the crime control constituency may well be in the offing.

Thus far a spirit of political pragmatism has allowed the child justice lobby to recognise, rather than dismiss, concerns about desert and retribution. In some instances there have been concessions (Skelton 1999). Yet many aspects of diversion and conferencing remain intact – sufficient for the reformers to claim that communitarian justice is far from dead. The child justice lobby has been encouraged by the unanimous acceptance within the committee of the bill's proposal to raise the age of criminal capacity from 7 to 10 years. In this instance, too, astute lobbying on the part of child justice activists has proved crucial.

In a fine display of critical introspection, Skelton (2002) warned against the pitfalls of too idealised a depiction of indigenous African justice in support of the restorative model as a solution to the problems of child justice; and too sharp a juxtaposition between the paradigms of restorative and adversarial justice. She emphasised the need for meshing restorative justice principles with crime control objectives. Pragmatism among the moral entrepreneurs may not, however, be enough to keep communitarian ideas afloat. As elsewhere in the criminal justice system, the gap between theory and practice, between social policy and bureaucratic implementation, may loom large. This may be the case despite the fact that the bill was placed before Parliament together with an implementation strategy and detailed costing (Barberton 2003). Notwithstanding such initiatives, the political will to sustain this model of child justice may prove to be fickle in the face of contradictory pressures to 'tough justice' elsewhere in the criminal justice system.

Conclusion

A superficial analysis of the current state of criminal justice in South Africa might lead to the conclusion that the idealism, both liberal and communitarian, that was shared by South Africa's reformers and their international allies in the first years of criminal justice reform, has been lost. One might argue that the initial optimism was misplaced in its hopes that a society in transition would provide greater opportunities for reform than would be available in a stable democracy. Certainly it is true that in South Africa, as elsewhere in the transitional world, reform of policing in its widest sense has been reduced to a much narrower reorganisation of law enforcement capacity. The grand alliance of state, market and civil society in pursuit of the 'governance of security' (Shaw and Shearing 1998), as originally anticipated, has failed to materialise. The integration of informal justice and policing structure with the formal machinery of state control has made almost no headway. Thus at the end of eight years of attempted criminal justice reform one is forced to note that while much has changed at the level of theory, not so much has changed in practice.

However, there is also much that is permanent in the changes that have been introduced. A new style associated with democratic policing has made serious inroads into the colonial-style policing that dominated under apartheid. The same applies to the demilitarised prisons. New legal and social rules are embedded in constitutional politics. Principles of accountability, demographic proportionality and equity of access are firmly part of the criminal justice discourse. The structures created to institutionalise new rules and principles look very different from those that operated under apartheid. Even the treatment of juveniles by the criminal justice system may improve.

Our conclusion is that the time not only for liberatory optimism but also for unprincipled pragmatism has passed. Both are arguably features of a society in transition. Perhaps to some extent South Africa has now become a stable democracy with reduced opportunities for fundamental reform. However, there are now new possibilities for thinking about criminal justice policy. As South Africans have lived through the extremes of both positions, the new debate about criminal justice need not be conducted at quite the same declamatory level. There is a new maturity in this debate and with it encouraging signs that imported ideas will be less uncritically accepted. The 'criminology of practitioners' that has dominated for the past five years or so is being subjected to re-evaluation. Criminologists, who might have been disillusioned by initial failures to have their ideas implemented, now have the opportunity to return to the fray. The challenge is to ensure that the innovations that are still being put forward by practitioners are evaluated both for short-term effectiveness and for the longer-term contribution that they can make to social justice.[13]

A further conclusion is that the impact of foreign donor assistance and of the ideas that they have brought with them about the institutions of the criminal justice system has varied greatly. When the recent history of imprisonment in South Africa is compared to that of policing there can be little doubt that prison policy has not been subjected to such intensive international influence. This may be simply because international donors that invested heavily in improving policing in South Africa have not been as interested in supporting prison reform. One reason for this relative lack of interest may be that policing is perceived as directly affecting interests of donor countries more, because they will be harmed if South Africa were to become a haven for organised crime or by a general decline in stability in South Africa. Even poorly run, inhumane prisons will not have such an impact on the material interests of the donors, in the short term at least. Prison reform also differs from juvenile justice reform in that South African reformers have not been able to portray it as an issue that should be addressed as a matter of urgency. Certainly improving conditions for ordinary convicted criminals does not have the same symbolic impact as alleviating the needs of 'innocent children' in conflict with the law, who are more easily portrayed as latent victims of the long years of apartheid injustice. For this reason too it is less likely to attract foreign funding. South African reformers will have to ensure that such donors' perspectives of what deserves priority do not overly affect their own judgements of those aspects of the criminal justice system most urgently in need of improvement.

Notes

1 The most prominent of these were the Institute for Security Studies (formerly the Institute of Defence Policy) and the Centre for the Study of Violence and Reconciliation.
2 South Africa ruled Namibia from 1921 to 1989, in theory in terms of a mandate from the League of Nations but in practice as a colony. The eventual liberation of Namibia and its emergence as a constitutional democracy following a process of transition under the auspices of the UN proved a valuable testing ground for South African constitutional reform in general and criminal justice initiatives in particular.
3 The Constitution of the Republic of South Africa Act, Act 200 of 1993. This Constitution, which was adopted as an interim measure by the old South African Parliament in 1993, was the product of the negotiation process that led to majority rule and formed the constitutional basis for the new South African government that came into power in 1994. It was replaced by a new constitution, which was adopted by the new South African Parliament sitting as a Constitutional Assembly, as the Constitution of the Republic of

South Africa, Act 108 of 1996. The two constitutions are referred to as the 'interim Constitution' and the 'final Constitution' respectively in this chapter.

4 The most important policy documents include the following: *Draft Policy Document* (Minister of Safety and Security 1994), the South African Police Service Act (Act 68 of 1995) and the *Community Policing Policy Framework and Guidelines* (Department of Safety and Security 1997).

5 Section 212 of the interim Constitution; ss. 18 and 19 of the South African Police Service Act.

6 Section 35(2)(e) of the Constitution of the Republic of South Africa, 1996. For further discussion of the full implications of the rights guaranteed to all prisoners in s. 35(2), see Van Zyl Smit (2001a: 592–3).

7 Internal compromises in the first Government of National Unity dictated that the Minister of Correctional Services would be a member of the minority Inkatha Freedom Party rather than the ANC.

8 See Government Notice 2103 of 2001; *Government Gazette* 22718 of 27 September 2001.

9 Misguidedly so, according to some critics. On the limited participation of the judges in the work of the Truth and Reconciliation Commission, see Dyzenhaus (1998).

10 Neither the prosecution nor the defence in the original criminal trial sought to bring the matter to constitutional finality, so the case was argued by counsel for the Minister of Safety and Security, who sought to demonstrate the continued constitutionality of the old provision, and Counsel for the Minister of Justice and Constitutional Development, who took the opposite view.

11 According to Muntingh (2003: 6) the number of children awaiting trial in prisons has increased six-fold since 1996. By 2001 the number of children awaiting trial in prison exceeded sentenced children in prisons. The number of children sentenced to imprisonment increased at an annual rate of 16 per cent between 1999 and 2000. The average length of prison sentences of children has been on the increase too.

12 The Child Justice Bill (B 49-2002) proposes 'to establish a criminal justice process for those children accused of committing offences so as to protect the rights of children entrenched in the Constitution and provided for in international instruments; to provide for the minimum age of criminal capacity of such children; to incorporate diversion of cases away from formal court procedures as a central feature of the process; to establish assessment of children and a preliminary inquiry as compulsory procedures; to provide that children must be tried in child justice courts and to extend the sentencing options available in respect of children; to entrench the notion of restorative justice in respect of children, and to provide for matters incidental thereto'.

13 For an example of the latter, see Dixon (2001) on the implications for contemporary South Africa of the ideas of Jock Young.

References

Barberton, C. (2003) 'Costing of the Child Justice Bill.' Presentation to the Justice and Constitutional Development Portfolio Committee, 20 February (http://www.pmg.org.za/docs/2003/appendices/030220barberton.ppt).

Bennett, C.J. (1991) 'Review article: what is policy convergence and what causes it?', *British Journal of Political Studies*, 21: 215–33.

Berg, J. (2001) 'Accountability in private corrections: monitoring the performance of private prison in South Africa', *South African Journal of Criminal Justice*, 14(3): 327–43.

Boister, N. (2003) 'Problems of legitimacy and respect for human rights in the globalization of penal norms: confiscation in South Africa as a case in point', in J. Sarkin (ed.) (forthcoming).

Brogden, M. and Shearing, C. (1993) *Policing for a New South Africa*. London: Routledge.

Cape Times (1996) 'Disused mine may become prison,' 23 August: 3.

Department of Correctional Services (1994) *White Paper on the Policy of the Department of Correctional Services in the New South Africa*. Pretoria: Government Printer.

Department of Correctional Services (2002) *Annual Report – 1 April 2001 to 31 March 2002*. Pretoria: Department of Correctional Services.

Department of Safety and Security (1996) *National Crime Prevention Strategy: Summary*. Pretoria: Department of Safety and Security.

Department of Safety and Security (1997) *Community Policing Policy Framework and Guidelines: A Manual for the South African Police Service*. Pretoria: Department of Safety and Security.

Department of Safety and Security (1998) *White Paper on Safety and Security: 'In Service of Safety, 1999–2004'*. Pretoria: Department of Safety and Security.

Department of Safety and Security (2000) *Strategic Focus: South African Police Service, 2000–3*. Pretoria: Department of Safety and Security.

Dixon, B. (2000) *The Globalisation of Democratic Policing: Sector Policing and Zero Tolerance in the New South Africa*. Cape Town: Institute of Criminology, University of Cape Town.

Dixon, W. (2001) 'Exclusive societies: towards a critical criminology of post-apartheid South Africa', *Society in Transition*, 32(2): 205–27.

Dyzenhaus, D. (1998) *Judging the Judges, Judging Ourselves: Truth, Reconciliation and the Apartheid Legal Order*. Oxford: Hart Publishing.

Geer, S. and Ngubeni, K. (2002) *Daai Ding: Sex, Sexual Violence and Coercion in Men's Prisons*. Johannesburg: Centre for the Study of Violence and Reconciliation.

Giffard, C. (1999) *Out of Step? The Transformation Process in the South African Department of Correctional Services*. Cape Town: Institute of Criminology, University of Cape Town.

Giffard, C. (2002) 'Restorative justice in prison – an option for South Africa?', *Track Two*, 11(2): 34–8.

Goyer, K.C. (2001) *Prison Privatisation in South Africa: Issues, Challenges and Opportunities*. Institute of Security Studies Monograph Series 64. Pretoria: Institute of Security Studies.

Justice and Constitutional Affairs Portfolio Committee (2000) *Directorate of Special Operations Bill Hearings*, 6 September (http://www.pmg.org.za/minutes/000906pcjustice.htm).

Justice and Constitutional Development Portfolio Committee (2003) Child Justice Bill: Deliberations, 14 March.

Kempa, M. and Shearing, C. (2002) 'Microscopic and macroscopic responses to inequalities in the governance of security: respective experiments in South African and Northern Ireland', *Transformation: Critical Perspectives on Southern Africa*, 49: 25–54.

Luyt, W. (1999) 'A perspective on the future of prisons in the new South Africa', *South African Journal of Criminal Justice*, 12(2): 223–8.

Minister of Safety and Security (1994) *Draft Policy Document*. Pretoria: Ministry of Safety and Security.

Muntingh, L. (ed.) (2003) *Children in Conflict with the Law: A Compendium of Child Justice Statistics: 1995–2001*. Cape Town: Child Justice Alliance.

Parmentier, S. (2001) 'The South African Truth and Reconciliation Commission: towards restorative justice in the field of human rights', in E. Fattah and S. Parmentier (eds) *Victim Policies and Criminal Justice on the Road to Restorative Justice: A Collection of Essays in Honour of Tony Peters*. Leuven: Leuven University Press.

Penal Reform Lobby Group (1995) *An Alternative White Paper on Correctional Services*. Cape Town (mimeographed report).

Rauch, J. (2002) 'Justice and security after apartheid: assessing police and criminal justice reform in South Africa.' Unpublished Paper, Johannesburg, CSVR.

Roche, D. (2002) 'Restorative justice and the regulatory state in South African townships', *British Journal of Criminology*, 42(3): 514–33.

Sarkin, J., Steyn, E., Van Zyl Smit, E.D. and Paschke, R. (2000) 'The constitutional court's bail decision: individual liberty in crisis?', *South African Journal of Human Rights*, 16(2): 292–312.

Schönteich, M. (2000) 'South Africa's arsenal of terrorism legislation', *African Security Review*, 9(2): 39–50.

Seekings, J. and Murray, C. (1998) *Lay Assessors in South Africa's Magistrates' Courts*. Cape Town: Law, Race and Gender Unit, University of Cape Town.

Sekhonyane, M. (2002) 'Showing its teeth: the Jali Commission on prison corruption', *SA Crime Quarterly*, 2: 27–30.

Shaw, M. and Shearing, C. (1998) 'Reshaping security: an examination of the governance of security in South Africa', *African Security Review*, 7(3): 3–12.

Skelton, A. (1999) 'Juvenile justice reform: children's rights and responsibilities versus crime control', in C.J. Davel (ed.) *Children's Rights in a Transitional Society*. Pretoria: Protea House.

Skelton, A. (2002) 'Restorative justice as a framework for juvenile justice reform: a South African perspective', *British Journal of Criminology*, 42(3): 496–513.

Sloth-Nielsen, J. (2001) 'The role of internatinal law in juvenile justice reform in South Africa.' Unpublished PhD dissertation, University of the Western Cape.

Van der Spuy, E. (1997) 'Regionalism in policing: from lessons in Europe to developments in Southern Africa', *African Security Review*, 6(6): 46–53.

Van der Spuy, E. (2000) 'Foreign donor assistance and policing reform in South Africa', *Policing and Society*, 10: 342–66.

Van der Spuy, E., Geerlings, J. and Singh, A.-M. (1998) *Donor Assistance to Crime Prevention and Criminal Justice Reform in South Africa, 1994–1998*. Report Commissioned by the National Crime Prevention Secretariat. Cape Town: Institute of Criminology, University of Cape Town.

Van Zyl Smit, D. (1987) '"Normal" prisons in an "abnormal" society? A comparative perspective on South African prison law and practice', *Criminal Justice Ethics*, 6(2): 37–51.

Van Zyl Smit, D. (1990) 'Contextualising criminology in contemporary South Africa,' in D. Hansson and D. Van Zyl Smit (eds) *Towards Justice? Crime and State Control in South Africa*. Cape Town: Oxford University Press.

Van Zyl Smit, D. (1992) *South African Prison Law and Practice*. Durban: Butterworths.

Van Zyl Smit, D. (1999) 'Criminological ideas and the South African Transition', *British Journal of Criminology*, 39(2): 198–215.

Van Zyl Smit, D. (2001a) 'South Africa', in D. Van Zyl Smit and F. Dünkel (eds) *Imprisonment Today and Tomorrow: International Perspectives on Prisoners' Rights and Prison Conditions*. The Hague: Kluwer.

Van Zyl Smit, D. (2001b) 'Tough justice: South African style?', in E. Fattah and S. Parmentier (eds) *Victim Policies and Criminal Justice: On the Road to Reformative Justice*. Leuven: Leuven University Press.

Van Zyl Smit, D. (forthcoming) 'Swimming against the tide: controlling the size of the prison population in the new South Africa', in B. Dixon and E. Van der Spuy (eds) *Justice Gained. Crime and Crime Control in South Africa's Transition*. Cape Town: Juta.

Villa-Vincencio, C. (1999) 'Different kind of justice: the South African Truth and Reconciliation Commission', *Contemporary Law Review*, 1(4): 403–28.

Weitzer, R. (1993) 'Transforming the South African police', *Police Studies*, 16(1): 1–10.

Zehr, H. (1997) 'Restorative justice: when justice and healing go together', *Track Two*, 6(3 & 4): 20.

Cases

August and Another *v*. Electoral Commission and Others, 1999 (3) SA 1 (CC).
Carmichele *v*. Minister of Safety and Security and Another, 2001 (4) SA 938 (CC).
Goldberg *v*. Minister of Prisons. 1979 (1) SA 14 (A).
Government of the Republic of South Africa and Others *v*. Grootboom and Others, 2001 (1) SA 46 (CC).
Minister of Correctional Services and others *v*. Kwakwa and another, 2002 (4) SA 455 (SCA).
Minister of Health and Others *v*. Treatment Action Campaign and Others (no 2), 2002 (5) SA 721 (CC).
Minister of Justice *v*. Hofmeyr, 1993 (3) SA 131 (A).
S *v*. Dodo, 2001 (3) SA 382 (CC).
S *v*. Malgas, 2001 (2) SA 1222 (SCA).
S *v*. Makwanyane, 1995 (3) 391 (CC).
S *v*. Walters and Another, 2002 (4) SA 613 (CC).
S *v*. Williams and Others, 1995 (3) SA 632 (CC).
Strydom *v*. Minister of Correctional Services, 1999 (3) BCLR 342 (W).
Van Biljon and Others *v*. Minister of Correctional Services and Others, 1997 (4) SA 441 (C).

Statutes

Constitution of the Republic of South Africa Act (Act 200 of 1993).
Constitution of the Republic of South Africa (Act 108 of 1996).
South African Police Service Act (Act 68 of 1995)

Chapter 10

Policy transfer in local crime control: beyond naïve emulation

Kevin Stenson and Adam Edwards

Introduction

This chapter examines the growing salience of policy transfer around issues of local crime control in advanced liberal democracies. Recognising the need for a detailed programme of further research, the chapter questions the transatlantic origins of local partnership approaches to crime control in Britain in the 1980s and 1990s. In this there was a particular emphasis on diagnosing the complex under-pinnings of volume crime and the need to shift resources and focus towards crime prevention, rather than focusing on more reactive and coercive forms of policing and criminal justice. It is noted that policy ideas have also been gleaned from Europe, Australasia and beyond.

Policy ideas about crime control were bound up with programmes for restructuring local governance, for urban renewal and community development with a particular neoliberal emphasis on the need for commercial leadership in urban regeneration. The applicability of this governing strategy was limited in the British context, where business had not, since the rise of the welfare state, accepted such a leading role in local governance. This led to significant modifications of the US models in creating approaches more suited to local conditions in the UK. Greater efforts were made in the UK by central government at first to bypass the role of elected local government, devising modes of governance to drive through reforms. Yet the failure of business to lead created a space for local, public authorities to reassert a leading role for themselves in partnerships for urban renewal.

Secondly, it is argued that this illustrates how policies and directives emanating from central ministries are dependent for the implementation of policy on actors at subordinate tiers of governance. This gives rise to the probability of an 'implementation gap' in the realisation of policy. This usually creates some space at local levels for resistance, avoidance and the reinterpretation of attempts to enact sovereign government locally. Hence, reinforced by the emergence of the fluid partnership modes of local governance of crime control, this produced discretionary space for local coalitions of political actors. This enabled them to diagnose, differentially, local issues of crime control and promote locally appropriate solutions favouring the viewpoints and interests of particular groups. This is illustrated by reference to studies of local coalitions involved in crime control and involves a full recognition of the choices, formation of alliances and the emotional and habituated character of ways of conceptualising problems of crime and responding to them. Moreover, at subnational levels, it is argued that there are considerable variations in the ways that national policies are appropriated and tailored for local use. However, the New Labour government in the UK has attempted to increase central control and limit the scope for local discretion.

Thirdly, despite this complexity and variation in the contexts in which policies are implemented, the chapter explores the way in which leading academic and policy discourses have constructed problems and solutions in depoliticised, 'technical' forms. These inhibit the capacity and willingness within official policy-making circles to recognise and debate the subtleties, variations in context, clashes of interest and culture that make up the local politics of crime control. This 'technical' discourse depicts a commonality in the problems facing the advanced liberal democracies. It also attempts to provide the discursive means to translate between the various professional discourses of the agencies tasked with crime control in multifarious ways. These discourses employ forms of rhetoric that, using research-based notions of acceptable evidence, emphasise the similarity of local conditions and the transferability of problems of government and solutions to them. This generates a key question for policy-makers, policing and criminal justice practitioners, and criminologists: to what extent can universal elements of policies be identified and then emulated irrespective of the diverse social contexts across which they are transferred? This requires us to open up new ways of conceptualising and analysing contexts.

Local politics of crime control

An awareness of processes of economic, cultural and political globalisation has influenced crime control policy principally by drawing attention to the purported 'threat' of transnational organised crime and attempts to control a range of cross-border crimes. These may include, for example, transnational policies and partnership policing initiatives to control illegal drugs markets, terrorism, the smuggling of contraband and illegal immigrants (Edwards and Gill 2003). However, there has also been an international trade in ways of understanding, and acting upon, more mundane, local, volume crimes. These include, for example, routine acquisitive crimes, crimes against the person, anti-social behaviour and criminal damage to the immediate environment with graffiti and other means. This has also been accompanied by a growing emphasis on shifting resources away from reactive policing and criminal justice responses towards crime prevention. Let us recognise two analytically distinguishable but, in practice, often intertwined forms of intellectual trade. On the one hand there are academic analyses and secondly those created by policy advisers and civil servants (sometimes drawing on academic knowledge) employed to provide politicians and ministers with governmental *savoir*: the intellectual instruments and substantive data that drive, shape and provide rationales for the governing process. These are the ideas and instruments, or technologies in the widest sense, which make problems, populations and targeted, risky geographical areas thinkable and measurable for the purposes of government (Stenson 1991, 1998, 1999).

Influential university-based theoretical narratives emphasise that in a range of 'late modern' societies there are common economic, cultural and political conditions that create problems of crime, fear and insecurity and the institutional determinants of penal responses to these problems (Taylor 1999; Young 1999). It is argued these conditions have created a 'culture of control' (Garland 2001). This is seen as marked by an increasing cultural sensitivity, reflected in the media and elsewhere, towards crime, insecurity and penality, and has lead to the rapid growth both in the political salience of crime control and the growth of the commercial security market. These institutionalised social control responses are seen as responses not to media exaggeration of everyday threats but to historically high crime rates and a declining faith in the ability of the institutions of the state and criminal justice system alone to manage crime, fear and insecurity. Governments have been faced with rapid inward demographic movements from poor countries and increasingly diverse, unequal, potentially disorderly and risk-prone populations. In these conditions, among the key governmental problems shared by governing elites at different spatial levels in a range of advanced societies, are how to assess and manage the new forms of risk posed by these changes and how best to restore government to disorderly areas and populations (Stenson 2001).

However, in response to these generalising academic narratives, there have been criticisms that the dominant academic explanations rely too much on vaguely defined structural forces or trends. This is at the expense of recognising the role of intentional political actors, since only human beings act, not structural forces. This refers to the role of calculating individuals and groups involved in interpreting problems, formulating goals and negotiating the complex, conflictual stages of the policy process from initial formulation to the apparent convergence in style and substance in these policy trends. These critics have emphasised that, in making sense, for example, of the transfer of policies relating to zero-tolerance policing or prison privatisation, there is a need to unpack what is meant by 'policy'. There may, for example, be much similarity between locations in the forms of policy style, symbols or rhetoric. Yet national and subnational differences may be more apparent when focusing on the substantive content and the specific regulatory, administrative, judicial and other policy instruments used in each setting (Dolowitz and Marsh 2000; Jones and Newburn 2002).

The institutions of policing and criminal justice perform manifold functions. Yet, mindful of this caveat, in focusing on the substance of crime control policy we emphasise three focal clusters of policy that have become increasingly salient in the last 20 years and which usually operate in varying hybrid combinations in local settings. These include liberal 'community security' initiatives involved in the 'turn to the local' in crime control: problem-solving and intelligence-led, community policing, crime prevention and community/restorative justice initiatives, usually bound up with programmes of urban regeneration. Secondly, there are target-hardening/situational crime prevention initiatives that strengthen the defences against the offender through the use of CCTV, environmental redesign and so on. This can be viewed as a counterpart to the increasing emphasis on risk assessment and management in judicial and ancillary penal practices, sometimes at the expense of retributive and rehabilitative measures. Thirdly, there is the familiar conservative lexicon of punitive means employed to maintain sovereign control over disorderly populations and neighbourhoods. This includes zero-tolerance/quality of life and SWAT squad, militarised policing, the war on drugs, 'three strikes and you're out' sentencing policies and, in the USA, the use of the death penalty (Stenson and Edwards 2001, 2003).

Let us explore this further by briefly examining the development of community security approaches since the early 1980s within the overall political and economic contexts, at different spatial levels, within which they operated in the USA and the UK. While there may be similarities in the form, rhetoric and styles of policies, their meaning and impact are likely to vary considerably in the light of these differences in context.

American borrowings: intervening at the local level

The new programmes, strategies and technologies of local regeneration and crime control developed during the 1980s draw on familiar themes, first developed by the Chicago Area Project in the 1920s and 1930s to foster greater communal self-organisation among poor immigrant communities. These were refined in many cities over the generations (Sampson *et al*. 1997). However, the new feature here was the shift in political and economic context provided by New Right national administrations on both sides of the Atlantic. In particular, these local policy strategies operated during the progressive withdrawal by state agencies from assuming *long-term* responsibility for the welfare of the generality of citizens, particularly through the use of demand management policies in the efforts to maintain full (male) employment. This shift in the wider context and the rise of New Right public administration were accompanied by demands for new, pluralistic forms of public governance that traversed the boundaries of statutory, commercial and not-for-profit voluntary agencies (Stenson 2000). This new climate also placed a heavy burden of expectations on what local agencies and initiatives may achieve. Hence, the principal modern exemplars for British urban regeneration and crime prevention models were developed in the USA during the administrations of Ronald Reagan and George Bush senior (Davis 1993; Hope 1995).

This period of neoliberal experimentation signalled a retreat (consolidated under Clinton's New Democrat presidency) from the traditional assumptions, established during Roosevelt's New Deal in the 1930s, about the responsibilities of the state to maintain full employment and safety nets for the poor. This heralded an attempt to open up the protected US economy to the global marketplace, offset by the development of pump-priming regeneration initiatives, many federally funded and sponsored by the National Institute of Justice. These were accompanied by apparently liberal/progressive strategies of problem-solving community policing, and targeted towards a token number of those areas and populations in the deindustrialising cities, which were the salvageable casualties of the new political economy (Goldstein 1990; BJA 1997; NIJ 1998). Hence, the goals were simultaneously to 'weed' crime and serious criminals from areas in decline, while 'seeding' optimistic regenerative initiatives for the future, in the hope that developments would be 'sustainable' in the longer term, through local citizen and business initiatives. As in other policy spheres, the new governmental discourses emphasise the need to loosen the boundaries and barriers between agency responsibilities in the development of entrepreneurial partnerships between statutory, voluntary and commercial organisations.

This is indicative of a general feature of policy frameworks in societies that have undergone neoliberal reforms. Universalism in public service provision and the pursuit of social justice are replaced by the logic of targeting. This involves getting scarce resources to high-risk problems, areas and population groups where they are allegedly needed most in such a way that does not alienate the majority (Hough and Tilley 1998). There is an increasing distrust of big government and reluctance to part with taxes in order to help the poor and the weak (Galbraith 1993). In Britain, targeted interventions were developed by Conservative administrations between 1979 and 1997. It is argued that the economic reforms of these administrations generated high unemployment, social disaffection and civil unrest (Benyon and Solomos 1987). In turn these were dealt with by the punitive use of policing and criminal justice to restore order. Yet, Lord Scarman's report into the riots of 1981 emphasised the need to supplement a tough enforcement of sovereign law with the amelioration of social conditions (Scarman 1981). The Conservative response must be understood in terms of the overall accompanying political and economic, as well as ideological, contexts.

It was argued, in key policy statements, that crime prevention cannot be left to the police alone, but is a task for the whole community (Home Office 1984, 1990). The publication of these policy statements can be regarded as a major symbolic turning point in helping to generate a substantial shift in the governance of crime. It was convenient for a Conservative administration wishing to distance itself from crime control policy failures, while maintaining its rejection of the welfare state. This was accompanied by reductions in central state grants to (predominantly non-Tory) elected local authorities and a reduction of their statutory powers and their capacity to raise local taxes. Direct local control over key services like education, social housing, youth services, the police and social services was steadily eroded and replaced by new 'quangos', organisations directed by compliant ministerial appointees, dispensing funding to partnerships of statutory, commercial and voluntary agencies (Loveday 1994; Jenkins 1996). A series of state-funded urban regeneration initiatives were developed.

At the heart of these initiatives was a preference for American-style urban development initiatives. For example, the London and Mersey-side Docklands Development Corporations were developed through the 1980s with state pump-priming funding. The premise of these corporations was that commercial entrepreneurs should assume the leadership of urban regeneration, encouraging ambitious professional people to recolonise urban centres, in the, as it turned out, misplaced hope that the fruits of growth would 'trickle down' to local poor populations (Jacobs 1992). Later examples of neoliberal, US-inspired urban development and crime reduction initiatives included City Challenge, Housing Action Trusts and Safer Cities. By 1994, Safer Cities had initiated more than 3,300 crime prevention and community safety measures, with Home Office funding totalling £20.4 million (Bright 1991; Home Office 1993; Tilley 1993; Hughes 1996). Its agenda included, for example, improvements in home, high street and neighbourhood security through architectural redesign and the installation of security cameras, courses in personal safety and diversionary activities for the young perceived to be at risk. The partnership-based programme initially provided a low-key role for local authorities in ways that reduced their discretionary power and retained organising power in the hands of Home Office officials and their proxies.

In the crime prevention sphere, two tax-funded quangos acted as proxies for the Home Office: Crime Concern and NACRO (the National Association for the Care and Resettlement of Offenders). They have played a key co-ordinating role, disseminating standards of perceived good practice nationally. This also formed part of the central government agenda to circumvent what was viewed as local government obstruction and stalling. In turn, the intellectuals in these organisations and Home Office officials were and still are locked into complex networks, or intellectual circuits of power (Stenson 1991), with their counterparts in other countries, in government departments, think-tanks and the Eisenhower and other charitable foundations in the USA. While trade in policy themes covered a wide range there was a bias towards target-hardening/situational crime prevention initiatives and the punitive sovereign initiatives associated, for example, with what was popularly known as 'zero-tolerance policing'. These intellectual themes focusing on crime reduction in the narrow sense were reinforced in numerous transatlantic exchanges in the 1980s and 1990s under both Conservative and New Labour administrations. These made senior American criminologists, political scientists, politicians and police chiefs like James Q. Wilson, George Kelling, Larry Sherman, Rudolph Giuliani and William Bratton favoured guests in the Home Office and other senior UK policy-making circles. Similarly, British criminologists like Leslie Wilkins and Ron Clarke, the first Director of the Home Office's Crime prevention Unit, were significant British influences in the USA.

These personal links were accompanied by institutional bonds linking, for example, the Institutes of Criminology at Oxford and Cambridge Universities and the Home Office with the National Institute of Justice and the Eisenhower Foundation in Washington, Rutgers University, John Jay College of Criminal Justice, New York City and the University of Chicago. Furthermore, these exchanges were reinforced by similar links within western Europe and between Britain and Australia, for example, under the auspices of the European Institute for Crime Prevention and Control, Affiliated with the United Nations (HEUNI) based in Helsinki (Graham and Bennett 1995; Stenson and Edwards 2003). Through these means they exchanged information about how to conceptualise problems and policy solutions, and how best to evaluate interventions. However, despite these transatlantic links, because of structural and cultural similarities between European societies, there remained a pull in the UK towards the formation of policies that tried to reinvent initiatives that are more European and social democratic in character. Under the auspices of the EU and the United Nations, the traffic of personnel and ideas is particularly strong between the UK, Europe and Australasia (Graham and Bennett 1995; Bright 1997).

However, in the UK, British corporations failed to match the public role performed by American corporations. By contrast with the UK, in the US corporations had for long played a fuller role in local urban governance, reinforced by fierce competition by urban managers for inward investment and the greater scope for local taxation (Logan and Molotch 1987; Stone 1989). By contrast, in the UK, there was limited scope for local taxation and hence locally directed, grand policy initiatives. Since the rise of the welfare state the business community had grown accustomed to expecting the state and municipal authorities to provide infrastructure and a congenial framework of governance for enterprise (Stoker 1998; Harding 2000). Hence, by the mid-1980s it became apparent that commercial firms were reluctant to take a long-term strategic view of regeneration and this created a space for local public authorities adopting the logic of targeted interventions.

In response to criticisms about fragmentation of initiatives and problems of leadership, a joint state ministries fund, the Single Regeneration Budget (SRB), was set up and administered by the regional offices of central government, dispensing £1.4 billion on a competitive bidding basis in 1994–5, its first year of operation. SRB allocation criteria emphasised that projects should recognise the interdependence of crime prevention and reduction with environmental improvements, training initiatives, programmes for youth and economic stimulation in a virtuous and *holistic* reform programme. The goals of these programmes were to provide short-term 'pump-priming' investment, rather than the provision – under the auspices of a solidaristic 'social' model – of long-term, routine, directly tax-funded services dispensed by salaried professionals. The goal of community-building policy rhetoric included a moral agenda: to boost the confidence and political and entrepreneurial skills of those perceived as poor, dependent and disadvantaged, so that they may take charge of their own lives and neighbourhoods in ways acceptable to authorities (Department of the Environment 1994; Stenson and Watt 1999a).

Sovereignty, power dependence and governance from below

Local authorities – particularly those led by the Labour and Liberal Parties – exploited this strategic space by shifting the emphasis in crime control away from reactive policing and criminal justice towards holistic crime prevention as an element of community building. In this the policy discourses generated by Crime Concern and NACRO covertly aided them. A major impetus for this was the deep disillusionment with the performance of the barely accountable police and other formal bureaucracies responsible for crime control and justice. This reminds us that the struggle for sovereignty is never complete. Even in the most coercive and hierarchical polity, commands require the active interpretation of signals and compliance of subordinate agents, and even more so in liberal polities. There is always an 'implementation gap' between legislative and policy commands emanating from above and governmental practice, given the necessary dependence of would-be rulers on subordinate actors for the actual exercise of their power (Latour 1986; Rhodes 1997).

It is in the interstices of this power dependence that local actors can resist, contest and manipulate central commands to fit their own agendas. Because of this, we need to transcend the general narratives that identify the common ingredients of the local governance of crime.

217

We need to develop, through empirical research, analytic tools that facilitate an understanding of local differences in the play of community governance, and the local forms of 'habitus' among political agents: the cultural, emotional and instrumental repertoires and dispositions for cognition and action. We can understand this at two levels. First, there is a local politics of crime control involving the statutory agencies. Secondly, there is a level at which official agencies blur into the more informal sites of governance, involving, for example, spontaneous, angry gatherings, residence associations, ethnic, religious and even criminal groupings. These sites of governance do not necessarily minute their meetings but may, none the less, play a significant role in local governance (Stenson and Watt 1999b).

At a national level, local authorities, for example, organised and lobbied to extend their scope of discretionary action and hence define and respond to issues in the light of local conditions. With their national policy-making bodies, the Association of Metropolitan Authorities and Association of District Councils, they broadened the ethos of and domain assumptions about crime control beyond target-hardening/ situational crime prevention to embrace community security technologies that focused on the social and economic causes of crime (Howett et al. 1994). This philosophy was usually labelled under the heading of 'community safety' and was articulated in the Home Office-commissioned Morgan Report published in 1991 (Home Office Standing Conference 1991). The Morgan Report was produced by a working group that was established by the Home Office Standing Conference on Crime Prevention but was independent of the Home Office itself and invited to appraise government policy on local crime prevention and make recommendations for the local delivery of crime prevention through the partnership approach. This advocated holistic approaches to community safety and community regeneration linking, for example, employment, drugs and health education, youth work and training programmes, community development programmes and neighbour-hood initiatives.

However, notwithstanding this progressive drive, local authorities usually stopped short of including white-collar crime and other crimes of the local powerful elites within their agenda of concerns. Though the Morgan Report was not endorsed by central government it provided a further stimulus to local authorities to develop policy and an embryonic cadre of community safety specialists at local levels. It should be emphasised that this creative, locally driven agenda coincided during the early 1990s with a sharp economic recession, high levels of unemployment, especially among young people, and tough, punitive policing responses to major public order disturbances in poor, predominantly white areas of social housing.

This impetus was not confined to traditionally left-wing areas. For example, in the Thames Valley, a heartland of neoliberal restructuring dominated by the Conservative Party, local coalitions of professional agents involved in the governance of crime had achieved surprising success in prioritising the conceptualisation of volume crime within the terms of a holistic, community safety framework. This provided some shielding from the narrow crime reduction targets set by central government and preferred by many local councillors (Stenson 2002). This illustrates the need for further accounts of the uneven ways in which political rationalities and governmental technologies are configured in different localities by competing coalitions of actors (Hughes and Edwards 2002).

Turning to the more immediately local politics of crime control, it is *misleading* to focus too much attention on elite policy networks, to see policies as principally their creation and local conditions important mainly as providing obstacles to the implementation of centralised, perhaps imported, policy handed down from the top. Such a view neglects the fact that policy agendas can also emerge from below through local political alliances and complex local conditions (Hancock 2001). These involve a variety of formal and less formal sites of governance and through upsurges in public opinion and even full-scale moral panics involving local and national communications media (Stenson 1999; Edwards and Hughes 2002). For example, where there are fierce, and often ethnically inflected, local struggles about issues like the impact of prostitution on local neighbourhoods, the siting of holding centres for 'asylum seekers', the release from prison of paedophiles into poor neighbourhoods, youth crime and illegal drugs markets, there are usually struggles to translate issues into forms that will disrupt and forge alliances.

These alliances involve attempts to construct and mobilise coalitions of supporters around preferred ways of defining and responding to problems of crime and other social harms (Stenson and Edwards 2001: 75–81). It is usually at the local level that the fiercest passions and disputes are played out, grabbing the attention of local and national politicians, and the media, eager to exploit swings in public sentiment. In addition, this is where we often find the greatest challenges for the establishment and legitimation of liberal sovereign authority. In this climate, in the mix of local crime control measures, punitive controls have become increasingly salient in recent years. This results not just from the strengthening of the top-down command and control capacities of central government. Indeed, the policy push from the centre manifests the increasing power and influence of the media at local and national levels in representing 'punitive-populist' sentiment about crime control. It also manifests the increasing ability of directly active local coalitions to set the agenda in demanding that the police and local and national governing agencies employ more coercive, punitive methods in dealing with those offenders granted folk-devil status (Stenson and Edwards 2001; Ryan 2003).

The dynamics involved in this can be further illustrated by research. During the 1990s Conservative national administration, in a study of community governance in Labour-controlled Leicester and Nottingham, in the East Midlands of England, it was found that, despite local political-economic similarities, conditions on municipal housing estates were apprehended differently in each case (Edwards 2002). These examples revealed two distinct approaches to policy-making, and in part were driven by, competing approaches to researching crime and disorder. In Leicester, coalitions prioritised problematisations of youth crime principally in terms of opportunity reduction, emphasising punitive sovereign law enforcement practices that, in effect, heightened the social exclusion of marginal groups. The knowledge base for the diagnosis of youth issues relied mainly on a standard quantitative research audit into patterns of 'hotspots' of youth crime and the interpretation of these patterns by elite policy-makers. On this basis, 'template', 'off-the-shelf' models of youth crime prevention were applied irrespective of the priorities of local people.

By contrast, in Nottingham, coalitions prioritised a problematisation that highlighted community safety and community security technologies in ways that were more inclusive of marginalised groups. In Nottingham local residents, parents and young people themselves were enrolled in the process of identifying, interpreting and responding to issues of juvenile delinquency from the outset of the crime prevention strategies adopted. The approach could be best described as that of 'participatory action research' (PAR) in which the particular knowledge and experience of local citizens were revealed and valued though qualitative interviews, discussion groups and meetings in addition to statistically based surveys. Rather than the detailed consultation and deliberation entailed in PAR being seen as an impediment to good crime control (cf. Liddle and Gelsthorpe 1994: 4–9), this very source of problems could be viewed as precisely the opportunity to reinvigorate democratic and liberal values, through bringing conflicts out into the domain of public struggle. Where the 'voice' of local citizens is subordinated to the top-down imposition of crime control strategies, these strategies are unlikely to be sustainable as the necessary participation of these local citizens is jeopardised by their alienation from the process of policy *formulation* as well as implementation.

Hence, we can see that the effective transfer of crime control policies is dependent on the capacity of decision-makers to translate problems of crime and disorder into terms which resonate with the interests and lived experiences of citizens in particular localities. Conceptually, this process of transfer implies the identification of those qualities of crime and its control that are genuinely generic, and therefore sufficiently robust to withstand transfer across diverse social contexts, and an understanding of those contingent qualities which are generated by locally specific social conditions.

New Labour: strengthening policy implementation from the centre

After the accession of new Labour in 1997 the ingredients of local crime control policy, with their locally tailored versions of US policy themes under the Conservatives, were retained and extended. Nevertheless, a key criticism of Conservative policy had been that their crime control policies were principally aimed to protect the affluent Tory suburbs (Rose 1996). In this context, there was now a particular emphasis on the struggle for local sovereign control and a greater effort to apply central, new public management, target setting and auditing controls to maximise the prospects of successful implementation. Despite, eventually, increased investment in the public services during the second term of office after 2001 and targeted support for poor families with family tax credit and other measures, major economic redistribution was ruled out. So, law and order policy assumed salience in the struggle to construct Labour's fragile electoral balance between its various constituencies; it had to discover new ways to ameliorate social dislocation and inequalities.

At the heart of this strategy was a commitment to use punitive sovereign technologies to re-establish control over poorer residential as well as central, public locations. A central promise made by New Labour was that disorderly areas, dominated by youth gangs, criminal networks and vigilante groups, must be reconquered for the respectable working classes. This would attempt to honour the Hobbesian contract for government to provide an inclusive security even for those unable to buy it as a commodity in the burgeoning commercial security market. Hence, New Labour endorsed US zero tolerance, and a range of other punitive sovereign approaches (Stenson 2001; Jones and Newburn 2002). These included, for example, anti-social behaviour orders restraining 'neighbours from hell' and curfew orders for young offenders, measures that were contained in the Crime and Disorder Act 1998.

Spurred by the vengeful tabloid press, populist punitive rhetoric has played a significant role in determining policy and sentencing trends in the courts. Tough policing was reinforced by a commitment to increase the prison population (at the time of writing to over 72,000 inmates and rising) and to taunt left, 'liberal' critics of such policies. The New Labour legislative programme announced in the Queen's Speech in November 2002 reinforced the punitive sovereign message. In essence the aim was to rebalance the criminal justice process more in favour of the rights of victims rather than offenders. This was to be achieved, for example, by toughening penalties for anti-social behaviour and sex offenders, limiting the rights to jury trial and informing juries about defendants' previous criminal records. This centralising tendency, whatever its inevitable limits, hence reduced the discretionary scope for the local tailoring of policy.

However, a range of community security initiatives has complemented tough technologies of sovereign crime control. They include, for example, restorative and community justice initiatives, community, problem-solving and intelligence-led policing and local urban regeneration strategies. These are complemented by preventive technologies in scope and aim. This was buttressed by the commitment to a communitarian morality, to investment in social entrepreneurship and social capital at local levels and to a greater role for the third, voluntary, not-for-profit sector. These initiatives range from parent support programmes for potentially criminogenic families at risk, funded under the SureStart (echoing the US Headstart) programme; the New Deal and other educational and training initiatives to get people from welfare to work; efforts to reduce school exclusion, domestic violence and autocrime; the introduction of drug treatment sentences first introduced in Florida; and the New Deal for Communities. The latter has invested not only in material infrastructure to regenerate poor, high-crime areas but also in the human capital of the local population.

The complex range of ingredients was developed principally in the Crime and Disorder Act 1998. In conjunction with a range of welfare and other reforms drawing heavily on models developed by the New Democrats in the USA, the new administration tried to recast policies to emphasise the interaction of tough and tender policies: 'tough on crime and its causes.' A key ingredient of the new ideological glue binding

New Labour policies is the attempt to retreat from narrowly egoistic, consumerist and rights-based values associated with the neoliberal right. The new direction draws from Christian socialism and Amitai Etzioni's version of communitarianism. Etzioni proved an effective US intellectual ambassador for these themes in visits to senior New Labour policy-makers in Britain. Just as under the US New Democrat adminis-tration in the 1990s, this philosophy emphasises duty, civic values, responsibility and good parenting, and was bound up with 'tough love' policies to limit and reorder the rights to welfare (Hughes 1996).

The new policy framework was also committed, as in health and other areas of social policy, to an evidence-based approach that involved social science in establishing the policy and cost-effectiveness of all inter-ventions. Accompanied by the announcement of a crime reduction budget of several hundred million pounds, with rich opportunities for criminological evaluation contracts, this perspective was crystallised in a key Home Office document, *Reducing Offending* (Goldblatt and Lewis 1998). This document attempted to bring together all that was known through high-quality (particularly in quantitatively based studies) research about the following:

- Preventing criminality among young people and investing in situational crime prevention measures to reduce opportunities for offending.
- Preventing crime in the community through effective policing and community development measures.
- Criminal justice interventions through changes in sentencing policy or extending the use of effective interventions with offenders and drug users.

However, recent commentators have argued that there are increasing tensions set up by the struggle to impose a uniform crime control policy agenda from the centre by means of target setting, auditing, the creation of performance tables and other instruments of the new public management. New Labour policy frameworks appear to offer less scope for local authorities and crime reduction multi-agency partnerships to construct local policy in the light of local conditions. Broader, holistic, joined-up 'community safety' agendas are giving way to an increasing emphasis on targeted programmes of crime reduction, with a focus, for example, on burglary, anti-social behaviour and street robbery (Hughes 2002; Stenson 2002).

Governmental *savoir*

The analysis we have presented emphasises the need to recognise the political, cultural and economic contexts within which internationally mobile policy ideas emerge and are applied and which can vary their meaning and impact. Crime control at every spatial level is not simply a technical, administrative application of black-letter law but is an increasingly central arena of political conflict. This may seem an unremarkable, even banal, claim to an audience of political science and social policy academics, or streetwise politically active citizens. It is, however, especially pertinent in a policy-making climate characterised by the downgrading by politicians and policy-makers of political analysis that may pose, for example, awkward questions about values, policy goals and unintended consequences. This has been replaced by a preference for the apparently neutral 'technical' work of state-sponsored criminological academics, promoting purportedly objective, 'scientific' criteria for 'what works, what doesn't and what's promising' in the transfer and emulation of 'best practice' in local crime control. A key moment in the consolidation of this governmental discourse of crime control came when the leading US criminologist, Larry Sherman, was asked in 1996, on behalf of the US congress, to provide a comprehensive evaluation of the effectiveness of the Department of Justice's grants to assist in the prevention of crime – through a systematic evaluation of 'what works' in crime control (Sherman *et al.* 1997). This knowledge base also provided an agenda for further policy-oriented research and provided a template for the aforementioned Home Office review in 1998 of evidence for what does and does not work in reducing offending (Goldblatt and Lewis 1998; Tilley 2002).

These policy-oriented forms of knowledge may draw on academic analyses but function primarily as governmental *savoir*, or the intellectual instruments of government (Foucault 1991; Stenson 1991, 1998; Stenson and Watt 1999a). They are conditioned by their role in helping the politician and civil service policy-maker create diagnoses of problems and tailor appropriate solutions, including the creation of operational indicators and targets in order to evaluate success or failure. These policy models have become increasingly important since the early 1980s with the rise of the neoliberal focus on the need for economy, efficiency and effectiveness in public service delivery: the use of market disciplines in the public services and the development thereby of a new public management ethos. Expenditure is expected to be directed to those policies that have been proved to have 'worked', as determined by research that has met the governmentally approved criteria for what may count as acceptable methodology, sample sizes, theoretical frameworks and so on (Hope 2002; Hope and Karstedt 2003).

Some of the discursive roots of the policy discourses of partnership-based local crime control have long provenance. Yet, since the early 1980s, there has been a pressing need for new ways of describing problems, driving forward the agendas and organisational forms of the new local governance. The different practitioner disciplines of policing, education, health, probation and so on had been used to describe and conceptualise issues in their own terms. The new emphasis on linking reactive with problem-solving policing and the various stages of crime prevention from parenting support to initiatives to divert youth from crime required new forms of 'joined-up-thinking'. Hence, one of the central features of this reconstruction of public government through crime control has been the effort to produce a lingua franca. The aim of this is to enable professionals in partner agencies to communicate with each other and, more significantly, provides rhetorical encouragement to partnership work (Ekblom 1996).

These developments have created continuities, in the UK, for example, between Conservative and New Labour administrations. The new emphasis, orchestrated by the Home Office's Crime Prevention Unit set up in 1983, on situational crime prevention, was accompanied by an attempt to provide an overarching theoretical rationale provided by rational choice theories, newly fashionable in cognitive psychology and other disciplines. In this case they were applied to offending behaviour and helped to shift – without wholly displacing – the policy emphasis away from older 'social' attempts to deal with the alleged psychological and socioeconomic root causes of, or dispositions towards, crime.

This was aided during this period in the UK by the (continuing) hegemony within the Home Office of criminologists whose original training and principal disciplinary allegiance was to psychology. This is a discipline in which, since the 1970s, cognitive psychology had achieved ascendancy, and which is intellectually ill-equipped to facilitate the critique of policy and practice. This derives from its tendency to picture the social world reductively as made up of interacting individuals. Approaches more commonly found in other social science disciplines are more likely to conceptualise social and economic relations as having an institutional reality beyond individual persons and visible groups and give rise to more subtle attempts to understand the links between human agency and the wider structural contexts that help to shape thought and action (Ritzer 1992: 427–56). This psychological bias gives rise to an inability to conceptualise the constraints upon and opportunities for action that are established by different policy environments. Hence, these criminologists prefer quasi-experimental models of policy analysis and institutionalised evaluation criteria that inhibit the exploration of the impact and the political complexity of problems embodied in the formulation, implementation and evaluation of programmes. These impoverished intellectual models retain a powerful hold on this and other areas of public policy (Hope and Karstedt 2003).

Using this psychological lens, for example, ambitious, comprehensive, social crime prevention initiatives appear difficult to measure and tend to be viewed as separate from crime reduction strategies, defined more narrowly. While high-profile grant-aid programmes, such as the New Deal for Communities, Surestart and Connexions, were introduced during the first term of office of the New Labour administration (1997–2001) with an explicit social crime prevention brief, the focus of Home Office expenditure remained upon reducing situational opportunities for crime and enhancing law enforcement operations. Indeed, it has been argued that while experiments in 'joining up' crime prevention with social policies on education, employment and housing, etc., progressed in many metropolitan community safety strategies during the Morgan Report era, they have subsequently been marginalised in guidance and funding criteria provided to the statutory crime and disorder partnerships established under the Crime and Disorder Act 1998 (Hughes 2000). The danger is that, notwithstanding rhetoric about the need for 'joined-up policy', crime reduction is seen as separate and relatively disconnected in organisation and delivery from strategies to deal with the deeper causes of crime. It remains to be seen to what extent the core local police/local authority partnerships downgrade dealing with deeper causes in the new policy climate.

In addition, it is important to understand the broader context of changes to public expenditure patterns in which the funds accorded to these grant-aid programmes at the national level are swiftly dissipated into highly targeted interventions in certain localities (Stenson and Edwards 2001, 2003). Not only is the impact of these interventions diffused by the relatively paltry funding they provide to local partnerships but their impact has also been further affected by key changes to the calculation of central government financial support to local government. This has resulted in a redistribution of support grant finance from the affluent district authorities of the south east of England, which include significant pockets of deprivation, to local authorities in relatively poorer districts in the north of England. There is, therefore, an effective net loss of public expenditure in southern districts where national government has retrieved more in core funding than it has given back out in competitive grant aid (Stenson 2002).

There is some awareness among policy-makers of the need to recognise diverse local conditions. The new message to local partnership crime control groups is to abandon a 'one size fits all' formulaic approach in favour of a bespoke one, tailored to local conditions (Bright 1997). This was, for example, the message to local crime reduction partnerships provided by the Home Office's guidance notes for the undertaking of crime audits and crime control strategy as required by the Crime and Disorder Act 1998 (Home Office 1998). Logically this should lead to enlarging the scope for local discretion and devolution of budgets for community safety. Yet, to reinforce the point that has already been made, central government has amassed a growing battery of centralising powers, which have curtailed the independent policy-making and budgetary powers of local police and municipal authorities. In addition, powerful central bodies like the Audit Commission and other regulatory agencies have been charged to monitor whether agencies at local level meet centrally set performance indicators. There are already indications that this 'action at a distance' control through 'performance culture' thus serves to shift the emphasis once more towards fostering a timid compliance with formulaic measures that are presented as benchmarks of good practice (McLaughlin and Murji 2001). At worst, this may pressure local policy-makers towards a naïve emulation of measures that in very different settings have, it is claimed, been shown to have 'worked'.

Conclusion: reconceptualising the contexts of government

Certain implications for the dynamics of policy transfer follow from the desire to avoid such naïve emulation. These can be usefully illustrated through reference to a basic conundrum of lesson-drawing in public policy. This refers to the 'fungibility' of policies. By fungibility we mean the extent to which lesson-drawing across diverse social contexts is both possible and desirable. At one extreme, policies are viewed as totally transferable, in the way that production plans for the assemblage of automobiles can be replicated in any locality whether Detroit, Dagenham or Cologne. At the other extreme, the transferability of policies is seen as totally blocked by the unique culture, history and institutions of a locality (Rose 1993: 34–40). It has been argued, however, that this polarity presents a false dilemma. In this view, total blockage, the idea that policy actors in one locality can learn nothing from those in another time or place, is as implausible as the idea that actors can simply emulate each other's 'best' practices irrespective of the diverse contexts in which these practices originate (Rose 1993: 40–4).

The question for intelligent transfer remains: how to distinguish the generic elements of a policy that will withstand transfer across social contexts from those elements that embody the political, economic and cultural particularities of the contexts in which they were originally developed. In the latter case, the attempted transfer of policies may not just fail but further exacerbate the very problems to which a policy is addressed. Although criminological research has begun to address this need for context-sensitive policy transfer with respect to the transferability of recent innovations, for example experiments in restorative justice (*British Journal of Criminology* 2002), research into the conditions for intelligent transfer is still at a very early stage of development. The desire among UK policy elites to transfer criminological ideas and practices from the USA, Australasia and other European countries for use in crime control in British localities is a defining characteristic of contemporary policy change, evaluation and learning. If, however, the naïve emulation of policies is to be avoided then greater attention needs to be given, in research on policy transfer, to the concept of 'social context' and its effect in filtering, if not 'blocking', the lessons that can be drawn about crime control practice elsewhere.

In this chapter we have suggested that the importance of context, while rhetorically acknowledged in much official criminological discourse on policy evaluation, has been effectively subordinated to the promotion of international standards of 'best practice' on 'what works, what doesn't and what's promising' (Sherman *et al.* 1997). Yet here there is a major tension between policy-makers being sensitive to context and, on the other hand, the promotion of standards that gloss over and forget the contextual qualities of governance (cf. Keith 1993; Lacey and Zedner 1995). This tension is clarified when the focus of research into policy transfer is shifted from exchanges among elite policy actors operating in *inter*national criminological networks towards the importance of *intra*national policy networks as sources of policy innovation. Once it is recognised that differences within nation-state territories can be greater that differences between them, then taking the nation as the basic unit of policy analysis for transfer and learning cannot be sustained.

Arguably, nation-states are taken as the default units of analysis in debates over policy transfer in crime control because criminal justice is used as the organising framework for understanding policy change. However, criminal justice is but one aspect of crime control, best viewed as a 'wicked issue' that segues across the social policy spectrum. It is a currently fashionable way of coding complex social issues that go well beyond crime. This encourages us to recognise other criteria for organising the spatial and temporal foci of research into policy transfer, beyond national, universal, criminal legal codes and the institutions through which they are implemented. A corollary of this argument is that context is understood in terms of local political, economic and cultural, as well as legal, histories. Consequently, understanding how policy is actually transferred and how, none the less, it could be transferred otherwise can be informed by a programme of comparative research. This would define context, first, in political terms, for example, in terms of the contrasts between unitary, federal governing systems, the forms of party political leadership and so on. Secondly, it would define context in economic terms, for example by reference to the role of different economic sectors such as industrial, financial, agrarian and so on. Thirdly, it would define context in cultural terms. These may include, for example, local sensibilities about place, perceptions of threat, risk and public insecurity, and the everyday cultural traditions and ethos of state police and other governing agencies. Sensitivity to these contextual characteristics would enable us to test for their effects in originating, enabling or blocking policy change and learning about crime control.

References

Benyon, J. and Solomos, J. (eds) (1987) *The Roots of Urban Unrest*. Oxford: Pergamon Press.

Bright, J. (1991). 'Crime prevention: the British experience', in K. Stenson and D. Cowell (eds) *The Politics of Crime Control*. London: Sage.

Bright, J. (1997) *Turning the Tide: Crime, Community and Prevention*. London: Demos.

British Journal of Criminology (2002) Special issue: 'Practice, performance and prospects for restorative justice', 42(3).

Bureau of Justice Assistance (BJA) (1997) *Revitalizing Communities: Innovative State and Local Programs*. Washington, DC: US Department of Justice.

Davis, M. (1993) *Beyond Blade Runner – Urban Control, the Ecology of Fear*. New York, NY: The Free Press.

Department of the Environment (1994) *Bidding Guidance: A Guide to Funding from the Single Regeneration Budget*. London: Department of the Environment.

Dolowitz, D. and Marsh, D. (2000) 'Learning from abroad: the role of policy transfer in contemporary policy-making', *Governance*, 13(1): 5–24.

Edwards, A. (2002). 'Learning from diversity: the strategic dilemmas of community-based crime control, in G. Hughes and A. Edwards (eds) *Crime Control and Community: The New Politics of Public Safety*. Cullompton: Willan.

Edwards, A. and Gill, P. (eds) (2003) *Transnational Organised Crime: Perspectives on Global Security*. London: Routledge.

Edwards, A. and Hughes, G. (2002) 'Introduction: The Community Governance of Crime Control', in G. Hughes and A. Edwards (eds) *Crime Control and Community: The New Politics of Public Safety*. Cullompton: Willan.

Ekblom, P. (1996) 'Towards a discipline of crime prevention: a systematic approach to its nature, range and concepts', in T. Bennett (ed.) *Preventing Crime and Disorder: Targeting Strategies and Responsibilities*. Cambridge: University of Cambridge Institute of Criminology.

Foucault, M. (1991a). 'Governmentality', in G. Burchell *et al.* (eds) *The Foucault Effect: Studies in Governmentality*. Hemel Hempstead: HarvesterWheatsheaf.

Galbraith, J.K. (1993) *The Culture of Contentment*. London: Penguin Books.

Garland, D. (2001). *The Culture of Control: Crime and Social Order in Contemporary Society*. Oxford: Clarendon Press.

Goldblatt, P. and Lewis, C. (eds) (1998) *Reducing Offending: An Assessment of Research Evidence on Ways of Dealing with Offending Behaviour. Home Office Research Study*. London: Home Office.

Goldstein, H. (1990) *Problem-oriented Policing*. New York, NY: McGraw-Hill.

Graham, J. and Bennett, T. (1995) *Crime Prevention Strategies in Europe and North America*. Helsinki: European Institute for Crime Prevention and Control, affiliated with the United Nations.

Hancock, L. (2001) *Community, Crime and Disorder: Safety and Regeneration in Urban Neighbourhoods*. Basingstoke: Palgrave.

Harding, A. (2000) 'Regime Formation in Manchester and Edinburgh,' in G. Stoker (ed.) *The New Politics of British Local Governance*. London: Macmillan.

Home Office (1984) *Circular 8/84: Crime Prevention*. London: Home Office.

Home Office (1990) *Partnership in Crime Prevention*. London: Home Office.

Home Office (1993) *A Practical Guide to Crime Prevention for Local Partnerships*. London: Home Office.

Home Office (1998) *Guidance on Statutory Crime and Disorder Partnerships*. London: Home Office.

Home Office Research and Statistics Directorate (1998) *Reducing Offending: An Assessment of Research Evidence on Ways of Dealing with Offending Behaviour*. London: Home Office.

Home Office Standing Conference on Crime Prevention (1991) *Safer Communities: The Local Delivery of Crime Prevention through the Partnership Approach*. London: Home Office Standing Conference on Crime Prevention.

Hope, T. (1995) 'Community crime prevention', in M. Tonry and D.P. Farrington (eds) *Building a Safer Society: Strategic Approaches to Crime Prevention*. Chicago, IL: Chicago University Press.

Hope, T. (2002) 'The road taken: evaluation, replication and crime reduction', in G. Hughes *et al.* (eds) *Crime Prevention and Community Safety: New directions*. London: Sage/Open University.

Hope, T. and Karstedt, S. (2003) 'Towards a new social crime prevention', in

G. Kury and J. Obergfell-Fuchs (eds) *Crime Prevention – New Approaches*. Weisse: Ring.

Hough, M. and Tilley, N. (1998) *Getting the Grease to the Squeak: Research Lessons for Crime Prevention*. London: Home Office Police Policy Directorate.

Howett, M., Atkinson, A. and Blackman, T. (eds) (1994) *Research for Policy: Proceedings of the 1994 Annual Conference of the Local Authorities Research and Intelligence Association*. Newcastle upon Tyne City Council: LARIA.

Hughes, G. (1996) 'Communitarianism and law and order', *Critical Social Policy*, 16(4): 17–41.

Hughes, G. (2000) 'In the shadow of crime and disorder: the contested politics of community safety', *Crime Prevention and Community Safety: An International Journal*, 2(3): 47–60.

Hughes, G. (2002) 'Plotting the rise of community safety: critical reflections on research, theory and politics', in G. Hughes and A. Edwards (eds) *Crime Control and Community: The New Politics of Public Safety*. Cullompton: Willan.

Hughes, G. and Edwards, A. (eds) (2002). *Crime Control and Community: The New Politics of Public Safety*. Cullompton: Willan.

Jacobs, B. (1992) *Fractured Cities: Capitalism, Community and Empowerment in Britain and America*. London: Routledge.

Jenkins, S. (1996) *Accountable to None: The Tory Nationalisation of Britain*. Harmondsworth: Penguin Books.

Jones, T. and Newburn, T. (2002) 'Policy convergence and crime control in the USA and the UK: streams of influence and levels of impact', *Criminal Justice*, 2(2): 173–203.

Keith, M. (1993) *Race, Riots and Policing: Lore and Disorder in a Multi-racist Society*. London: UCL Press.

Lacey, N. and Zedner, L. (1995) 'Discourses of community in criminal justice', *Journal of Law and Society*, 22(3): 301–25.

Latour, B. (1986). 'The powers of association', in J. Law (ed.) *Power, Action and Belief*. London: Routledge & Kegan Paul.

Liddle, A.M. and Gelsthorpe, L.R. (1994) *Crime Prevention and Inter-agency Co-operation*. London: Home Office.

Logan, J.R. and Molotch, H. (1987) *Urban Fortunes: The Political Economy of Place*. Berkeley, CA: University of California Press.

Loveday, B. (1994) 'Government strategies for community crime prevention', *International Journal of the Sociology of Law*, 22: 181–202.

McLaughlin, E. and Murj, K. (2001) 'Lost Connections and New directions: neo-liberalism, new public managerialism', and the "Modernization of the British Police", in K. Stenson and R. Sullivan (eds) *Crime Risk and Justice: The Politics of crime control in liberal democracies*. Willan: Cullompton.

National Institute of Justice (NIJ) (1998) *What can the Federal Government do to Decrease Crime and Revitalize Communities?* Washington, DC: US Department of Justice.

Rhodes, R.A.W. (1997) *Understanding Governance: Policy Networks, Governance, Reflexivity and Accountability*. Buckingham: Open University Press.

Ritzer, G. (1992) *Contemporary Sociological Theory*. New York, NY: McGraw-Hill.

Rose, R. (1993) *Lesson-drawing in Public Policy: A Guide to Learning across Time and Space*. Chatham, NJ: Chatham House.

Rose, D. (1996) *In the Name of the Law: The Collapse of Criminal Justice*. London: Jonathan Cape.

Ryan, M. (2003) *Penal Policy and Political Culture in England and Wales*. Winchester: Waterside Press.

Sampson, R.J., Raudenbush, S.W. and Earls, F. (1997) 'Neighborhoods and violent crime: a multilevel study of collective efficacy', *Science*, 277(15 August): 1–7.

Scarman, Lord (1981) *The Scarman Report*. Harmondsworth: Penguin Books.

Sherman, L.W. and the National Institute of Justice *et al.* (1997) *Preventing Crime: What Works, What Doesn't, What's Promising: A Report to the United States Congress*. Washington, DC: US Department of Justice Office of Justice Programs.

Stenson, K. (1991) 'Making sense of crime control', in K. Stenson and D. Cowell (eds) *The Politics of Crime Control*. London: Sage.

Stenson, K. (1998) 'Beyond histories of the present', *Economy and Society*, 29(4): 333–52.

Stenson, K. (1999) 'Crime control, governmentality and sovereignty', in R.C. Smandych (ed.) *Governable Places: Readings in Governmentality and Crime Control*. Dartmouth: Ashgate.

Stenson, K. (2000) 'Crime control, social policy and liberalism', in G. Lewis *et al.* (eds) *Rethinking Social Policy*. London: Sage.

Stenson, K. (2001) 'Some day our prince will come: zero-tolerance policing and liberal government', in T. Hope and R. Sparks (eds) *Crime, Risk and Insecurity: Law and order in everyday life and political discourse*. London: Routledge.

Stenson, K. (2002) 'Community safety in middle England – the local politics of crime control', in G. Hughes and A. Edwards (eds) *Crime Control and Community: The New Politics of Public Safety*. Cullompton: Willan.

Stenson, K. and Edwards, A. (2001) 'Crime control and liberal government: the "third way" and the return to the local', in K. Stenson and R.R. Sullivan (eds) *Crime, Risk and Justice: The Politics of Crime Control in Liberal Democracies*. Cullompton: Willan.

Stenson, K. and Edwards, A. (2003) 'Crime control and local governance: the struggle for sovereignty in advanced liberal polities', *Contemporary Politics*, 9(2): 203–17.

Stenson, K and Watt, P. (1999a) 'Governmentality and the "death of the social"? A discourse analysis of local government texts in south-east England', *Urban Studies*, 36(1): 189–202.

Stenson, K. and Watt, P. (1999b) 'Crime, risk and governance in a southern English Village', in G. Dingwall and S.R. Moody (eds) *Crime and Conflict in the Countryside*. Cardiff: University of Wales Press.

Stoker, G. (1998). 'Public–private partnerships in urban governance', in J. Pierre (ed.) *Partnerships in Urban Governance*. London: Macmillan.

Stone, C. (1989) *Regime Politics: Governing Atlanta, 1946–1988*. Lawrence, KS: University Press of Kansas.

Taylor, I. (1999) *Crime in Context: A Critical Criminology of Market Societies*. Oxford: Polity Press.

Tilley, N. (1993) 'Crime prevention and the safer cities story', *Howard Journal*, 32: 40–57.

Tilley, N. (2002) 'The rediscovery of learning: crime prevention and scientific realism', in G. Hughes and A. Edwards (eds) *Crime Control and Community: The New Politics of Public Safety*. Cullompton: Willan.

Young, J. (1999) *The Exclusive Society*. London: Sage.

Chapter 11

Containment, quality of life and crime reduction: policy transfers in the policing of a heroin market

David Dixon and Lisa Maher

This chapter provides a case study of how international developments in policing policy and practice (particularly in New York City) impacted on the policing of a heroin market in Cabramatta, an outlying suburb of Sydney, Australia. Attempting to provide the kind of empirical study suggested by Jones and Newburn (see Chapter 7) which links structure, culture and agency, we seek to show how transferred policies are implemented, how elements of them may conflict and how the crucial transfer may be not so much of particular policies but, rather, of less specific perceptions and attitudes, in this case a confidence in the ability of the police to reduce crime and an elision of the distinctions between community policing, harm minimisation and law enforcement.

Cabramatta is a working-class suburb in Sydney's sprawling south west, located some 20 km from the centre. Its inhabitants are poorer, younger and less likely to be employed than the state average. A long-standing point of arrival for Sydney's migrants, since the 1970s Cabramatta has been Sydney's Asian city (Maher *et al.* 1998). Three of every five residents were born overseas. In their homes, 32 per cent speak Vietnamese and 27 per cent speak a Chinese dialect, while only 23 per cent speak English (Legislative Council 2001: 6). It is not an area that fits usual Australian stereotypes: the busy streets, shops and restaurants of Cabramatta's central business district (CBD) resemble those of a south east Asian city. In the 1990s, Cabramatta became known as Australia's 'heroin capital', a potent symbolic location in which fears about the connections between ethnicity, drugs and crime were played out. The heroin market began as a freelance street activity. It subsequently developed off-street operations and more organisation and sophistication, not least in response to police crackdowns. Along with these developments, a substantial cocaine market also emerged (Maher *et al.* 1998).

This chapter draws on our research since 1995 which has employed ethnographic and other methodologies to study drug markets, public health, homelessness, crime and policing in Cabramatta (Coupland *et al.* 2001; Dixon and Maher 2002; Maher 2002; Maher *et al.* 1997, 1998, 2001, 2002; Maher and Dixon 1999, 2001; Sargent *et al.* 2001). Specifically, the second and third sections draw on a study of policing policy in which officers at every level from constable to deputy commissioner were interviewed.[1] Otherwise unattributed quotations below are from officers interviewed in this project. In 2000–1, Cabramatta's policing became the subject of a bitter political dispute in which there was extended public debate about what policy was, appeared to be and should be. The third section draws on a parliamentary committee's investigation which played a key part in this episode (Legislative Council 2001). While, as will be shown below, its process and conclusions were questionable, its investigation and report were influential and, in themselves, form part of the subject matter of the chapter.[2]

We seek to trace the origins, development and transfer of policing policy in three stages: a period of denial and containment in the late 1980s and early 1990s, a period when displacement of the drug market was attempted in the mid and later 1990s in an attempt to improve quality of life in Cabramatta's CBD, and a concerted crackdown since the turn of the century which was designed to root out the drug market.

Denial and containment

Cabramatta's heroin market emerged in the late 1980s. By the mid-1990s, it had overtaken a traditional red-light district nearer Sydney's centre as the country's premier heroin market (Dixon and Maher 1999). The initial response of the police was to downplay its significance. In part, this was a traditional response to problems for which they could be blamed. Also, the police were slow to appreciate the scale of the emerging problem because their intelligence gathering from and contact with the local community were inadequate. However, there was also a concern that publicity would worsen the situation, attracting new customers to the cheap, high-quality heroin readily available in the thriving street retail market. From this perspective, crackdowns could operate counter-productively 'like a marketing exercise' attracting people into the drug market. In retrospect, an officer commented:

[W]e've got a suburb that's been allowed to become the heroin distribution capital of Australia, and quite simply that is because the media had always published how much heroin is available in Cabramatta, it's always the best quality, and it's the best place to go and get it, so people go there and get it.

When police activity in response began to grow, its public face varied according to the personal preference of the local chief officer: while the commander from 1991 to 1995 expressed community policing commitments, his successor was more law enforcement oriented. They shared a commitment to the use of discretionary law enforcement and order maintenance designed to exert whatever control over the market was possible. Neither had any ambition that the drug market could be eliminated. In the mid-1990s, success meant no more than preventing the problem from getting worse:

[Y]ou've just got to try to contain them rather than stop it, ... it's too far gone now to ... remove the problem.

We wouldn't have any hopes at all or any expectations of eradicating the problem ... It's a no-win situation.

Various metaphors were used to express this strategy, such as 'stemming the tide', 'managing' it and 'trying to keep a lid on it. Stop the fires from spreading'. Another officer argued that:

It wasn't a winning situation ... it was a matter of trying simply to limit it ... It's really important for police and ... the community to understand exactly what it is police can do. Too many times the [NSW police] service takes on responsibility for things over which they've got no control.

Other senior officers made clear the limits of drug policing and the need to define 'realistic' objectives:

I never imagined that at the end of my time ... there would be no heroin available in Cabramatta, 'cause there are forces, economic forces, that are absolutely beyond my control, in fact beyond the control of governments influencing this process, so if that's what's in people's minds then – I'd guess I'd like that too, but in realistic terms, that's not going to happen. Therefore, if anything short of that is failure, then we were going to fail before we started.

To 'win the war on drugs' is an absolutely absurd comment because we can't do that.

There was modesty about the direct, indirect and long-term effects of police intervention. The limited direct effect of punitive sanctions was acknowledged:

We can keep locking people up 'til the cows come home, but they're going to use gear: it will always be a revolving door effect ... [T]he users are going to go in and come straight out again and go straight on the street to buy again ... they're not going 'Oh the cops have locked me up so I'm going to stop this behaviour', and so it will be with the street suppliers.

This perception was encouraged by the regenerative capacity of the drug market. Arresting street-level dealers simply created market opportunities for others, literally, to take their place:

[A]s soon as you knock one lot over, another lot bobs up.

[O]n a good day we were charging 20 suppliers ... by the time we'd finished, say 5 or 6 o'clock at night, we'd drive past the locations where we lifted them and there was people back there taking their spots selling again.

[A]rresting low-level street users and suppliers ... doesn't make a great deal of difference. It just generates a lot of arrests, a lot of paperwork, people go to jail for 5, 6, 12 months for selling caps at Cabramatta, but ... the numbers are just being filled by new people, and [the police] are not *stopping* it.

From this perspective, problems which, it was recognised, seriously affected the quality of life of people living in Cabramatta (overdoses, discarded needles and syringes, visibility of people shooting up or 'nodding off' on the street) could only be dealt with by 'an absolutely disproportionate level of response out there which might create other problems'. Implicit in the commitment to containment was an acceptance that, as the drug market could not be suppressed, it should be localised. From this perspective, geographical displacement as a result of vigorous enforcement would be undesirable.

The best that policing could achieve was to employ 'a policy of disruption' of the market by lengthening the 'search time' for drugs

(Drug Programs Co-ordination Unit 1996). But even this was seen as being of limited positive value: drug market participants 'may well be a little more cunning, they may be a little bit more desperate', but they would continue to sell and buy heroin.[3] Efforts were concentrated on the lower end of the market: even specialist DEA officers found themselves assigned to buy/bust operations against street-level user dealers.

There was some attempt to justify this as 'climbing up the pyramid', using street-level enforcement to gain intelligence about suppliers. However, the Commander of Cabramatta police between 1991 and 1995 claimed that he was unable to focus operations above street level because of lack of local resources and his distrust of the regional drug squad which he 'threw ... out of my command'.[4] He believed that street-level law enforcement was effective in itself: it had 'a deleterious effect on the supply network right to the top ... It is like any business: if you start hacking away at the cash flow you are going to feel somebody squealing somewhere along the line. Someone is not going to get paid'. The approach was hardly sophisticated:

> If I were to place a police officer outside every newsagency in a particular location and stop people buying particular newspapers, it would not be very long before certain media moguls would make noises about the distribution of newspapers. It works roughly along the same lines; you do have an impact.[5]

This was an example of indirect policy transfer: the commander was 'guided by inferences' from a report by the NSW Bureau of Crime Statistics and Research (BCSR) on heroin user/dealers. In the Preface, the Bureau's Director stated that the 'report, dealing as it does with the lower strata of [the] distribution network suggests that these levels may be more vulnerable to intervention and disruption by law enforcement than those higher up the chain. Such a finding has great relevance to current law enforcement policy' (Dobinson and Poletti 1988: vii). These policy implications were, in fact, not explicated in the report.[6] However, both the report and the conclusions drawn from it by the Director were strongly influenced by US research, notably Mark Moore's *Buy and Bust* (1977) and Johnson *et al.*'s *Taking Care of Business* (1985), and the general shift of emphasis in US drug law enforcement 'from wholesale to retail trafficking' (Uchida and Forst 1994: 82; Kleiman 1988).

By 1997, senior detectives were critical of the 'bottom-up' policy. The problems of relying on pyramid models were acknowledged: 'planning operations at street-level are just a waste of time because the product in terms of drugs seized and information produced did not justify the cost:

all it's doing is tying up police at court.' Indeed for this group, starting at the street level was not by choice, but because they were directed to do so in response to a political imperative for visible, active policing: 'we haven't really thought that, you know, … if we just start at the street level and away we go. We always wanted to target that upper level … but it was just that we had to do that street level stuff before, more by direction than anything else.' Indeed, the effectiveness of such strategies was questioned in an influential official report (Sutton and James 1995).

Merely maintaining a situation which was acknowledged to be unacceptable was not satisfying for many police officers. By mid-1997, there was a feeling of considerable frustration among senior police at local and district level about their lack of impact on the drug market. However, a more senior officer disagreed with this assessment, describing their efforts as 'an outstanding success … Ultimately [if] it doesn't look much different when you leave as to when you arrive, you do have a sense of failure'. However, stopping the situation escalating was regarded as 'probably the most outstanding success [the local commander] could have achieved'.

This pragmatic approach was an expression of the broader approach to policing which had emerged from empirical studies of policing in the USA and which was still prevalent in the early 1990s. It included scepticism about the potential impact of police on crime, concern for counterproductive effects of aggressive crime fighting and emphasis on the need to tackle social problems through co-ordinated strategies in which policing is but one part (Bayley 1994). Its routes of influence on Australian policing were wide ranging, but included the US and UK research literature on the limits of police effectiveness in crime control and the Alderson/Scarman approach to community policing. The influence of more specific research is shown, for example, in the reference quoted above to Moore's concept of 'search time' (1990).

As the scale of the drug market grew, so police attempts to control it intensified. In a context of loosely defined police powers, political pressure for results and a racial folk devil (the 'Vietnamese drug dealer') as prime target, nobody with any knowledge of drug policing would be surprised that the outcome was problematic. Persistent and credible allegations of misconduct and low-level corruption by officers emerged. Abuses in stop/search practices and in dealing with confiscated heroin were the prime source of complaint (Dixon and Maher 2002).

Within Cabramatta's southeast Asian communities and business organisation there was considerable concern about police operations. The recipients of this hard-line policing were very often not (as police and media presented them) from outside Cabramatta, but rather were the sons, daughters, brothers, sisters, nieces or nephews of those observing stop/searches and arrests (Maher and Dixon 1999, 2001; Dixon and Maher 2002). At the same time, these and other communities in Cabramatta wanted the drug trade stopped, and argued publicly that the 'containment policy' sacrificed Cabramatta or put the interests of other areas above Cabramatta's 'because the concerns of its non-English speaking background can be more easily ignored by authorities than other areas' (Legislative Council 2001: 13).

Quality of life

In 1997, new regional and local commanders introduced a different strategy to the policing of Cabramatta which was heavily influenced by contemporary developments in New York City. In his 'Strategic and Tactical Action Plan', the newly appointed Regional Commander stated:

> The illegal use of drugs is a major social and economic problem facing the community of Cabramatta. Despite the fact that Police are proving their effectiveness in terms of increased arrests for trafficking and drug seizures, it is evident that the extent of the drug problem has never been greater. New initiatives need to be found to reduce the demand for drugs as well as to control the supply (Evans 1997).

Intensive enforcement was recommended as a means of disrupting the drug market by deterring buyers and sellers alike. The aim was not, as before, to contain the market: on the contrary, now the police set out to drive drug sales and drug use out of Cabramatta's CBD. The major expression of this approach was 'Operation Puccini II' (and its numerical successors), described by a senior officer as 'a high profile, beat policing operation, saturation policing' which was designed to 'try and reclaim certain parts of Cabramatta to start with, disperse the dealers, discourage the itinerant travellers coming in and buying'. Puccini involved a tactical shift from relying primarily on undercover officers engaged in buy-bust operations to using large numbers of uniformed police stopping, questioning and searching suspected drug market participants, and deploying a range of legal resources, including not only drug offences but also numerous minor offences including train-fare evasion, goods in custody and offensive behaviour or language:[7] 'It's got to be high profile, we've got to ... discourage them from working, we've got to discourage the drug users and the drug suppliers from supplying in Cabramatta. The only way to do that is to be right beside them.'

Constant pressure was required. As a senior commander commented: 'Saturation policing works whilst ever it's saturated. Take away the resources and it invariably reverts back to what it was ... I can't pull the cops out of Cabramatta. Within a day, it would be back to what it was.' Maintaining continuous saturation would, inevitably, be a draining commitment for the police service. Puccini was supplemented by CCTV in the CBD: compared to the UK, CCTV is in its infancy in Australia, and Cabramatta was one of the first sites for intensive surveillance (Maher *et al.* 1997).

The criterion of success in this approach was distinctive. As under the containment policy, there was no expectation that the drug market could be suppressed. However, 'cleaning up' the CBD by moving the drug market out of central Cabramatta was regarded as a worthwhile goal because of the potential improvement in 'quality of life' in the area. While the first approach regarded displacement as a potentially problematic effect of intensive policing, the quality-of-life initiative regarded it as necessary and desirable:

> [W]e've driven it from the CBD, we've driven it underground and to other locations ... Puccini has certainly had the effect of removing the obvious blatant heroin dealing on the street ... and that's what we set out to do.

> [T]he displacement effect was anticipated, was hoped for. That was the whole aim of it, to move them out, to break them up and fragment them so that all the police could deal with the problem, not just Cabramatta police.

When asked if displacement was a problem, one officer responded: 'Certainly not for Cabramatta, and ... my job is to provide a policing service for the people of Cabramatta.' Displacement was regarded as beneficial as long as similar law enforcement efforts were directed at emergent, smaller drug markets in surrounding areas:

> [I]f you start off with 100 and you displace 40 and it becomes 20 in those two locations then you've effectively reduced your problem by 20%.

> [Puccini] will of course move the problem but if you move it to other areas the problem becomes smaller and more manageable

problems rather than one massive big problem which … can't be managed.

Once dispersed, drug problems could be addressed by various local commands which, in turn, could 'break things down into very manageable pieces':

> We've been given a massive problem to remove this boulder in the middle of the street. Now we probably need 200 people to carry it, but we just can't do it. So we've got to chip a little bit away and then carry bits of it away. So we're doing the same with the drug problem.

> Displacement was one of the things that we tried to achieve … That was the plan, that we get it out of the one community and spread it about a bit.

Displacement was regarded as allowing more effective control and as equitable both for the local community and for the local police. A senior commander drew an analogy with a problem of great contemporary concern to Sydney's residents:

> It's a bit like aircraft noise, most people are prepared to accept their share provided it's equitable.

> I don't believe it should fall to 150 police in Cabramatta to police the entire drug use. There's 13000 police that can police it if it is separated from just one central point.

While most interviewees spoke mainly about displacement to other suburbs, some also favourably mentioned displacement within Cabramatta: 'If we do move these drug sellers … out of the CBD, will it be into a residential area? But … even a couple of blocks off the main street, there's no hustle and bustle as there is in the main CBD, so people can't get lost as easily.'

These positive comments about displacement reveal a problematic narrowness of perspective. While Puccini had some effect in improving the 'quality of life' in the CBD, it had the opposite effect in surrounding residential areas to which drug users and user dealers resorted. Improving 'the quality of life' sounds like an indisputably desirable objective: the difficulty is that improving the quality of life of one section of the community may mean reducing that of another. There is also the danger that a displaced drug market will adapt in undesirable ways (Maher and Dixon 2001).

This 'quality of life' initiative bore the strong imprint of policies implemented in New York City from the mid-1990s (Kelling and Coles 1996; Bratton 1998). Cabramatta police were now seeking not the limited, negative goal of containment but, rather, the positive improvement of 'quality of life'. This was, in part, merely pragmatic: 'we're not going to stop people using drugs, so let's do the best we can with what we've got'. Cabramatta's 1997–8 'Command Plan' had three objectives: it set out 'to reduce the number of break and enter offences [and] of robbery offences', but its ambition was only 'to target street level heroin supply'. This marked a reordering of police priorities. Restoring or improving 'quality of life' was regarded as an appropriate and significant aim of policing. It was argued that the public were more concerned about public disorder and incivilities than about more serious offences. Success was defined in specific and local terms: law enforcement was to be used in the interests of the local community. This was seen as going 'back to basic policing'. The priority was cleaning up the streets:

> Our objective is to improve the quality of life for the business people, for the shoppers who use the CBD and for the people who use the railway station ... We can't stop the drug industry ... But we have to do something in Cabramatta to improve the quality of life.

Another familiar influence from the USA and UK came in the acknowledgement that, as regards crime and disorder, subjective perceptions were as significant as objective realities:

> The problem they've had here in the past is that it has just been so blatant, there's been needles all over the street ... the whole aim of [Puccini] is to remove the major drug problem in the Cabramatta area ... [and] to make sure that the people of Cabramatta feel safe.

> The whole idea of Puccini was to make the CBD a safe place or make – let people believe that it was a safer place and that's actually been achieved.

> It's really encouraging when you stand out in the street ... and see a dear old lady walking up and down the street with two shopping bags and they'll say 'G'day' to you and they'll say 'Thanks very

much … this is the first time I've been out in three months'. You know … you say well, even if we don't achieve anything else but to restore the confidence of those poor old ladies.

People are generally offended by, not so much the drug dealing, more about the drugged druggies lying around the place and wandering around the place … and evidence of use.

An officer suggested that if the drug market moved out of the CBD:

it will tend to go underground a bit which is really what the public wants, they just don't want to see it.

The high profile of the drug dealer's gone and that's certainly moved them out into a number of back streets … [W]e know where they are, and they're out of the CBD and that was the whole aim of Puccini.

Interviewed officers did not claim that less heroin was being bought and sold than before. This was not the criterion of success:

The drug dealing is not decreased, the quality of life for the people has improved, but still drug trafficking continues.

What the community wants is not drug law enforcement but cleaner streets … we can clean the streets and make it visually presentable. It's unrealistic to think we're going to get rid of junkies and dealers.

What this community really wants, they want a clean town, that's all.

The public's greatest concern is … they can see this happening. I think if the public didn't see it happening, they wouldn't be concerned about it, so if it was hidden behind a back wall and there was exactly the same amount of people dealing and using, if the public didn't see that, they wouldn't really be too concerned about it.

The primary beneficiaries of Puccini were seen to be the retail businesses in the CBD:

> Most people don't really care if people sell heroin – go ahead but don't do it outside my shop.

> If there's a junkie flaked out on the footpath, people are not going to step over them to go into a shop. So it was the presence of these filthy-looking, tat-covered, earring … you know … that they perceive as a turnoff to customers. And so our main strategy … [is] clean the streets up and make it visually presentable.

This was reported to be successful: 'the majority have noticed an increase in business … And they've all noticed basically what we're doing'. Similarly, police saw the introduction of CCTV as something that 'gives the people a feeling of security'.

A secondary, but significant, element of the strategy was to use legal resources instrumentally. Again, the influence of the New York experience was clear. Laws were to be enforced, warrant checks were to be made, stop/searches were to be carried out, not just for their own sake, but to facilitate further police intervention and thereby, possibly, to lead to detection or clear up of more serious offences. This, of course, was an attempt to apply Wilson and Kelling's 'broken windows' thesis (1982) transmitted via its implementation in New York City in the mid-1990s. While the influence of New York was clearly acknowledged, NSW officers were keen to distinguish their approach from the much-publicised slogan, 'zero-tolerance policing': 'I don't class what we're doing as zero tolerance at all. That is just saturation policing to target everything: we're targeting drugs only.' However, targeting drugs involved more than drug law enforcement: enforcement of other laws was used as a means of facilitating drug policing, not as some general commitment to zero tolerance. A characteristic and significant tactic was to use trespass charges against drug users who were found on private property such as garages, apartment stairwells and gardens. Similarly, police examined the tickets of incoming travellers at the railway station, thereby providing an opportunity to stop, check and (where deemed appropriate) search. Such activity could be productive:

> We are getting a lot of first instance warrants because we speak to people and they're wanted, they come here to buy drugs and are wanted on another unassociated matter … we're finding a lot of people with property on them that they're bringing in here to pawn as well.

Puccini was a focused crackdown which did not aspire to zero tolerance, but which drew substantially upon broader related concepts in terms of methods and objectives.

A senior commander (who had visited the NYPD) made explicit the connection between policing in New York and Cabramatta:

> [The NYPD's] philosophy is that people who commit felony crimes are not specialists. So they rob, they steal cars, they do all sorts of things, but they also commit the quality of life offences – urinating in the streets, swearing in the street, public street drinking. Their philosophy is that if we tackle people in the street, first off, if they commit a quality of life offence we have the opportunity of searching them and we'll probably find a weapon, probably find they're wanted on warrant and once we take them back to the police station … we'll probably find they're a felon and may well be wanted for a felony crime. That's their philosophy.

It was thought that this approach could be beneficially applied in Cabramatta. This influential officer suggested 'it's the same here' and described the NYPD's strategy as 'the answer'.

The policy of using law enforcement to improve 'quality of life' was the product of multiple factors. First, it accorded with the hypothesis that law enforcement may encourage users to seek treatment (especially methadone maintenance) by driving heroin's price up and its purity down, and disrupting the market so that the 'search time' is increased (Moore 1990). Here, law enforcement could be presented as a tool of harm minimisation and interagency co-operation. Secondly, intensive law enforcement responded to local demands for the area to be 'cleaned up': it was law enforcement as a tool of community policing. Thirdly, law enforcement responded to political pressure at state level for significant action against illegal drugs. In the context of recurrent law and order campaigning and the identification of drugs as a fundamental threat to society, calls for police action against the drug market tripped easily off politicians' tongues. Fourthly, police leaders were influenced by the growing body of studies which emphasised the importance of responding to subjective fears as well as realities of crime and disorder. Fifthly, law enforcement slotted neatly into the growing commitment of police to strategies usually collected (inappropriately and to considerable police discomfort) under the banner of 'zero tolerance' in which the policing of 'quality of life' offences is reconceptualised as a central tool in the war on more serious crime. Finally, it fitted with contemporary concerns for proactive, intelligence-led policing which targets high-risk groups, notably repeat offenders such as street-level user dealers. In such a context, it would be naïve to look for (or expect interviews to produce) a simple account of rational, instrumental policy formulation. The significant point is that law enforcement policing in Cabramatta was produced by various factors outlined above against the background of a clear message from New York City that police could take action which would improve 'quality of life'.

From quality of life to crime reduction

In 1998, Sydney's tabloid daily newspaper announced that the quality-of-life strategy had succeeded: zero tolerance had won the war on drugs in Cabramatta. The police service described police operations in Cabramatta as 'an outstanding success'.[8] This was not just police rhetoric: a prominent Vietnamese community leader subsequently described 1997–9 as a 'time of promise and hope when there was a great deal of attention paid to the area by people from the Premier down … [S]treet crime was brought under control' (cited in, Legislative Council 2001: 72). However, this satisfaction was to be short lived. Very soon, the wheel came off in spectacular fashion, and Cabramatta was transformed from an outstanding success into a disaster which became the subject of an intense political dispute and led to the development of a new strategy.

Exactly what happened is a matter of controversy. The publicly accredited account given by a parliamentary committee (Legislative Council 2001) and, subsequently, by the State Premier was that the police 'took their eye off the ball' of drug-related crime[9] which, consequently, spiralled out of control with a spate of shootings in early 2000.

Somewhat ironically, it was our clearest example of 'transferred policy' which was held to be responsible. This was the Operations and Crime Review (OCR), a process of managerial examination of local police commands' performance which was introduced in 1998 as a direct local application of the NYPD's Compstat (Henry and Bratton 2002). Three senior NSW officers had conducted a study tour of New York. The group included the regional commander for the Cabramatta area and the police service's key reform strategist. Their report (Evans *et al.* 1998) commented favourably on the NYPD's programme and was decisive in shaping the OCR programme, which was directed by the reform strategist. In addition, there had also been extensive publicity within and outside policing circles about the impact of Compstat.

In the OCR, the NSW version of Compstat, local commanders appear at a meeting at the Sydney Police Centre where they are called to account for their officers' performance (Davis 2002). In a direct echo of Bratton's mantra ('accurate and timely intelligence; rapid deployment; effective tactics; relentless follow-up and assessment'), police are told that crime will be reduced by 'Good information and intelligence; good tactics and strategies; rapid response; and relentless follow-up' (NSW Police 1999). While the atmosphere is less confrontational than in Compstat, it was somewhat incongruous to see a deputy commissioner who had long been an advocate of community policing demanding local commanders to promote more 'in your face' policing.

As in Compstat, much use is made of computerised performance indicators. This is said to be where the problem arose. The police service had developed a 'crime index' of five volume crimes (assault, burglary, robbery, stealing and motor vehicle theft) which would allow comparisons to be made across commands at OCRs. Drug offences and homicides were not included, the former because clear-ups are a product, rather than a measure, of police activity, the latter because of their comparative rarity and because they were primarily the responsibility of specialist task forces rather than local commands. According to the accredited account, the local commander became so concerned about being able to demonstrate success on crime index performance indicators that resources were diverted from drug policing into crime index offences (Legislative Council 2001: 38–45). Between October 1998 and September 2000, narcotics possession charges declined by 40 per cent and dealing arrests declined by 52 per cent in Cabramatta (Legislative Council 2001: 16).

In what was to become a notorious 'league table' of the most crime-affected areas, Cabramatta came in at 51 out of 80 local commands, prompting the Commissioner to claim that the police had had 'such a success at Cabramatta that it's no longer regarded as dangerous or as difficult a place as it used to be' (cited in, Legislative Council 2001: 73). As critics quickly pointed out, the index suggested that Cabramatta was less crime prone than the prosperous suburb where the Commissioner lived. Cabramatta was downgraded to a level-2 command, drawing a lower level of resources. Disagreements about this policy (and other disputes) produced a series of conflicts within Cabramatta Police Station, leading to a debate on a motion of no confidence in the local commander (who was soon transferred), a consequential slump in performance and morale, and dissatisfaction from sections of the public. Reports of serious gang-related violence next to reports of police internal feuds were the catalyst for public complaints about policing in

Cabramatta which led to the investigation by the parliamentary committee.

This committee reported that 'the Crimes Index had a critical and damaging impact upon Cabramatta policing' (Legislative Council 2001: 131):

> Significant harm was caused to policing in Cabramatta because of the way the Crimes Index was used in the allocation of resources by management within the Cabramatta LAC ... The priority in allocation of tasks and resources within the station became based around improving the Command's performance in Crime Index category offences, rather than the area's number one problem, drug crime (Legislative Council 2001: 41–2).

> [N]ew style management tools, such as the Crimes Index, were introduced on top of an unchanged authoritarian command and control culture. The result was a demoralised local command, a decline in effective policing and a breakdown in community trust and relationships (Legislative Council 2001: 167).

> The people were told crime was under control and that the streets were safe at a time when it was obvious to anyone in the area that drug crime and violent crime was [sic] at completely unacceptable levels (Legislative Council 2001: 72).

As the final comment suggests, the episode exemplified the police service's inadequate contact with and knowledge of the local community. Once again, people came to express the view that police policy was containment in order to limit the political damage caused by the drug market (Legislative Council 2001: 75). The committee emphasised that the police problem was not mere local mismanagement but, rather, the slavish application at local level of departmental policy: 'What went wrong in Cabramatta is that poor management, driven by inappropriate centrally imposed performance measures, prevented front line police in Cabramatta from focusing on effectively policing the aspects of crime which was [sic] most important to residents of Cabramatta' (Legislative Council 2001: 68)

The end result was presented as a gross example of how managerialist nostrums – notably the reduction of every function to quantifiable performance indicators – which have swept through policing (Waters 2002) can produce counterproductive results. The specific criticism of the OCR in relation to Cabramatta chimed with a damning critique of

249

the process generally in a crucial report (Hay Group 2000; Dixon 2001) on the progress of reforming the police service in the wake of a highly critical royal commission into police corruption (Wood 1997; Dixon 1999b).

We have doubts about the accuracy of this accredited account. Both declining productivity in drug policing and increasing violence in the drug market were, in part, measures of police *success* rather than failure. Puccini had affected the market which, predictably, had adapted to police crackdowns. It became more organised, hierarchically differentiated and sophisticated – a hardened target. The street market declined in favour of dealing via mobile phone and/or from so-called 'drug houses' – residential properties beyond the CBD which required more organisation and protection and were harder to police. The amateurs in the freelance market were replaced by people who were tougher and better connected. Ironically, the authorities strengthened what they feared most – gangs and organised crime. Those left in the marketplace were more willing to take risks and more inclined to use violence (Maher and Dixon 2001). This unfortunately coincided with increased use of cocaine (with its attendant problems) and a growing black market in illegal handguns. Coupled with internecine disputes between groups involved in the drug market, the result produced a series of well publicised violent incidents, including several homicides.

Over-politicisation distorted the issues: just as the state government had been quick to claim credit for the success in Cabramatta, its political opponents were equally quick to exploit the political opportunity provided by the embarrassment over the index. The Police Commissioner had become politically identified with the government. His vulnerability to attack over Cabramatta was seized on by the government's opponents in Parliament and the media. The Commissioner became the target of a concerted campaign which eventually forced his removal from office in 2002.

Meanwhile, the local political pressure was due at least as much to the level of activity of local business people as to changes in drug-related crime. Both business associations (divided principally into European and southeast Asian) became more vocal. Key alliances were made between local politicians, influential media commentators, local police and other critics of the Commissioner who used the apparent crisis in Cabramatta to embarrass and criticise the government.

The disputes within Cabramatta police station owed much to clashes of personality. As the subsequent Region Commander commented: 'There were [sic] a myriad of issues at the centre of the dispute, including the approach to the drug problem, overtime, motor vehicles and relations between management and at least some staff' (cited in, Legislative Council 2001: 68).

While OCRs may have focused on index offences, doing so meant considering drug-related crimes, if not drug offences specifically. They certainly took account of other performance indicators (use of stop/ search and move-on powers) which were indirect measures of drug policing activity. Finally, the committee's investigation was inadequate in a key respect: somewhat bizarrely, neither the local nor regional commander were called to give evidence. Consequently, neither of the police managers who were directly responsible for what had happened in the policing of Cabramatta provided their account of events.

Whatever the truth of the matter, it was the government's and the media's acceptance of the committee's account which counted. Local and regional commanders were replaced. A new strategy for policing Cabramatta was introduced. Again, it was influenced by the New York example, but this time a different lesson was taken from the USA: its priority was not quality of life but crime control, and its objective was not displacement but substantial reduction. In the new Region Commander's 'Seven-point Action Plan for 2001', it was announced that 'tackling the drug problem is our number one operational priority'.[10] This was to be done by reorganising dedicated operational units into an 'action group' and building 'an increased response capability to major crime'. In 2002, the plan was amended to include the targeting of 'those risk factors that can be reasonably targeted by police and that contribute disproportionately to our crime and disorder problems: drugs, the small group of people who account for most offences, gangs, truancy, alcohol and crime, domestic violence, crime hotspots, and organized crime'. The new command team set out to tackle drug retailing in Cabramatta directly, with the clear expectation that it would not just be contained but radically reduced. It was this confidence that police could be effective in fighting crime through law enforcement which, more than anything else, the NSW police drew from international experience in the 1990s.

The new strategy involved an intense police crackdown, first on what was left of the street market, then on the 'drug houses'. In April 2002, the government reported that 75 drug houses had been 'eliminated', 2,487 move-on directions had been issued in the previous nine months and drug supply charges had increased by 50 per cent (NSW Government 2002: 9). Drug houses were tackled first by use of civil remedies,[11] then by specific criminal legislation (see below). In a series of operations, the centre of Cabramatta was flooded with uniformed and undercover police, with sniffer dogs, on horses and on bicycles. Police made extensive use of their expanding legal resources. Move-on powers were deployed: backed by the offence of 'refusing direction', these were a potent means of excluding suspected drug market participants (and sometimes innocent residents) from the CBD. The less intrusive interventions of issuing a summons, court attendance notice or on-the-spot fine were abandoned for 'drug offenders', all of whom were arrested and charged. Doing so greatly expanded police control: bail conditions were used to apply 'banning orders', requiring people to keep out of Cabramatta (or of specific streets). Breach of bail made the person liable to be remanded in custody. This was widely used 'to disrupt the local drug markets, reduce visible drug using and dealing, improve the conditions for local residents and, for the drug dependent user, to try to coerce them into treatment'.[12]

Participants in a study of homelessness in the area (Bessant *et al.* 2002: 45) commented:

> [Y]ou don't have to be doing anything wrong. If you're suspected of being a drug user even if, like I'm doing my shopping and they'll tell me out get out of Cabramatta. Now I've lived here all my life. I was born here. What right have they got to tell me to get out?

> [Y]ou can be walking along the road and a police car will stop beside you and ask you your name. They check their computer and if you've got a record they tell you can't go to Cabra for seven days or ever. They do this even when you aren't doing anything.

Similarly, a participant in a related study of youth homelessness and drug use in Cabramatta commented:

> The cops harass you because they don't want you lying there on the seat. But, you know, what can you do? You've got nowhere to stay … They'll expect you to move. [T]hey say 'Get away'. If you don't they'll charge you for … not following police instructions and that's … a \$500 fine. And when you're on the streets you don't have money to eat you know? How can you pay a fine that big? (Coupland *et al.* 2001: 58).

As in New York City, warrant checks were used extensively: intervention is notionally justified by, at best, the minimal suspicion required for stop and search, thereby opening the way to more serious matters. A study of 102 young people's experiences and perceptions of policing in 2002 found most (84) had been stopped and over half (52 per cent) had been stopped more than ten times in the last year. Some 85 said they had been searched in the last year. Just over a quarter (27 per cent) said they had been searched more than ten times in the last year. Nearly half (44 per cent) had been told to move on more than ten times (Maher *et al.* forthcoming).

During 2000–1, there were significant declines in (often drug-related) offences such as car theft, stealing from vehicles and robbery. Other indicia of drug activity also fell: possession/use offences, distribution of needles and syringes, drug-related deaths and ambulance call-outs to overdoses all reduced dramatically. It was claimed that this 'evidence indicates that increased policing and law enforcement activity in the Cabramatta area has reduced the availability and use of heroin' (NSW Government 2002: 9).

The confounding factor – and great fortune for the senior officers involved – was that the new strategy coincided with a remarkable disruption of the supply of heroin from late 1999 to mid-2001 which came to be known as 'the drought'. Why this happened is the subject of controversy: there are as many explanations of why heroin almost dried up in Australia during this period as of why crime in the USA declined in the 1990s. As in the USA, explanation is usually tied to sectional interest: not surprisingly, state and Commonwealth law enforcement officers claim that their activities were responsible (ABCI 2002; NSW Government 2002: 10–11). Whatever its origin, the significance of the drought is that it gave the police the chance to get a grip on the market. As the market was thinned out by limited availability and higher prices, so the police cracked down on what was left of the street-level dealers. The crackdown had a considerable incapacitative effect: many Cabramatta regulars (users and user dealers) were incarcerated (Bessant *et al.* 2002).

The specific case of Cabramatta has to be placed in a broader context of law and order politics in which it played a crucial role. Crude law and order 'auctions' have become a regular feature of electoral politics in NSW, as rivals seek to outbid each other in crime control rhetoric. However, around the turn of the century such politicking achieved a new intensity as crime and public security shifted from the margin to the centre of political debate. The significance and the structural and cultural sources of such shifts have been compellingly analysed by Garland (2001). In this specific case, the process operated through another example of indirect policy transfer. Inspired by the apparent success of the NYPD and encouraged by the heroin drought, the NSW police shifted from the cautious pessimism of containment to an optimistic exploration of what might work in crime control. The government shared this confidence, and greatly assisted by providing the police with an array of new powers and offences.

The NSW Labor government has promoted crime control as a key element of its strategy for electoral success. It has ruthlessly countered the conservative opposition by outflanking it to the right, leaving very little room for conventional conservative critique of Labor's policies as 'soft' and 'civil libertarian'. The sources of Labor's strategy are the cost to US Democrats of being perceived as 'soft on crime' in the 1980s and the benefit to the UK's New Labour of promising to be 'tough on crime, tough on the causes of crime'. This slogan has become a mantra for Labor in NSW. This transfer must be set in the context of the extensive policy interaction between the Australian and British labour parties (Scott 2000).

The specific outcome has been a willingness, or perhaps rather an enthusiasm, to provide extended police powers and to create new offences in NSW. The State Premier flaunts his commitment to a relationship between police and government which is of doubtful propriety in a democratic society:

If police can identify another power they need to protect order and public safety, they will get it.

It the police commissioner ever comes to me and says 'I need additional powers to arrest drug dealers', it goes without saying he gets those from the Carr Government.[13]

The statute book was expanded to include, *inter alia*: an offence (punishable by 20 years' imprisonment) of 'ongoing dealing', i.e. the supply of a prohibited drug in whatever quantity on three or more separate occasions; power to 'move on' suspected drug market participants; powers to enter 'drug houses'; a raft of offences associated with drug houses, in some of which elements of the burden of proof are shifted to defendants, requiring them to establish that they have a lawful reason for being in the house in order to avoid conviction; powers to impose non-association and place restriction orders; power to detain suspects in order to search for drugs within their bodies by means of medical imaging, such as X-ray or ultrasound; and increased penalties for illegal possession of firearms. On occasions, it appeared that the police were like a spoilt child asked to produce a list for Santa: they were hard pressed to think of something that they lacked.

The drug house legislation was very wide, and was added to existing practice, again copied from the USA, of using civil law, notably encouraging landlords to eject tenants suspected of drug market involvement (Green 1996). Some premises treated as drug houses in

Cabramatta were at odds with the description of armoured fortresses resistant to police entry. One was an abandoned house used as a squat and injecting room by homeless heroin users, rather than a retail outlet: police raided it, ejected occupants and arranged for the owners to demolish it (Coupland *et al.* 2001). Other 'drug houses' under the statutory definition included cars used for deliveries of heroin.

It is a considerable irony that Cabramatta led to the Police Commissioner's demise. Far from downplaying crime control, he had promoted it as the centrepoint of his strategy (Dixon 2001). Doing so set him directly at odds with the Royal Commission's vision for reform (Wood 1997). The Royal Commission had reflected what was once accepted wisdom among police researchers: the ability of police to control crime is limited, single-minded commitments to crime control produce unfortunate consequences, and criminal statistics are a poor test of police efficiency. The Royal Commission did not succeed in (the very difficult task of) specifying how a reform-oriented service would work. This left the political space for the Police Commissioner to justify replacing the Royal Commission's prescription with his own (Dixon 2001). Again, his confidence in his ability to tackle crime must be related to observation of apparent police success in tackling crime in the USA and UK.[14] For a Police Commissioner to set him or herself up to be judged on success in reducing crime would once have been regarded as foolhardy: around the turn of the century, it seemed appropriate.

The sources of the new approach are indicated by its use of the language of risks, hotspots, repeat offenders and crime reduction, and 'what works'. It is no coincidence that Lawrence Sherman has been a frequent visitor to Australia (e.g. appearing as plenary speaker at a NSW Police 'What works in crime control?' conference for senior officers in 1999). The message is that crime can be reduced if police use intelligence sources and concentrate on risks – risky suspects, risky victims, risky places, risky times, risky property.

The media have also played an important role in refracting international influence. Comparing Sydney with New York and calling for 'zero tolerance' have become as much a feature of journalistic stock as, not long ago, claiming that New York exemplified the fate into which uncontrolled crime would lead us. Now the message is very different. According to Sydney's tabloid press: 'The shining example of New York mayor Rudolph Giuliani and commissioner Bill Bratton's "Zero Tolerance" policies is hailed by law and order advocates as a universal panacea to all policing problems.'[15] Indeed, Bratton was promoted as an adviser to the NSW Police Commissioner: he was said to be the 'man to fix Sydney'.[16]

Such advocacy had a paradoxical effect. Police were in a difficult position because, while they drew much inspiration from the NYPD, they also acknowledged the critique of 'zero tolerance', and the NYPD and zero tolerance were (frequently and inaccurately) tied in media coverage of policing. At one level, police and related authorities hurried to disassociate themselves from 'zero tolerance'. The regional commander for the Cabramatta area insisted 'Our approach ... is not zero tolerance. I do not intend to get into the mess that they got themselves into in New York'.[17] A leading exponent of the new crime control strategies criticised a paper by one of the present authors (Dixon 1998) for suggesting that the NSW police's strategies were anything but home grown (Darcy 1999). Meanwhile, the government's Bureau of Crime Statistics and Research claimed that Dixon's article:

> saw the introduction of OCR panels as tantamount or akin to the adoption of 'zero tolerance policing'. As such ... [the OCR] represented a threat to civil liberties, had the potential to further inflame race hatred and was potentially inimical to the restoration of public confidence in the integrity of police (Chilvers and Weatherburn 2001: 12).

This was bizarre, as the offending article had *praised* OCRs. Its critique specifically distinguished 'zero tolerance' from the NYPD's programme of intelligence-led, managerially reformed policing, including Compstat. It commended the NSW police for developing programmes drawing on Compstat (Dixon 1998: 101–2). Far from condemning the OCR, Dixon's article was praising it. This misrepresentation was not just sloppy scholarship: it reflected an imperative that any suggestion that the NSW police practised zero tolerance was to be challenged. Similarly in 2002, the NSW police reacted sharply to references to zero-tolerance policing in the auditor's draft third report on the reform process (Hay Group 2002).

Harm reduction and policy implementation

No study of policy transfer in relation to street-level drug law enforcement would be adequate if it did not acknowledge that implementing policy can be particularly difficult where the discretionary realm of low-visibility street policing is involved (Grimshaw and Jefferson 1987). Policies may be transferred, but they may go no further than operational plans, strategy documents and glossy leaflets produced by headquarters. One senior officer in our interview study commented circumspectly: 'There are some problems in philosophy out there between the philosophy applied at the control end and the philosophy applied from central area.' Others were more blunt: 'It's clear what [the local commander] wanted [officers] to do but they wouldn't have a clue what anyone else wants them to do.' Mid-level commanders in our study felt frustrated in attempting to communicate the realities of policing practice to headquarters: 'frankly, they don't want to know me, they see me coming and they usually run for it, but they don't want to hear what I have to say'. Far from being rational and consistent, policy was regarded by some officers as always being vulnerable to short-term crisis management.

From the perspective of both officers and drug users on the street, constancy is more notable than change in policing. Some policies are easier to implement than others. If a commander's policy is that officers should do something that they are keen to do (such as crackdown on street-level user dealers), then the policy is likely to be implemented. If a commander is able to implement policy by setting priority targets or using rewards and punishments, and directing resources (e.g. allocating additional officers for undercover buy-busts, assigning patrols to particular areas), then policy can be implemented. However, police institutions are not rational bureaucracies (Dixon 1997: 3–8). As the Cabramatta example in 1999–2000 shows, there may be intense opposition to policy direction. More generally, it is very difficult to push street-level law enforcement in directions contrary to the imperatives of police culture. The lack of congruence between the NSW police service's harm minimisation policy and its harm maximisation practice provides an excellent example (Maher and Dixon 2001). Minimising harm was seen by many police as, at best, a marginal concern: 'There is a big push from our headquarters to deliver a more active harm minimisation proposal. That's ok, there's nothing wrong with that, but what are you going to do about the fucking assaults and the murder and the people who still wish … to live there?'

However, in the context of drug market crackdowns, harm minimisation provided the intellectual and policy justification for law enforcement. Again, this represents a significant example of transferred policy: the work of researchers such as Moore (1990), Pearson (1992) and Dorn and South (1990) on drug law enforcement has been absorbed into NSW police policy via its popularisation by the NSW Bureau of Crime Statistics and Research (BCSR) in a series of papers and reports arguing that law enforcement can be a tool of harm minimisation when it is used to 'push' drug users into seeking treatment, particularly methadone maintenance. A senior officer explained in an interview that:

what guided our strategy to a very large degree was [work] done by the Bureau of Crime Stats which in essence proffered the view that ... street level law enforcement combined with a 'ramp' ... into the methadone program was at least a viable way of addressing the larger problem ... [T]here would be some good done if we could push people up to that ramp, push them, make it just too hard so that they would resort to some other occupation in a sense of move right off drugs altogether.

A fundamental problem with this argument is the assumption that drug treatment is effective and available. As regards the latter, police may push drug users up 'the ramp' into methadone maintenance in the name of harm minimisation, but in the absence of sufficient treatment beds, the ramp is more likely to lead to conventional punishment.

Both the quality-of-life and crime control strategies were articulated with a rhetorical commitment to using law enforcement as a tool of harm minimisation. According to the then regional commander, the 2001 crackdown was intended 'to create a crisis in the life of the drug user. They will have to make the decision: seek treatment and we will give you every support, or go to gaol'.[18] The Deputy Commissioner with responsibility for police operations cited BCSR as authority for the view that 'the Police Service is a little like the sheepdog: in order to get people serious about rehabilitation, police ... pursue them ... [and] put pressure on people, to force them either convert to rehabilitation programs or alternatively bear the consequences' (cited in Legislative Council 2001: 22). Unfortunately, reality does not conform to such neat dichotomies of choice. While considerable investment in treatment facilities has been made or promised, treatment facilities in southwest Sydney were manifestly inadequate throughout the study period (Maher and Dixon 1999). Of particular concern is that ethnicity affects access to treatment. Several studies have found that Asian heroin users are less likely to have experience of treatment than respondents from other ethnic groups (Louie *et al.* 1998; Higgs *et al.* 2001; Maher *et al.* 2001). All too easily, 'pushing drug users into treatment' becomes a euphemism for pushing them into prison. In analysing such initiatives, there are real problems of disentangling rhetoric and commitment (not least because exponents may not be aware of where one stops and the other starts).

Conclusion

What does the case study of Cabramatta suggest about how policy travels? As noted above, policy in policing is not a simple import.

The transfer of policy from New York to Sydney has certainly been facilitated by the attractiveness of the former as a destination for 'study tours'. Australian police (and politicians, journalists and academics) have flooded to New York in a notable case of 'policy tourism'. It is no coincidence that there has not been the same rush of 'study tours' to Hartlepool, England's primary zero-tolerance experimental site. Conversely, the attractions of Sydney have encouraged academic and police visitors from the USA including J.Q. Wilson, the Director of the FBI, and the Commissioner of the NYPD.

Policy transfer has also been assisted by the role of the Internet in facilitating access to policy-related studies and documents. The NIJ and the NYPD in the USA, and the Home Office, HMIC and the Audit Commission in the UK, all have influential material easily available online. None the less, in domesticating policy from overseas, local institutions play a key role by simplifying and contextualising international research findings through briefing papers and reports. Such official agencies can have a closer relationship with police and government than university-based academics. As noted above, in a series of papers, BCSR has relayed the message from US and English researchers that policing can challenge drug markets and that law enforcement and harm minimisation can cohabit. The bureau has also sponsored influential visitors from the USA, notably Jonathan Caulkins (2002). It has played a more important role than the kind of 'think-tank' that has been so significant in the UK, although the right-wing Centre for Independent Studies did host a visit to Australia by J.Q. Wilson in 1997. Negatively, such institutions can play a gate-keeping role. The influential Australian Institute of Criminology consistently marginalises critical qualitative and quantitative empirical studies of local drug markets in favour of studies of captive populations or household survey data (e.g. Makkai 2002) which offer little useful guidance to policy-makers concerned with 'hotspots' like Cabramatta.

It has been significant that drug policing is a specialism. Drug policing is, it was stressed by several interviewed officers, a very specific, specialised form of policing which involves specific legislation, methodology, resources, sophistication of suspects, proactivity, international focus and contacts. Practitioners are consequently more likely than otherwise would be the case to look to what their equivalents are doing elsewhere and to attend drug policy conferences.

There is also what might be clumsily called non-policy transfer. A defining characteristic of contemporary drug policy is the increasing marginalisation of commitments to harm reduction which were once the foundation of Australia's drug strategy. The Commonwealth Government seems to be increasingly concerned to show its policy subjection to US government dictates (e.g. in opposition to trials of safe injecting rooms or heroin prescribing). Not developing certain policies (or even allowing research which would provide a scientific basis for assessing their desirability) has been a significant result of influence from the USA.

It is important to resist an efficient bureaucratic model of policy transfer and implementation. As noted above, perception may be more important than reality: for example, there was the impact of the mistaken belief that the police were committed to containment, when their policy was dispersal. Policy may diverge into mutually opposing elements: for example, in New York quality of life, performance indicators and aggressive enforcement were part of same strategy. However, in Sydney, aggressive enforcement was presented as the solution to problems caused by misplaced quality-of-life and performance measure initiatives.

Conversely, apparently opposed policies may in practice overlap, not least for presentational reasons. Everything, it seems, has to be done in the name of 'community'. For example, the 'Seven-point Plan for Cabramatta' was presented as 'community problem oriented policing' (Legislative Council 2001: 88), even though the then Police Commissioner had made known his preference for a 'policing-oriented community'.[19] If drug crime is defined as being 'the problem' (rather than, for example, the socioeconomic conditions which foster it), then law enforcement is easily seen as the solution, and problem-oriented policing produces little that is different from more conventional law enforcement models. Here, in a distinctive example of broader contemporary trends in policing (Dixon 1999a), the conventional antithesis between law enforcement and community policing is made redundant. Intensive law enforcement activity is carried out in order 'to deliver a community-desired outcome'. Police engage in extensive interagency consultation and express commitment to a broad problem-solving approach. However, the way in which the problem is defined, as well as the practical complexities of interagency activity and constraints on other state services (Maher and Dixon 1999), mean that, in practice, policing appears more like a traditional law enforcement crackdown than as something new.

Policies may have short spans of life unless they are immediately effective. Whatever else went wrong in Cabramatta in 1999–2000, there was also the simple fact that sections of the local community were becoming dissatisfied with what Puccini had achieved. The drug market may have been reduced, but it had not disappeared. There were new sources of related complaint, such as increasing numbers of homeless people, particularly around the time of the Olympic Games which led to pressures on the homeless to leave Sydney's city centre. Senior officers felt they were in a dilemma of having to respond to local pressure, but that, as one put it, 'the problem with the local community ... is there's unreal expectations on what the police are going to do'. The police found it very hard to explain to local people the limits of what could be achieved: 'that doesn't cut much ice when you learn that [when you try to sell your] $300,000 home, the best offer you get is $150,000.' If police talked about harm minimisation rather than law enforcement, 'you're gonna get belted, you're gonna be written up in the local rag, "The cops have thrown in the towel" '. The police perception was that nothing would satisfy the local audience other than 'locking up and locking up and locking up'.[20]

A problem in clearly identifying the influence of policy developed elsewhere is that, understandably, local officials are often ambivalent about acknowledging that policy is being transferred. While learning the lessons of New York is attractive at one level, it is less so if it means just doing what others have done. Kudos and promotion come from having your own ideas which are implemented successfully. More specifically, there is a characteristic Australian ambivalence about following the lead of the USA or the UK. On one hand, there is a deference or 'cultural cringe' which overvalues anything from overseas. On the other, there is a resistance to following the lead of either the old or new imperial master. A solution is often to insist that one's policy is simple, common sense or (the police version thereof) 'going back to basics'. However, one should not underestimate some police officers in our study, whose abilities went beyond merely copying others.

Throughout the period examined here, various policies, tactics and concepts have been borrowed and adapted from the USA and UK, including 'search time', quality of life, intelligence-led policing, crackdowns and drug house legislation. However, these are less significant than the transfer of confidence (held by both police and politicians) in the ability of the police to reduce crime. This is complemented by the ability of leading policy entrepreneurs such as William Bratton to convey this confidence. Bratton confidently reported 'the good news ... if you can make it in New York, you can make it anywhere' (1997: 42). Australian politicians returning from their study tours echoed: 'Whether you're talking about New York, Darwin, Melbourne, the lessons are the same'.[21] The popular press provided a repeated chorus: the police would be able to control crime if only they followed the NYPD's example.[22] Such positive messages were inevitably attractive to committed and ambitious police officers in the wake of a demoralising, disruptive Royal Commission inquiry.

The key lesson taken from the experience of New York in the 1990s is that, in contrast to the previous decade's mantra, some things work: rightly or wrongly, it is believed that targeted, intensive, intelligence-led policing can improve quality of life and/or reduce crime. It was only on the basis of this confidence in the ability of the police to influence public order and effect crime control that the specific policies and strategies which were borrowed and adapted since the mid-1990s could find fertile soil in Cabramatta.

Notes

1 This project was funded by the NSW Police Service (see Dixon and Maher 1998).

2 We draw on this as part of a broader project, 'From zero tolerance to the "new policing": strategic change in Australian law enforcement', ARC grant A59917112.

3 Subsequently, it would be acknowledged that increasing users' search time had counterproductive effects. Their increased visibility impacted upon quality of life and upon the public's perceptions of police effectiveness: see Assistant Commissioner C. Small, in *Report of Proceedings before General Purpose Standing Committee No. 3: Inquiry into Police Resources in Cabramatta*, 27 February 2001: 22.

4 As Alan Leak said, a subsequent Royal Commission on police corruption (Wood 1997) found that he 'was well and truly justified', in *Report of Proceedings before General Purpose Standing Committee No. 3: Inquiry into Police Resources in Cabramatta'*, 18 December 2000: 19.

5 *Ibid.*: b,21–2.

6 The report went no further than pointing out that user dealers were 'the most visible aspect of heroin distribution for law enforcement' and noting five interviews with undercover police for whom a common method was getting user dealers to introduce the officer 'to a dealer higher up in that particular network. If possible, this process would be repeated until the highest level was reached' (Dobinson and Poletti 1988: 112, 86).

7 Between July 1997 and March 1998, Operation Puccini produced 63 per cent more GIC/receiving charges, 86 per cent more resist/hinder/assault police charges, 100 per cent more traffic offences, and 306 per cent more 'street offences' than in the previous 12-month period (memorandum by Inspector John Stanioch, Commander Operation Puccini, 1 May 1998).

8 See 'Police win war in drug capital', *Daily Telegraph* (Sydney), 20 April 1998; 'Outstanding success of Operation Puccini', *Police Service Weekly*, 1 June 1998: 4–5.

9 'No excuses: Carr demands senior police do a better job', *Daily Telegraph* (Sydney), 13 July 2001.

10 'Greater Hume: keys to success', *Police Service Weekly*, January 2002.

11 Small in *Report of Proceedings before General Purpose Standing Committee No. 3: Inquiry into Police Resources in Cabramatta,* 11 May 2001: 8. This was clearly influenced by strategies developed in the USA (see Green 1996).
12 Small, *op cit.* note 3, p. 6.
13 'Carr gives go-ahead to roadblock', *Sydney Morning Herald,* 3 November 1998; 'No mercy for drug dealers, says Carr', *Sydney Morning Herald,* 12 December 1998.
14 The fact that he had previously been an English chief constable was significant.
15 'Is it time for zero tolerance?', *Daily Telegraph* (Sydney), 12 April 2002.
16 'Man to fix Sydney?', *Daily Telegraph* (Sydney), 12 April 2002.
17 Small, *op cit.* note 3, p. 22.
18 Cited in 'War on drugs the top priority, vow Cabramatta police', *Sydney Morning Herald,* 9 February 2001.
19 'Commissioner Peter Ryan launches police-community video in Cabramatta', *Australian Current Law News,* 3 December 2001.
20 In fact, this was the view only of a vocal section. 'Locking up' was not seen as a solution by other (less influential) sections, particularly in Cabramatta's Asian communities (Coupland *et al.* 2001).
21 Shane Stone (then Chief Minister of the Northern Territory), *ABC Lateline,* 4 June 1998.
22 For example, *op cit.* note 15.

References

ABCI (2002) *Australian Illicit Drug Report 2000–1.* Canberra: Australian Bureau of Criminal Intelligence.

Bayley, D. (1994) *Police for the Future.* New York: Oxford University Press.

Bessant, J., Coupland, H., Dalton, T. Maher, L., Rowe, J. and Watts, R. (2002) *Heroin Users, Housing and Social Participation: Attacking Social Exclusion through Better Housing.* Melbourne: Australian Housing and Urban Research Institute.

Bratton, W. (1997) 'Crime is down in New York City: blame the police', in N. Dennis (ed.) *Zero Tolerance: Policing a Free Society.* London: Institute of Economic Affairs, 29–42.

Bratton, W. (1998) *Turnaround.* New York, NY: Random House.

Caulkins, J.P. (2002) *Law Enforcement's Role in a Harm Reduction Regime.* Sydney: Bureau of Crime Statistics and Research.

Chilvers, M. and Weatherburn, D. (2001) *Do Targeted Arrests Reduce Crime?.* Sydney: Bureau of Crime Statistics and Research.

Coupland, H., Maher, L. and Thach, M. (2001) *Every Day's the Same: Youth Homelessness in Cabramatta.* Sydney: NSW Premier's Department, Fairfield City Council and NSW Department of Youth and Community Services.

Darcy, D. (1999) 'Zero tolerance – not quite the influence on NSW policing some would have you believe', *Current Issues in Criminal Justice,* 10: 290–8.

Davis, E. (2002) *Operations and Crime Reviews in the NSW Police Service*. MGSM case 2002–1. Sydney: Macquarie Graduate School of Management.

Dixon, D. (1997) *Law in Policing: Legal Regulation and Police Practices*. Oxford: Clarendon Press.

Dixon, D. (1998) 'Broken windows, zero tolerance, and the New York miracle', *Current Issues in Criminal Justice*, 10: 96–106.

Dixon, D. (1999a) 'Beyond zero tolerance.' Paper presented to the third National Outlook Symposium on Crime in Australia, Australian Institute of Criminology, Canberra, 22–23 March. Available at http://www.aic.gov.au/conferences/outlook99/dixon.html

Dixon, D. (1999b) 'Reform, regression and the Royal Commission into the NSW Police Service', in D. Dixon (ed.) *A Culture of Corruption*. Sydney: Hawkins Press, 138–79.

Dixon, D. (2001) '"A transformed organization?" The NSW Police Service since the Royal Commission', *Current Issues in Criminal Justice*, 13: 203–18.

Dixon D. and Coffin, P. (1999) 'Zero tolerance policing of illegal drug markets', *Drug and Alcohol Review*, 18: 477–86.

Dixon, D. and Maher, L. (1998) 'The policing of drug offences', in J. Chan *et al.* (eds) *Policing in Cabramatta* (unpublished).

Dixon, D. and Maher, L. (1999) 'Walls of silence', in G. Hage and R. Couch (eds) *The Future of Australian Multiculturalism*. Sydney: Research Institute for Humanities & Social Sciences.

Dixon, D. and Maher, L. (2002) 'Anh hai: policing, culture, and social exclusion in a street heroin market', *Policing and Society*, 12: 93–110.

Dobinson, I. and Poletti, P. (1988) *Buying and Selling Heroin*. Sydney: NSW Bureau of Crime Statistics and Research.

Dorn, N. and South, N. (1990) 'Drug markets and law enforcement', *British Journal of Criminology*, 30: 171–88.

Drug Programs Co-ordination Unit (1996) *Cabramatta Drug Harm Minimisation Strategic Plan*. NSW Police Service (unpublished).

Evans, C. (1997) *Drugs in Cabramatta: A Strategic and Tactical Action Plan*. NSW Police Service (unpublished).

Evans, C., Ireland, S. and Crumlin, S. (1998) *Key Decisions and Recommendations Arising from an Examination of the New York Crime Reduction Strategy*. NSW Police Service (unpublished).

Garland, D. (2001) *The Culture of Control*. Oxford: Oxford University Press.

Green, L. (1996) *Policing Places with Drug Problems*. New York, NY: Sage.

Grimshaw, R. and Jefferson, T. (1987) *Interpreting Policework*. London: Allen & Unwin.

Hay Group (2000) *Qualitative and Strategic Review of the Reform Process. Part 1* (unpublished).

Hay Group (2002) *Qualitative and Strategic Review of the Reform Process. Part 3* (unpublished).

Henry, V.E. and Bratton, W.J. (2002) *The Compstat Paradigm*. New York, NY: Looseleaf Law Publications.

Higgs, P., Maher, L., Jordens, J., Dunlop, A. and Sargent, P. (2001) 'Harm reduction and drug users of Vietnamese ethnicity', *Drug and Alcohol Review*, 20: 241–7.

Johnson, B.D., Goldstein, P.J., Preble, E., Schmeidler, J., Lipton, D.S., Spunt, B. and Miller, T. (1985) *Taking Care of Business*. Lexington, MA: Lexington Books.

Karmen, A. (2000) *New York Murder Mystery: The True Story behind the Crime Crash of the 1990s*. New York, NY: New York University Press.

Kelling, G. and Coles, C. (1996) *Fixing Broken Windows*. New York, NY: Free Press.

Kleiman, M. (1988) 'Crackdowns', in M.R. Chaiken (ed.) *Street-level Drug Enforcement*. Washington, DC: NIJ, 3–34.

Legislative Council (2001) *Cabramatta Policing. General Purpose Standing Committee No. 3 Report* 8. Sydney: NSW Parliament.

Louie, R., Krouskos, D., Gonzalez, M. and Crofts, N. (1998) 'Vietnamese-speaking injecting drug users in Melbourne: the need for harm reduction programs', *Australian and New Zealand Journal of Public Health*, 22: 481–4.

Maher, L., Crofts, N., Kelsall, J and Le, T. (2002) 'Don't leave us this way: ethnography and injecting drug use in the age of AIDS', *International Journal of Drug Policy*, 13: 311–25.

Maher, L. and Dixon, D. (1999) 'Policing and public health: harm minimization and law enforcement in a street-level drug market', *British Journal of Criminology*, 39: 488–512.

Maher, L. and Dixon D. (2001) 'The cost of crackdowns: policing Cabramatta's heroin market', *Current Issues in Criminal Justice*, 13: 5–22.

Maher, L., Dixon, D., Hall, W. and Lynskey, M. (2002). 'Property crime by heroin users', *Australian and New Zealand Journal of Criminology*, 35: 187–202.

Maher, L., Dixon, D., Lynskey, M. and Hall, W. (1998) *Running the Risks: Heroin, Health and Harm in South-West Sydney*. Sydney: National Drug and Alcohol Research Centre.

Maher, L., Dixon, D., Nguyen, T. and Travis, G. (forthcoming) 'Experiences and perceptions of the "new policing" in Cabramatta' (unpublished).

Maher, L., Dixon, D., Swift, W. and Nguyen, T. (1997) *Anh Hai: Young Asian Background People's Perceptions and Experiences of Policing*. UNSW Faculty of Law Research Monograph Series. Sydney: UNSW Faculty of Law.

Maher, L. and Sargent, P. (2002) 'Risk behaviours and hepatitis C infection among Indo-Chinese initiates to injecting drug use in Sydney, Australia', *Addiction Research & Theory*, 10: 535–44.

Maher, L., Crofts, N., Kelsall, J. and Le, T. (2001) 'Risk behaviours of young Indo-Chinese injecting drug users in Sydney and Melbourne', *Australian & New Zealand Journal of Public Health*, 25: 50–4.

Makkai, T. (2002) 'Illicit drugs and crime', in A. Graycar and P. Grabosky (eds) *The Cambridge Handbook of Australian Criminology*. Cambridge: Cambridge University Press, 110–25.

Moore, M.H. (1977) *Buy and Bust: The Effective Regulation of an Illicit Market in Heroin*. Lexington, MA: Lexington Books.

Moore, M. (1990) 'Supply reduction and drug law enforcement', in M. Tonry and J.Q. Wilson (eds) *Drugs and Crime*. Chicago, IL: Chicago University Press, 119–57.

NSW Government (2001) *Cabramatta Anti-drug Strategy*. Sydney: NSW Government.

NSW Government (2002) *Cabramatta: A Report on Progress*. Sydney: NSW Government.

NSW Police (1999) *Operations and Crime Review* (video).

Pearson, G. (1992) 'Drugs and criminal justice: a harm reduction perspective', in P.A. O'Hare *et al.* (eds) *The Reduction of Drug-related Harm*. London: Routledge.

Police Service Weekly (1996) 'Drug harm minimization and practical policing applications', *Police Service Weekly*, 9 December: 3.

Sargent, P., Maher, L., Higgs, P. and Crofts, N. (2001) 'Initiation to injecting drug use among Indo-Chinese young people', *Health Promotion Journal of Australia* 12: 242–7.

Scott, A. (2000) *Running on Empty: Modernising the Australian and British Labour Parties*. Sydney: Pluto.

Sutton, A. and James, S. (1995) *Evaluation of Australian Drug Anti-trafficking Law Enforcement*. Payneham: National Police Research Unit.

Uchida, C.D. and Forst, B. (1994) 'Controlling street-level drug trafficking', in D.L. MacKenzie and C.D. Uchida (eds) *Drugs and Crime*. Thousand Oaks, CA: Sage, 77–94.

Waters, I. (2002) 'Quality and performance monitoring', in F. Leishman *et al.* (eds) *Core Issues in Policing*. Harlow: Pearson, 264–87.

Weatherburn, D. and Lind, B. (1999) *Heroin Harm Minimisation: Do we really have to choose between Law Enforcement and Treatment?*. Sydney: NSW Bureau of Crime Statistics and Research.

Weatherburn, D., Lind, B. and Forsythe, L. (1999) *Drug Law Enforcement: Its Effect on Treatment Experience and Injection Practices*. Sydney: NSW Bureau of Crime Statistics and Research.

Weatherburn, D., Topp, L., Midford, R. and Allsopp, S. (2000) *Drug Crime Prevention and Mitigation: A Literature Review and Research Agenda*. Sydney: NSW Bureau of Crime Statistics and Research.

Wilson, J.Q. and Kelling, G.L. (1982) 'Broken windows', *The Atlantic Monthly*, March: 29–38.

Wood, J.R.T. (1997) *Final Report of the Royal Commission into the New South Wales Police Service*. Sydney: Royal Commission.

Index

'transfer', concept 6
transformation, general formulas of 81
Transformation Forum 194, 195
translation of concepts 7–8, 10–11, 20, 80, 82–3
transnationalisation 153
travel *see* global travel
Trevi group 51
Truth and Reconciliation Commission 22, 161, 184

UK
    implementation of international conventions on youth justice 165–6
    policy convergence in crime control 123–46
    prison privatisation 135–6
    as a provider and exporter of institutional models 16–17
    sex offender registration 137–9
    zero-tolerance policing (ZTP) 131–4
    see also England; Scotland
underclass
    in America 35–6
    in Australia and New Zealand 37
    in the UK 37
United Nations Convention on the Rights of the Child (1989) 164–5
United Nations Guidelines for the Prevention of Juvenile delinquency (1990) 165
United Nations Standard Minimum Rules for the Administration of Youth Justice (1985) 164
universalisation 153
urban regeneration initiatives 215
USA
    lesson drawing from 5
      reasons 9–10
    actuarial justice in 31–2
    and cross-border police co-operation 50
    cultural traditions of punishment 84–90
    drugs policies 39, 40, 44
    imprisonment rates 83, 90, 92, 124
      variables associated with 94–7
    policy convergence in crime control 123–46

political and institutional structure 20
prison privatisation 134–5
sex offender registration 136–7
and youth justice 157
see also New York City policing reforms

Van Biljon v. Minister of Correctional Services (1997) 196
'Varieties of Capitalism' approach 11–12
violent crime in South Africa 190–1, 192
'vocabularies of punitive motive' 93
Voltaire 16

War on Drugs 140
    and harm minimisation 39–41
warehousing 31, 33, 38
Wedderburn Report 111–12
welfare to work 126, 133, 160
welfarism
    critique 155
    in youth justice 156, 169, 171
westernisation 153
White Paper on the Policy of the Department of Correctional Services in the New South Africa 194
women, imprisonment of *see* imprisonment of women
Women's Policy group (WPG) 110, 111, 112, 113, 115

young offender institutions 165
youth custody 157, 165, 167–9, 170f
    in South Africa 200, 201
    in the USA 157
youth justice 152–77
    from welfare to neoliberal governance 155–9
    international conventions 164–6
    local governance 174–6
    national cultures and legislative sovereignty 167–74
    policy transfers 159–64
    in South Africa 200–1

zero tolerance, history of 140
zero-tolerance policing (ZTP) 19, 25, 131–4
    process of policy convergence 139–42, 162–3